GEORGE LONDON

Of Gods and Demons

by

Nora London

GREAT VOICES
9

BASKERVILLE
PUBLISHERS

Baskerville Publishers, Inc.
2711 Park Hill Drive
Fort Worth, Texas 76109

www.baskervillepublishers.com

Library of Congress Cataloging-in-Publication Data

London, Nora, 1924-
George London : of gods and demons / by Nora London.
    p. cm. — (Great voices ; 9)
ISBN 1-880909-74-X (alk. paper)
1. London, George, 1920- 2. Singers—Biography. I. Title. II. Series.

ML420.L865L63 2005
782.1'092—dc22

                              2005001808

Manufactured in Canada

First printing, 2005

Table of Contents

Acknowledgments

This book owes a great deal to the many friends who encouraged me and helped me to secure important facts about George London's life.

I am especially indebted to Dr. Howard Gotlieb, Director of the Howard Gotlieb Archival Research Center at Boston University, who had the foresight to collect George's papers while he was still alive. He is always ready with help and advice, and thanks to Howard, over one-hundred letters from George to his parents, as well as George's correspondence with Wieland Wagner have been preserved for posterity.

I also express all of my gratitude for the invaluable assistance of Gottfried Kraus. He has been a devoted friend of our family for over fifty years, and his knowledge of the musical life of Vienna is unsurpassed. And to Edgar Vincent for his work with George and his friendship.

Also, a special mention of Simon Bourgin of Time Magazine, who covered George's meteoric rise in the opera world and remained a friend for life. And I thank H.C. Robbins Landon, one of the world's leading musicologists, for his letter. He recognized George's talent from the very beginning and became a close friend.

I give many thanks to Maria Bedo, Executive Director of the George London Foundation, who spent many hours copying my text and preparing the chronology of performances, and cite the perfect work of Robert Baxter who prepared the discography.

Most importantly, I must express my deep appreciation for Ronald Moore's enthusiasm and love for opera and its great singers. Without him, this book would not have been possible.

George London: Of Gods and Demons

PREFACE:

Two decades have gone by since George London's death, and thirty-six years have passed since he stopped singing. Yet, his influence on a new generation of baritones and bassos of all nationalities continues to grow. The artistry of this performer whom the famous music critic and composer Virgil Thompson once described as "the greatest singing actor of our time" is now preserved in over fifty compact disks, as well as videos and DVDs, providing aural and visual evidence of his extraordinary voice and artistry to a new generation of opera fans who never heard him in person.

After World War Two, George London was the first American opera singer to have major success in Europe. For eighteen years, he was unique among Americans, becoming a star in both Europe and the United States. He was identified with the great bass-baritone roles of the repertoire and performed in all the world's opera houses and concert halls.

Coming from daunting poverty, he fulfilled all the dreams of his youth and paid the ultimate price with a catastrophic illness. He *was* the characters he interpreted on the stage: Don Giovanni, The Flying Dutchman, and in the end Amfortas with "the wound which never heals"

Dedication

For my children and grandchildren

They are the present and the future

This is the story of their past

Introduction

It was over half a century ago, precisely 1949, that the personality of George London burst upon musical Vienna.

George had the impact he did for three reasons: his magnificent bass voice, his innate musicality, and his handsome appearance in opera (who can forget his appearance while clad in white as the protagonist in Mozart's "Don Giovanni" at the Theater-an-der-Wien?)

I had the good fortune to use George as bass solo in two hitherto unrecorded pieces of eighteenth century Church Music: Haydn's "Missa in Augustiis (Lord Nelson Mass) and Mozart's Mass in C Minor K427. We recorded in Vienna in 1949 for the Haydn Society, and I was the producer. His performances electrified us, as well as thousands of others, when the records appeared. George's career was indeed meteoric and deservedly so.

H.C. Robbins Landon

Chapter 1
Childhood in Montreal

George London's career may have seemed "meteoric" to his new friends in Vienna, but the road to success was long and arduous. He was born George Burnstein in Montreal, on May 30, 1920. His parents Louis Burnstein and Bertha Berdichevsky came independently to America from Russia at the beginning of the century. An adventurous young girl, Bertha had traveled widely in Russia and Poland before taking the big step of coming to the new world. Louis had settled in the United Stated in New Jersey, and became an American citizen in 1911.

Throughout his life Louis was involved in left wing causes. At eighty, feeling nostalgic, he described his youth in a letter to a second cousin in London: "I wanted to relate to you some part of the story of our family. I am the oldest in the family at present, (I had a first cousin) who was about one year younger. We were born and raised in the same house together with our grandparents, (my father and grandfather were shoemakers) in a town called Shirvint in Lithuania, Russia. We studied in the same "chedar" (Jewish School) where we were taught by my uncle. At about the ages of 12 and 13 we left our hometown. My cousin was sent to a distant Yeshiva (school for higher learning of the Talmud). I went to Vilna, a short distance from Shirvint, where I entered a school for the learning of Talmud and Russian subjects." Louis did not forget the village where he was born, and every so often until his death, he talked about going back there to visit.

Louis's cousin left the ghetto to go to America, where he became editor of newspapers in Yiddish in New York and Montreal. Louis followed his cousin to New York, hoping to work with him. But both ventures failed for lack of readers, and his cousin soon departed for England, where he eventually made a living and settled down. The two would never see each other again.

Meanwhile, Louis remained in New York and met Bertha, who was working as a milliner. They decided to go to Montreal, where she had many relatives in the garment business. In 1919, Louis and Bertha were married. Although they were not very religious, they were married by a rabbi, partly because they were deeply aware of their Jewish background, and partly out of consideration for Bertha's devout Montreal relatives. Louis was thirty nine, and Bertha twenty nine. They entered into the business of manufacturing ladies' hats. They were good workers, and soon had their own thriving millinery business, the Mabelle Hat Company, which they owned and operated until 1935.

Their only child, George, was born on May 30, one year after their marriage. He was a big, healthy baby, according to existing photographs, obviously well groomed and well fed by his mother and a housekeeper, who took care of him while his parents were working. His mother often recounted that the birth was so difficult that she never wanted another child. There are just a few photographs of the young George after the baby pictures; the last one portrays a sweet-looking five-year-old dressed up in a sailor suit for a special occasion.

The family lived in Montreal in the district of Outrémont, a residential area beginning above Park Avenue near Mont Royal. Most Jews rarely ventured outside this neighborhood, for this is where they worked, shopped and socialized with their relatives during weekends. From the 1920's to the 30's, the Jewish population constituted the most important ethnic group, second only to the French Canadians in Montreal; however, the governmental affairs were conducted in English as befitted a British Dominion.

George rarely spoke about his childhood. When asked about his home and about his schooling, he avoided the subjects. It was painful for him to speak about this lonely, stifling period of his life. He went to the Strathcona Academy in Outrémont. The school was a strict English-style co-ed institution, and the majority of the students were Jewish. However, the school board and teachers were Protestant. On weekends, the boys relieved the harsh discipline of school by playing rough games in the streets near their homes.

Felicia Bonaparte, a professor of comparative literature who went to the same school as George writes:

> Yes, George London went to Strathcona Academy, or so we were told nearly every day, though, as I said, I don't believe he went through all (of) his high school years there. I should add that seeing his picture all over our high school and hearing him often over our loudspeakers in the auditorium got a lot of our high school people interested in opera. For many, it was the first time they had ever heard classical music and/or opera altogether. Ms. Bonaparte recalls huge numbers of students going down to the big hockey stadium in the middle of town ("hockey, of course, being the national religion,") which had been transformed into an opera house for one of the great opera companies that passed through Montreal almost every year. She states, "I often think this should be a lesson to modern educational institutions, so many of which cater to the music they think students want to hear."

During a speech to young singers in 1968, George told this story, which he repeated many times as if it was the only important event of his first fifteen years:

> I grew up like a typical Canadian boy interested in hockey and sports of that kind. There was no special musical

3

background in my family, except for a wind-up Victrola.
My mother had been a music lover in her youth and had
heard Caruso. We had a number of records, and I knew
these records backwards before I could talk. A big change
came into my life in 1931, I was just a young boy then
[eleven years old] and that was the year the Metropolitan started broadcasting on Saturday afternoon. When
I heard my first opera, I was simply overwhelmed. Now
this caused an enormous upheaval in the neighborhood
because I was a cherished left-wing player on the neighborhood hockey team on Saturday afternoons. I stopped
going to the hockey matches. I was listening to the opera. Can you imagine what this did to my reputation? I
was strictly a 'geek.' But I persisted. I read up on opera.
I read all the stories. I knew all about the singers. I wrote
out for autographed pictures.

In this way, George received an operatic education. He
heard and remembered all the singers of the 1930's. On Sun-
days, he played baseball or went skating in the winter, but on
Saturdays he always listened to the radio. His childhood was
cheerless; he lacked close friends even among his many cousins. He did not seem to fit in with anyone.

Once he was invited for the weekend to New Jersey by an
aunt on his father's side. There was no extra room, and he
slept on the couch in the living room. During the night, he
woke up with an uncontrollable urge to go to the bathroom.
When he saw a large plant standing in a corner, he relieved
himself in it. The plant died within days, and his aunt, guess-
ing the truth, never invited him again. But he still laughed
when he recalled this prank years later, hiding his lasting bit-
terness about most of his relatives lack of affection and support.

He had a big family in Canada mostly on his mother's
side. There were over twenty cousins, tall handsome young
men who were all the offspring of short Russian émigré parents. This miraculous transformation was attributed to the

virtues of the North American soil and more realistically to the abundance of good food. Under the influence of his more religious relatives, George did his Bar Mitzvah in Hebrew, and in spite of ups and downs, he retained a solid belief in God and a pride in being Jewish throughout his life.

George grew into a boisterous, lanky adolescent, and his Mother doted on him. However, his parents' business became less and less successful, while at the same time his Father's health became more precarious. They lost all of their savings in the crash of 1929. Their finances would never recover, and George's parents remained bitter about this forever. By 1935, the doctor told them that Louis would not survive if they stayed in the harsh Canadian climate.

So they sold the business, and with what little money they had, bought a car, hired a driver, and after a short stop in New York to visit Louis's brother and nephews, they drove to Los Angeles, California looking for a warmer climate and better opportunities. George was fifteen years old.

Chapter 2
Youth in California

The family settled in Hollywood, in a modest apartment on Russell Avenue near Hollywood Boulevard. Thanks to the excellent Canadian schools, George was able to skip a grade in Hollywood High School, and he graduated when he was seventeen. He said later that there were many great-looking girls in his class, one of them Lana Turner. George was very tall and terribly skinny and burning to ask Lana out, but he had no money at all and could not even offer her a soda. She never even looked at him. At this time, in order to contribute something to the family's dwindling financial reserves, George worked part-time selling fruits and vegetables in a giant market, and later he worked as a shipping clerk in a dry goods establishment. By late 1938, the family fortunes had dried up irrevocably, and at the ripe old age of 18, he found himself to be the sole breadwinner.

George soon attempted to change his career path by auditioning for the chorus of the WPA music project. However, he was instead assigned to a ditch-digging unit. According to George he "was still too young to be demoralized by this type of work. Luckily, after one day, as a result of some 'pull' at the top, I was rescued and transferred to the music project." The pay of $94.00 a month was enough for a family of three to live on and occasionally go to the movies as well. Unable to afford anything else, he had to be content with going to the movies, where he could watch gorgeous girls to his heart's content. He went as often as he could, and years later, he could still remember the names of all the stars and supporting actors of the 1930's.

At about that time, a neighbor heard George singing in the shower. The neighbor told his mother that she thought he had a beautiful voice and should take singing lessons. George was thrilled by this advice. He recalled

> To my amazement, when my voice changed it sounded like something serious, something whereby people would say 'my goodness, he should sing, he should study.' For me to study opera, which I already was in love with, was just about the most wondrous and miraculous thing that could ever have happened.

The kindly neighbor recommended Nathan Stewart, a well-known baritone with a beautiful top voice who not only sang for the San Francisco Opera, but also had established a successful vocal studio in Beverly Hills. Nate had a solid technique and a gift for teaching, and his wife was an accomplished pianist who accompanied the students. The tall young man who auditioned for him was totally unschooled, but Nate detected a dark quality in the voice that he liked. He agreed to teach George and started lessons twice a week at the going price of $5.00 an hour (later to go up to $7.00). To pay for his lessons, George worked at a fruit market and took long bus rides to get to his teacher's house. However, he felt that the results were well worth the sacrifices. George took lessons with Nate on and off over a period of five years. Little by little, he learned the basics of a reliable vocal technique that would serve him well in the future. His teacher was delighted with his progress, yet George was never satisfied, always feeling it could be better. He was always ready to repeat an exercise again and again, displaying from the very beginning an obsession with perfection which would eventually lead him to search for other teachers. But he did not forget his first mentor, and the Stewarts would have the satisfaction of being present for George's Metropolitan Opera debut in New York.

In the fall of 1937, he matriculated at Los Angeles City College, which he attended for two years. Feeling somewhat prepared by his voice lessons, he wanted a chance to perform. So George auditioned for the director of the first opera workshop in America, Dr. Hugo Strelitzer. Dr. Strelitzer, who had fled Nazi persecution in Germany, was able to bring his vast experience to young singers through this program. Forty-three years later, three years before his death, Hugo wrote of his first meeting with George.

He was one of more than a hundred students who came to audition for me and qualify for acceptance in this new unit. When he sang for me he was terribly nervous—who isn't? He was so terribly eager to be accepted, and like most young and inexperienced auditioners, he sang a song that was too high for his voice; and he cracked at the top and felt miserable. He asked me if he could audition a second time, go to some room, practice some more and then sing again for me. (Then and there I felt his burning ambition and some of the inner drive that has characterized his entire career.) Something in this young boy moved me. I liked him at first sight and felt his great sincerity. After some time, he sang again for me with the same results. He cracked on the top notes but revealed in his middle range and in the lower part of his voice some extraordinary quality, a natural and God-given velvet quality that could lead this youngster to untold heights. So, I accepted him into the opera workshop.

When he came to us, he was, musically speaking, absolutely untrained, without any musical experience during the years of his childhood, not playing any instrument, and (having) no artistic environment in his parental home that could have developed his innate musical instincts. As a matter of fact, when he sang in our chorus, he sweated blood to keep up with the rest of the group. He sang at that time—in order to make some money—at the WPA Music Project in the chorus—and a few of the chorus members who later sang with George in my Hollywood Bowl Chorus told me how hard George had to work to learn music, up to that date, totally unknown to him. In other words, George had to work from scratch—the gods did not drop the musical 'goodies' into his lap. But something else happened in those first few years when he was at the opera workshop—he outgrew his young adulthood and became a thinking human being, with an ever growing love for the tasks set for him and a genuine love for the music to which he devoted every bit of his life. He was ambitious as all talented men are—but with him there was more than that ambition—it was an almost missionary zeal to build and develop his many talents and setting for himself the highest goals. His first roles in our opera productions were small, but he grew very fast into bigger and then even leading parts in which he revealed an amazing sense for the stage and a dramatic instinct that was in his blood and cannot be taught. I believe that those years with me at City College laid all the foundations on which, years later, a man named George London conquered the musical and operatic world.

It can be argued that Hugo wrote with hindsight because he knew all about George's career when he wrote this letter. But having had a long operatic career in Germany before he came to California in the early 1930's, Hugo knew what he was talking about. He did teach George an invaluable repertory of music, languages, and interpretation; and George studied with him for close to eight years. George said later that he was immensely indebted to Hugo Strelitzer and the opera workshop.

In 1968, George recalled that he had sort of become the local bass-baritone around L.A. Then came the glorious moment when he made his debut, his first solo appearance before the public. It was in a production of *The Vagabond King* by Rudolf Friml. It opened on Christmas night 1939, and George had been assigned the role of the Herald of Burgundy, who had a short but energetic scene in which he comes in with a huge broadsword and announces to François Villon and his followers that the Duke of Burgundy is just going to burn the hell out of them unless they surrender. This was all done very forcefully with all of the power and conviction of a nineteen-year-old. George also became interested in makeup during this time because he had to wear a beard and a moustache that had been put on by the makeup artist. From that day on, he realized the importance of makeup because he was transformed from a callow youth of nineteen into somebody with a beard and a moustache looking at least twenty.

During the performance of the *Vagabond King*, George's acting did not go quite as planned:

> I entered, and I planted my broadsword firmly down onto the stage, and I thundered out my lines; and then I had to leave. Now, in order to leave I had to take my sword with me, but what had happened, this is God's honest truth, the sword went into a crack between two planks; and I couldn't get it out. It took at least twenty seconds to get it out and that seems like two hours when you are in a spot like that. Of course, the audience collapsed in gales of laughter, but this was the baptism of fire because it prepared me for all the horrors that would happen to me in opera later on.

That same year George decided to give up his solo career for financial reasons. He was better paid for singing in the chorus at the Hollywood Bowl than he was for the solo job. This job also gave him wonderful experience. George sang in the chorus of *Prince Igor*; he sang in *Aida;* he sang in *Carmen*. George recounted this experience during the production of Aida in which he was a priest: "I remember waiting for the moment of my entrance and the part of the basso, the part of Ramfis, was sung by a young American bass by the name of Douglas Beaty. He was a tall imposing man. He had a fine voice, and with the kind of a studied bonhomie that an arrived singer sometimes displays toward a tyro, he said, 'What is your ambition?' And I said, 'My ambition is one day to sing the title role of *Boris Godunov*.' He replied rather wistfully, "Ah! That is the ambition of us all." Little did George realize that approximately ten years later in Vienna, he would indeed have the honor and the thrill of singing *Boris Godunov*.

While he was at City College, and for a long time after, George was in endless financial difficulties. After the family moved to California, his father would never work again. He tried various jobs without success, but soon became very bitter and obsessed with a variety of extreme diets he believed would preserve his health. George's mother took up sewing and various other jobs to keep them going, and George was forever grateful to her. She told him that she stayed with his father because of him, her beloved son. This laid the foundation for what he called "my Jewish guilt feelings," which he carried throughout his life.

Perhaps these feelings of guilt had something to do with his total dedication to his work from the very beginning. He set out to "make it" against terrible odds: he had to take lessons, had to support his parents from the time he was eighteen, had to get more musical experience, and at the same time had to accept whatever paying jobs he could get. He never forgot his struggles and later did everything possible to provide help for other young singers.

He resented having so little money most of all because he could not afford dates with girls. He felt awkward, too thin, and unattractive; and since he could not take his date to a decent restaurant or pick her up in a car, he knew that he did not have a chance with the girls who appealed to him. He was most self-conscious about his ill-fitting clothes and his somewhat protruding lower teeth. He resented his parents' neglect of this problem when he was younger. With his first sizable check, he bought a new suit and had orthodontic work done as soon as he could afford it.

He never wavered in his determination, and after ten years of struggle, in October 1947, he wrote to his parents: "I have something different and unusual to offer as a singing actor. I feel so certain that within a year or two I will be in the Met and in a position to make a real career for myself."

During the decade between his audition for Strelitzer and the writing of this letter, George developed from an ignorant, albeit earnest, young man into a knowledgeable, cultured, and accomplished singer. When the opportunity was finally given to him, he was completely prepared.

It is not unusual to take this long to become a major artist. To be an important opera star it is necessary to combine many skills that take years to perfect. Of course, to start with, the voice has to have a unique and beautiful timbre, preferably of a velvety, dramatic, bell-like, or stirring quality that will distinguish it from all others. The voice has to be uniformly well produced throughout the range - high, middle, and low notes alike. This alone often takes years of study. The singer has to be able to project this voice, and he or she has to have a perfect knowledge of the words and music of a number of operatic roles in their original languages. In addition, he has to be able to act and to perform these roles in a way that will have a strong emotional impact on the audience. Then there is a physical aspect, and a charisma that is inborn. However, years of practice and an inner faith in the self will magnify these to such an extent that the artist will project from the stage and reach out to the audience in a powerful way.

Even with God-given gifts, great singers do not happen by chance. George was determined to be successful. He did not only want a "career." He wanted to be a great singer, as well as a great musician and well-rounded artist. He worked out in gyms to develop his narrow, lanky frame and grew into a powerful six-foot-two young man with a dashing figure. He decided that his name would be an impediment in the world of opera and changed it first to Burnson in October 1942, then to George London on February 21, 1949. The second name change was on the advice of Arthur Judson, president of Columbia Artists Management, who thought "Burnson" was not glamorous. He refused to take an Italian sounding name, as was the fashion then, because he thought it did not suit him. Instead he chose London because it sounded right, and Judson approved.

In the meantime, in order to survive in California George accepted any kind of job. Because he had no money for a car, he took buses in the early mornings to get to movie studios in the hope of getting work as an extra. It happened that he was hired for a chorus job in the 1942 movie "Casablanca." He can be seen in a French Foreign Legion uniform singing the "Marseillaise" in a very famous scene in Rick's cafe. He toured for some months in the chorus of the Ice Follies and fell in love with a graceful figure skater. He was required to skate out at intermission, throw a few single axels, and collect money for war bonds from the audience. But he became so ill with bronchitis that he had to quit.

Later on, George gained a good deal of stage experience through appearances with the Civic Light Opera. This company was founded by Edwin Lester in 1938. Lester's goal was to produce Light Opera in the Grand Opera manner and introduce it to Los Angeles, which he did successfully for half a century. He produced operettas like *Red Mill, Rose Marie,* and *Gypsy Baron.* He was like a father to the artists and took a liking to George. He gave him a small role in *Gypsy Baron* with John Tyer, a well-known baritone who had the lead. John Tyer remembers that George, who was engaged for the supporting role of Rudy, was so nervous that he vocalized endlessly before his short appearance.

Even with this success, London knew that he had to move to the East Coast. Since the 1940's to the present, New York has been known as the epicenter of classical music in the United States. No one could hope to launch an important career without the help of a prominent manager, and prominent managers worked out of New York.

Without money, George's only hope to get there was to be hired as a cast member in a show that would tour the United States and make it to New York. So he was thrilled when Lester engaged him to play Ali-Ben-Ali in a touring company of *The Desert Song,* an operetta by Sigmund Romberg. He said good-bye to his parents and promised to his distressed mother that he would write often. He kept his word, and for the rest of his life he wrote to his parents every week without fail.

In a 1968 speech, George recalled:

> I came to New York in 1946 in a touring company of *The Desert Song.* Don't assume that I played the lead, nothing of the kind. I played the second lead, an Arab chief called Ali-Ben-Ali, and I had one song. I did pretty well with it. I got good notices, and when we came into New York I got very good notices, though the show it-self was not so well received. The headline in *The New York Times* was 'Deserted Song.' That gives some idea of the production and the condition it was in after six months playing one-night stands. Arthur Judson, the powerful President of Columbia Artists Management happened to hear me in this performance. God knows whatever took him to the City Center to hear *The Desert Song* but he did, and he signed me to a contract with Columbia Artists.

This represented an enormous step forward. George was no longer alone, hoping for a possible engagement. He now had his own manager and was backed by a large and well-established organization that was working for him. Columbia Artists Management was one of the most important talent agencies in the United States and was known all over Europe as well. Arthur Judson and the Vice-President Bill Judd were feared and respected in the music business.

At first, engagements were slow to come, and his father's

brother, Nat Burnstein, lent him some money against his future earnings. George would say later, "Uncle Nat was the only person who had confidence in my future, and the only one willing to help me." No one else ever helped.

Thanks to the loan, he was able to take lessons with a famous Italian teacher, Enrico Rosati, and get coaching lessons with Peter Herman Adler, a conductor with great experience in a wide repertoire who also happened to be a refugee from the Nazis.

Little by little, there were sporadic appearances with orchestras, like a Verdi *Requiem* in Dallas conducted by Antal Dorati on November 25, 1946. This was George's first important engagement, and he received a good review. George wrote to his parents:

> The review should do me no harm. Columbia should be pleased, since they attached a lot of importance to this appearance. There was a small fire under the stage which the critic mentioned, but I sat through the whole thing without realizing anything was wrong. The other soloists all smelled the smoke. I smelled nothing. I guess I was too absorbed in the music.

Toni Dorati had engaged a well-known Hungarian bass to sing the part, but he could not get his visa in time so George got the part. Dorati was so impressed and fascinated by the young American that he did not have the heart to send him back, even when the Hungarian arrived after all. He did not regret it, for the concert was a great success. Toni and George remained close friends throughout their lives.

George also sang a few recitals with the Community Concerts, a part of Columbia Artists that arranged concert series throughout the United States long before the arrival of television. These concerts were sponsored and financed by local organizations that wanted to increase the musical life in their town on a nonprofit basis. Leading citizens formed an association and raised money by subscription. Then Columbia

Concerts came and sold a series package to the Community Concerts Association in each city. Because most cities did not have very large budgets, Columbia sold them a package of three or four events, including well-known names and talented newcomers. This was a way to introduce new artists to the concert circuit.

George recalled that before he was given a contract with Columbia Artists, Arthur Judson had also just signed another young tenor by the name of Mario Lanza, and Judson didn't know what to do with him at the time. George had met Mario Lanza in Los Angeles in 1944, where they became good friends and remained in touch for years although their lives would take different paths. Judson also managed a young soprano from Vancouver by the name of Frances Yeend from Vancouver, a girl with a glorious voice. Somebody in the corporation got the bright idea to put these three youngsters together, and they were dubbed the Bel Canto Trio. The Trio toured the United States, Canada, and Mexico for one entire season in a repertoire consisting of some of the great operatic trios, duets, and solo arias. During the season of 1947-48, the trio sang over a 86 concerts from coast to coast, from just south of the Arctic Circle down to the heart of Mexico. This seems almost impossible, but when you are that young and that ambitious, nothing is too difficult.

Mario refused to fly, and while the soprano and accompanist were winging their way to various destinations, George would be sweating out horrid train and bus trips with the tenor. One of these was a journey in a dilapidated bus from Torreon in the north of Mexico down to Mexico City. The heat was intolerable, the interior stank, and the bus became more crowded after each stop because of an increasing number of passengers who traveled with livestock, including goats, pigs and chickens. Mario and George were fortified with a gallon of the local wine and, as the journey progressed, they began to become more and more oblivious to their surroundings. They proceeded to get roaring drunk and gave vent to

spontaneous operatic outbursts that were greeted with enthusiastic applause by the peasants. The two reached Mexico
City in a state of euphoria and staggered into the lobby of
the hotel to the horror and dismay of Miss Yeend and the
pianist, who were nervous about their late arrival just one
hour before the concert. The concert was not a total disgrace,
but it was not the trio's finest either. Furious, Frances refused
to speak to the men for several days after that.

In 1948 at the end of that tour, Mario decided to pursue
a career in the movies, and he was snapped up immediately.
Frances went on to operatic activities, and George decided
that the time had come to get down to serious work on his
operatic career. Until then he had sung only sporadic performances of opera, although he had quite a good deal of experience on the stage.

The success of these talented young people still in their
mid-twenties and with exceptionally beautiful voices was extraordinary, and to this day people who heard them cannot
forget these concerts.

Unfortunately, there are no recorded tapes of any of the
recitals except an unsuccessful short excerpt from *La Boheme*.
This was taken from an audition by the three for a television
show. During the tour with the Bel Canto Trio, George at last
made some money, although as the baritone and least known
of the three he was also paid the least. He received two hundred and fifty dollars per performance, the tenor received five
hundred, and Frances Yeend seven hundred and fifty dollars. The fee of the pianist, Joseph Blatt, who was also their
coach, is not recorded. The three had great times and a lot
of fun together. They enjoyed their success, yet all of them
knew this was just a first step. George was happy to be able
to send $100.00 with his weekly letter to his mother from
one of the stopovers in the hope that "she could manage until
the end of the month."

He continued to improve his knowledge of repertoire. In
1948, he sought out a Russian bass-baritone by the name of

George Doubrovsky. He was a younger colleague of Chaliapin, a legendary Russian bass, and he was a product of a school of acting that was typical of the Russian Lyric Theater and also of the Moscow Art Theater. George went to Doubrovsky and studied *Boris Godunov*, Scarpia in *Tosca*, and also Mëphistophélès in *Faust*. In these, George worked with Dubrovsky on every movement and every gesture. George knew exactly what the people working with him were going to do, and he was ready to do these parts. He was ready to work the next day if it was necessary.

One of the parts that he studied prior to leaving for Europe was the part of Escamillo in *Carmen*, but this was a less successful venture. For his part, George went to a Spanish ballet master to study the toreador. He thought that most Escamillos were decidedly un-Spanish in their deportment, and he wanted to be authentic. According to George:

> Well, my ballet master got carried away with this; he had never worked with a singer before so he showed me how to walk and to gesture like a Spaniard, like a bullfighter, and this was all to the good. However, he studded the aria with so many leaps, lunges, twists, and turns that at the end of each session I was a candidate for an oxygen tent.

When he sang Escamillo for the first time in Vienna, his Carmen was the distinguished Italian-American soprano Dusolina Giannini, and she didn't hesitate to tell George, the younger colleague, that he was making his life unnecessarily difficult. She told George to cut out a lot of the business and stand there and sing. She instructed him to think and not carry on like a crazy man. So George cut out a lot of the calisthenics, and as a result, his vocal performance improved considerably.

He was well aware that he would get ahead only if he went to Europe and auditioned for opera houses there, primarily in Germany and Austria. In the 1940's, more than today when there are a number of regional companies in the United States and Canada, opera singers could obtain experience in their craft only by being engaged by one of the numerous opera houses in Germany, where performances were given every night throughout the year. Every large city in Germany has an opera house. Singers had the opportunity to perform several times a week in a variety of repertoire. Moreover, George was convinced that he would only get a good offer for principal parts at the Metropolitan Opera if he was successful in Europe.

So once again he borrowed money from Uncle Nat - a thousand dollars, which he added to two thousand dollars that he had saved. He then booked a passage to Europe on the SS Caronia in June 1949.

Chapter 3
Europe

The weather during the crossing was unusually stormy for the season, but George, not hampered by seasickness, spent most of the time in the dining room sampling the great food. The only other family, who regularly came for meals with their young son, had heard that the tall young man was a singer, but the boy did not dare to speak to him. Years later the young boy, Martin Bernheimer, would become a Pulitzer Prize winning journalist, and the two men's paths would cross again as performer and music critic.

George arrived in Paris, well nourished and rested. He remembered in a speech to his students that he called an agent in Vienna who had been recommended by his brother, who was an accompanist in the United States. George called this agent, Martin Taubman, and said, "I know you have heard about me from your brother. I am in Paris and I would like to sing for you. Shall I come to Vienna?" Taubman replied, "No, stay in Paris. I am going to be there in two days."

So Martin Taubman came to Paris. George auditioned for him and evidently Taubman liked his audition. He said:

> The Vienna Opera is doing a series of guest appearances in Brussels currently. I suggest that we get on the train tomorrow and go over. Let's see if I can arrange an audition for you. I can't promise a thing; but I think it is not a big trip, and there is not a great risk.

The next day Taubman and George went to Brussels and

ended up at the Palais des Beaux Arts where the company was giving their performances. They entered a rehearsal room where they were rehearsing *The Marriage of Figaro*.

By 1949, many people had heard about the fabulous Mozart ensemble of the postwar Vienna State Opera. The big opera house had been bombed out in the closing days of the war in 1945, but no sooner had the last shot been fired than the company moved into the small eight-hundred-seat Theater-an-der-Wien. This theater was famous because Beethoven's *Fidelio* was first performed there, as well as many of the first performances of the famous operettas by Franz Lehár. Several of the great singers from eastern countries fled ahead of the Red Army and some Austrian and German singers of the highest quality were in Vienna and couldn't get out, so together they formed an ensemble, one of the greatest operatic ensembles in the history of Vienna and certainly in the history of the operatic world.

> It was a rehearsal of just such an ensemble that I witnessed that June afternoon in 1949, and it was a revelation for me. I couldn't imagine that Mozart could be done that way. I was just bowled over, enchanted. When the rehearsal was over, Mr. Taubman got up and went over to Karl Bohm, the great conductor, and he said, 'I have a young American baritone here; I know you are very tired but could you hear him?' Well, Böhm indeed was tired, but he said, 'All right, I will hear him'.

In the meantime, the artists had left the rehearsal room and George started to sing. The first thing he sang was the Toreador song, and he had sung about ten measures of it when the door opened and all of the great singers of the Vienna Opera ensemble came back into the room and stood in a semi-circle facing him. When George got through the aria, they all applauded. Taubman said that he was certain that no matter how many years George sang, he would never receive a greater compliment, and that was true.

George was asked to perform one aria, then another, and then every piece he had prepared. He was feeling rather good but couldn't help noticing that Dr. Franz Salmhofer, the director of the Vienna Opera who sat next to Karl Bohm, kept shaking his head. He became seriously worried and wondered what could be wrong. "It can't be that bad if the other singers like me," he thought. When the audition was over, he asked Taubman about this, and he replied: "Salmhofer was just shaking his head and mumbling, 'What a voice, what a voice,' and they are offering you a contract with the Vienna Opera for four months starting with the opening of this season in September."

George was incredibly excited and wrote to his parents: "This is the first time in Mr. Taubman's memory that an American singer was offered an engagement simply on the basis of one audition. I am the only American singer who will sing with the Vienna Opera in the five years since the war."

As soon as his contract was signed, George went to Vienna and settled down in the cozy Pension Schneider, not far from the Theater-an-der-Wien, the theater where he would soon perform. He started intensive coaching of all the roles that he was scheduled to sing in the upcoming season and also took a crash course in German, which he did not know at all.

One of his favorite stories from this time was about a short vacation he took in Salzburg some weeks before the Vienna opening. Feeling good about the future, he decided to have a few days of rest. With his friend Bobby Halmi, he drove the short distance from Vienna to Salzburg. The two young men were determined to have a good time, and so they went to a well-known nightclub. They made the acquaintance of a pretty blonde. Right away, to impress the young girl, Bobby, who was acting as interpreter, boasted about George's future at the Vienna Opera. When the girl expressed some doubts, Bobby went over to the orchestra and convinced them to play for George. So George got up and gave a stentorian and impassioned rendition of Tosti's "Mattinata." There was tremendous applause, the girl was overcome with admiration, and the evening was a huge success.

Encouraged by their good fortune, the two young men decided to go back to the same restaurant on the next day. They met another pretty blonde and enacted the same scenario. However, when George launched into the first phrases of an equally fervent "Mattinata," he saw to his horror that the girl from the previous night was sitting at another table with a huge grin on her face. These youthful pranks eased some of the tension that was building up as the date for his debut approached.

George London's "marriage" with the Vienna Opera would be a happy one for both. The young American did not expect that his wish to be engaged in a European opera house would bring him directly to the Vienna State Opera. He was coming to a city where a special artistic experience was extremely important to the people, even more important than during times of affluence. The wounds of the Second World War were present everywhere. Austria was still a defeated, occupied country even though it had become a separate state again. The victorious allies had divided Austria into four Zones: the western part was occupied by the Soviets and the rest of the country was occupied by the Americans, the English, and the French. There was a strictly controlled border in between these zones. Vienna, the capital, was administered by the four victorious countries together, and the population had grown accustomed to the sight of the legendary "Four in a Jeep," soldiers from each of the occupying countries patrolling the city. Little by little, life had returned to normal, but there was still a lack of many daily necessities; many items were simply not available. Only a few motels or restaurants were open, and most Austrians would not have been able to afford them anyway. There were hardly any private cars; people got around in streetcars or very old-fashioned taxis.

In contrast, the cultural life was thriving. The theaters were sold out and the concert halls were packed. Vienna was once again the capital of the music world. Many famous artists found their way to Vienna, proving that little Austria was once again on the way to becoming an important cultural power. Thus, the great conductor Bruno Walter took the Vienna Philharmonic on a tour to London and Edinburgh, and there were also performances in Paris, London, Brussels, and Italy that were greeted with huge success.

The Vienna Opera was not only very rich in tradition, but it was also one of the last important ensemble theaters. There was a performance every day for 10 months from September until June. It was a company with the greatest singers of that time and with a diverse repertoire. The operas by Mozart, Wagner and Richard Strauss were the mainstay along with the big German operas from *Fidelio* to *Palestrina*; but Italian, French, and important Russian repertoire was also performed regularly. However, all of these operas were always sung in German.

Since the singers came from a variety of European countries, it created an interesting mix of voices and temperaments. The highest aspiration for a European singer was to be engaged at the Vienna State Opera. There were guest appearances at times, but they were the exception. Unlike today, there was no constant international travel for the artists. The aim of the opera house was to be able to cast the important repertoire with its own roster, to have its own style, and to have an unmistakable artistic identity. This was also achieved by the conductors who worked in the opera house, who were committed to the quality and special style of the company. During the postwar years, the conductors were mostly Joseph Krips and Rudolf Moralt and, of course, Karl Böhm, who had been General Manager since 1942. In 1947, Clemens, Krauss, and Hans Knapperstbusch returned to the Vienna Opera. After the war, Franz Salmhofer and Egon Hilbert became the directors of the opera house.

When George London came to Vienna, the State Opera was in a special situation because of another circumstance. The opera house, which had been inaugurated in 1869 on the Ringstrasse, was hit by bombs during the war and burned down on March 12, 1945. Although there had not been any performances since 1944 because of the war, the destruction of the opera house touched the Viennese deeply. The proud building had always been more than just a theater; it was a symbol of identity. The house's reopening became the first and most important goal after the occupation of Vienna by the Russians. Even before the Second World War was officially ended, the curtain came up in the Volksoper, Vienna's second opera house, on May 1, 1945 with Mozart's *Marriage of Figaro* conducted by Joseph Krips. The Viennese celebrated the resurrection of opera and the beginning of a new era in their destroyed and occupied city.

The reconstruction of the big opera house seemed impossible, but situated not far from it was the Theater-an-der-Wien, which had a historic past. Emanuel Schikaneder, the author of the libretto of Mozart's *Magic Flute*, had built this theater at the beginning of the nineteenth century. At that time, it was known as the most beautiful and modern theater in the Austrian Empire. Throughout the years it had been the home of important performances including the first *Fidelio* in 1805 as well as the operettas of Franz Lehar. Now, with some necessary renovations, it would become the makeshift quarters of the Vienna State Opera. The opening of *Fidelio* on October 6, 1945 was the beginning of ten "temporary" years, which were without a doubt, one of the most extraordinary chapters of Vienna's operatic history.

The size of Theater-an-der-Wien (800 seats) required more inventive productions, for both the stage and the orchestra pit were small. Because of the hardships during the postwar times, they could not afford complicated staging or expensive scenery and costumes. This had some advantages, for it forced simplicity, concentration, and attention to the basics.

Since many amenities were missing, the happenings on the stage and in the orchestra were more important. There was no need for great gestures, but for personal intensity, truth, and immediacy. Because life outside of the theater was so difficult and full of problems, it seemed to be even more important for the artistic experience to be meaningful.

George made his debut at the Vienna State Opera (in the Theater-an-der-Wien) in September of 1949 as Amonasro in *Aida*, a role which he had never sung before in his life. His repertoire was pretty sparse at the time, so when they asked what he could do, George mentioned Amonasro as a part that he knew. And the director said, "Marvelous, we need an Amonasro right at the beginning of the season. It will be your debut role." George had no stage rehearsal. He did have one short rehearsal with a pianist in a room; this was all the preparation he had to make his debut with one of the great opera companies in the world.

Nobody knew the truth except George's few close friends. During the second act there was some stage confusion some of the time, the chorus and George did not have the same idea about where they should be. But the way George behaved the audience would have thought that the chorus was wrong.

One of the old-timers of the Vienna Opera, a character singer who had been there many years, came backstage afterwards, took George aside, and said, "You dog, you could only have done that with your American nerves." But London knew his way around the stage, and the stage experience that he had had in the past, even though it was not in that particular role, came in handy.

Friend and music critic Gottfried Kraus wrote:

Later on, George London often said that he understood immediately the special atmosphere of the Theater-an-der-Wien. The young American had never experienced an opera company of this kind. Youthful, slender, elegant, and somehow exotic, he looked not only different than the singers that the Viennese knew, but his voice also had a different, foreign timbre. He moved differently and everything that he did seemed confident and natural. He always seemed spontaneous and relaxed towards his colleagues and towards his fans, who soon besieged the artist's entrance after each performance. Many of his colleagues were a little jealous of his laidback style, but when they knew him better, they soon realized how much discipline, training, and hard work was hidden behind this casual exterior. It was remarkable that each role he sang during those early weeks were his first performances of the parts.

My first impression in *Aida* remains unforgettable. Amonasro's "Suo padre" was performed with an incomparable mixture of warmth, pride, and menace. This was not only a new, unusual voice, but a new sound and a new presence with fascinating gestures and articulation. Just a few days later, George London's youthful, elegant, and virile Escamillo made a similar impression. He sang in perfect French during a routine repertoire performance of *Carmen*, sung in German as was the custom by the rest of the cast.

During the following weeks George London conquered role after role and a firm place in the ensemble and in the favor of the Vienna public, which did not begrudge him the fact that he alone sang his parts in the original languages. On the contrary, we were fascinated that he knew how to vary his characterizations with his voice and language style and delineate his figure's stage presence down to the smallest gestures.

After Amonasro and Escamillo, came Galitzki in Borodin's *Prinz Igor*, a gripping character study. And at the beginning of October, for the first time, George London sang the four villains in the *Tales of Hoffman* and coined for years a performance which became one of the unforgotten highpoints of the Vienna ensemble.

During that first season in Vienna, London became the

darling of the fourth balcony, which were the cheapest seats, occupied by the youngest fans. He sang quite a variety of parts. He sang *Méphistophélès* as well as the four villains in *The Tales of Hoffmann*, all with great success. In the Venetian act, he had rehearsed with a wonderful singer by the name of Sena Jurinac, who happened to be slim and beautiful. George rehearsed thoroughly with her and the night of the performance he sang his aria. Then the orchestra came in with two brisk chords. He turned to face his beautiful soprano and instead entered a small, heavy cruiser dressed up like a woman. According to George she was

> the fattest soprano I had ever seen in my life! Nobody had told me about her. Sena had gotten sick and there she was. It really almost threw me.

On the recommendation of Martin Taubman, who became George's European manager, George was invited to dinner by Henry Pleasants and his wife Ginny, who were some of Taubman's compatriots in Vienna. Henry was then liaison officer between the U.S. High Commission and the Austrian government, as well as the musical correspondent for *The New York Times*. Henry and George discussed singing and opera, and George (who had yet to make his debut) proceeded to talk in detail about his future plans. He spoke of *Don Giovanni, Boris Godunov*, all the parts he was going to sing and about "the voice" that he had been given. He always spoke of "the voice" in the third person. When he was gone, Henry, irked but impressed, turned to Ginny and said: "The cocky little bastard! You know, he might just do it all."

Through Henry, George met other Americans working in Vienna, most of them journalists. George loved to talk politics with them and entertain them with jokes. Henry, Ginny, Simon Bourgin, and Franz Spelman (the latter two being correspondents for *Time* and *Newsweek* respectively) witnessed his amazing success and became his close friends.

The entire American press corps attended his performances and applauded their young compatriot.

In November 1949, he gave his first recital in Vienna. It was a triumph. He wrote to his parents:

> I've never in my life experienced anything like the applause, the shouting and the stamping of feet that I received at the end of my program. I had to take so many bows I lost count of them.

Gottfried Kraus describes his own view of the recital:

> Then I got to know George London as a recitalist. He gave a demonstration of his diversity in the Brahmssaal of the Vienna Musikverein, the most venerated hall for lieder. The program consisted of three Baroque arias, a Schubert group sung in flawless German, several songs by Duparc, and ended with Negro spirituals. Scattered throughout were arias with promising, impressive interpretations of forthcoming opera roles: Boris, Prince Igor, and Iago. The critic of the *Vienna Daily* proclaimed 'Triumph of a voice.' With the effect of this flowing dark voice, whatever was promised by George London's opera performances was confirmed in the concert hall. It is a revelation to once again meet an unforgettable voice after so many years.
>
> There was no question anymore; Vienna understood that an extraordinary career had begun. The management of the Staatsoper was smart and enlightened enough to give George London the opportunity to prove himself in the great bass-baritone roles. In the course of one week in December, London sang for the first time the title part in *Boris Godunov* at the Theater-an-der-Wien and Mephistopholes in *Faust* at the Vienna Volksoper. A greater contrast seems almost unthinkable. George London's Mephisto was not just a mere stage devil, performing in French, he transformed himself into an elegant seducer who took a hellish pleasure in dazzling

not only Faust and Marguerite, but also Dame Marthe Schwerlein with his craft. Then came (the opera) *Boris Godunov* and he created a completely new interpretation of the role. Here again his diction, the original language, and his dark voice, equally expressive throughout all registers, a huge impact. But above all, you were moved by the human dimension which London gave to the character. His Boris was not a cruel, unpredictable despot, but a profoundly lonely, grief-stricken man who became guilty for political reasons and was destroyed by his guilt.

Success did not corrupt George and never would. Again he wrote to his parents:

> I can't really believe that I deserve that kind of success and ovation. This is not false modesty on my part. It's just that my demands upon myself are even much greater; I am very, very far from being able to sit back and be satisfied at all. In any event I am very happy and very fortunate and feel even more the need to work and study and constantly improve.

George remembered this period in the program notes that he wrote in 1964 for the *Boris Godunov* recording: everywhere he went his steps were dogged by autograph hunters. He had quickly become somewhat of a sensation. It was this unusual state of affairs which gave London the courage to request a performance of *Boris Godunov* at the Theater-an-der-Wien. It was pointed out to him that priority for the principal role in this opera went to either of two distinguished senior colleagues of the company, Ludwig Weber and Paul Schöffler. So George waited patiently, though without much hope; however, early in December he was called in by the director and told that on Christmas night he would sing his first Boris.

In those early, critical days, George was surely protected

by a most indulgent providence. He sang his first Boris with only one orchestra rehearsal and little help from the stage director (whose name he managed to forget). He was honored at the performance by the presence of the American minister (later ambassador) Walter Donnelly and his staff, as well as the entire American press corps. Since Vienna was then still occupied by the Four Powers, someone quipped that had the Russians decided that night to take over the city, there would have been no Americans around to report on it. As George made his lengthy entrance in the Coronation Scene, he saw that the two front rows of the Theater-an-der-Wien were filled with Russian officers in white dress uniforms. After the performance, a group of Russian officers and civilians came backstage and congratulated him enthusiastically in Russian. They seemed chagrined when he explained, through an interpreter, that his knowledge of their language was pretty much confined to the Pushkin libretto.

It was after this performance that George decided that he would someday sing *Boris Godunov* in Moscow. Gottfried Kraus writes:

> I never forgot my first impression after his Boris and even now, half a century later, I can hardly understand how a twenty-nine-year-old without a stage director could achieve such a degree of maturity and conviction in this role in his first stage interpretation. No doubt, George London had a special connection to this role due to his origins and his nature. Boris was not an opera character for him, but a sort of lifelong assignment which culminated in his historic performance at the Bolshoi Theater in Moscow. But even then, in the December 1949 performance, there was a foreboding of this event.

The success of this debut which was celebrated enthusiastically by the public and also by the critics was the highpoint of these first Vienna months. The young singer became a star in the shortest possible time, and his success was soon talked about elsewhere. In the summer of 1950, he performed *Figaro* in Edinburgh. Previously in June of the same year, Herbert von Karajan had engaged him to record this same opera with the Vienna ensemble, this time in the role of the Count. This recording with Elisabeth Schwarzkopf, Irmgard Seefried, Sena Jurinac, and Erich Kunz remains to this day a landmark in the opera catalogue.

During the previous weeks, London had sung his repertoire at the Theater-an-der-Wien. According to his contract, he was not paid by the performance, but by the month. In those days, like every true member of the ensemble, he was obliged to perform small parts as well.

Therefore his first Mozart role in Vienna was not in *Figaro*, but in a performance of the *Magic Flute* in September 1950, in which he sang the "Sprecher." In October, the Opera produced *Eugene Onegin*, which had been absent from the repertoire for many years, especially for George London. The staging was simple, but with real atmosphere, three singers dominated the performance with their great personalities: Ljuba Welitsch, retuning from her triumph as Salome in New York; the incomparable Mozart tenor Anton Dermota; and, as the star of the evening, George London as Onegin.

Gottfried Kraus wrote:

> No one who saw and heard him in this role can ever forget it. The fact that he was so young conformed exactly to the description of Pushkin. His elegance and virility made the romantic young girl's letter completely believable. But above all he managed to make his transformation into a tragic figure and his passionate declaration at the end plausible.

During following years, the Theater-an-der-Wien programmed *Eugene Onegin* only when George London was in Vienna, and Ljuba Welitsch was usually the Tatiana. But in one of the early performances a very young soprano, aged

24, took the place of the ailing Welitsch. Her name was Leonie Rysanek, and her beautiful, exciting performance was the forerunner to their many great appearances together.

London performed his varied repertoire in Vienna until the end of 1950. In addition, he sang the Verdi Requiem with Karajan in the *Musikverein*, another recital and two arias from *Figaro*, and Leporello's Aria from *Don Giovanni* during a Mozart Concert. These were probably the last quiet Vienna months before the demands of his international career. 1951 would be the year of the Amfortas in Bayreuth, his debut in *Fidelio* at La Scala with Karajan, and the debut at the Metropolitan with Amonasro in November. But in October, under the baton of Clemens Kraus, George London became the owner of another role, the title part of *Don Giovanni* of which he gave the definitive interpretation of his generation.

Gottfried Kraus continued:

My first impression remains the decisive one. George London's Don Giovanni was young, elegant, enthusiastic, an aristocrat who loves life and does not accept any rules. He is a man who loves women. Mozart's Don Giovanni is not a show off macho, not a cad, and definitely not a cynic. His fate is that he likes every woman, young or old, beautiful or not as Leporello says. There is room for every woman in his heart, and he wants to experience how each one will react to his courtship. Otherwise how can one understand the tenderness with which Mozart shows the Don's meeting with Zerlina. Even when he meets Elvira without recognizing her, his voice vibrates with warmth and tender expectation at first. There has never been another interpretation of Mozart's incomparable figure which made me understand his character the way it was back then at the Theater-an-der-Wien.

The newspaper "Neues Osterreich" wrote: "This is the

way that Mozart's first Don Giovanni might have looked; London shows him as a youth, a bewitching gentleman whose thousand and three conquests are believable in spite of his youth"

London's life in Vienna was not restricted to opera. With success on the stage there also came social rewards. At long last he could live comfortably. He rented an apartment in a stately private house; he bought a small car. Above all else, he could finally afford to take out members of the opposite sex. Gone were the days when he had trouble finding a date. The Viennese loved the tall, dark American, and he certainly responded. The years of study and yearning gave way to an explosion of *joie de vivre*. He had an active social life, made many friends, and plunged into a number of love affairs. Eventually he settled down with an attractive young soprano from the Vienna Opera with whom he had a long relationship. Very soon he acquired a command of German; he could not only speak with a perfect Austrian accent, but could also imitate the Viennese dialect.

However his career remained the focus of his life and he made sure that he was always ready and prepared for his performances. As he recalled during a master class:

> It was during my second season at the Vienna Opera [in 1950] that Rudolf Bing heard me. He heard me in *The Tales of Hoffmann* and in *Boris Godunov*, which I sang on successive nights. It is the kind of thing you do only when you are very young, and he invited me to join the Metropolitan Opera for the opening-night performance of *Aida* of the season 1951-52. So as it turned out Amonasro was my good-luck role; it was my debut role in Vienna and also at the Metropolitan. The great Italian tenor Mario del Monaco made his debut that same night, and the soprano was the incomparable Zinka Milanov.

Chapter 4
The Career Takes Off

The spring of 1950 proved to be a turning point in George London's career. Not only did Rudolf Bing have the opportunity to hear George sing in *The Tales of Hoffman*, but the great Wagner conductor, Hans Knappertsbush, also attended a performance of this opera. He was impressed and recommended George London to Wieland Wagner, who was looking for singers to perform at the re-opening of the Bayreuth Festival.

So on September 10, 1950, London was on his way to audition for the grandson of Richard Wagner. George described this extraordinary experience in a letter to his parents on the following day. He was met in Munich and driven the 100 miles to Bayreuth. He was greeted at the door by Wieland Wagner, the grandson of the composer, and the man who would be in charge of next year's Bayreuth Festival. Wagner was a vital and charming man who looked to be about 35 and of a sympathetic nature. George was entertained in "Haus Wahnfried" which Richard Wagner built many years before, and it still bears the imprint of his personality and of the colorful figures that passed through those rooms.

After a chat and tea, George was driven to his hotel where he took a bath, rested up a bit, and was then driven to the famous "Festspielhaus," the theatre that had seen the presence of so many great singers of the past. The theatre had housed all of the Bayreuth festivals since the 1870's. The house was not unusually large and ideal to sing in, but the acoustics were marvelous. During the performances, the orchestra played in a deep pit in front of the stage, but could not be seen by the audience. In spite of his long journey, George felt in good voice and rested, having slept well on the train from London.

In a Saturday Review article from 1967 about Wieland Wagner, George tells the rest of the story:

I found myself on the stage of the Festspielhaus excited and awed, singing a long audition of arias and monologues of Wotan, Hans Sachs, and Amfortas. Afterward, Wieland invited me for supper at the "Eule," a restaurant located in an alley of the old part of Bayreuth and frequented by the artists of the festival since its inception. We ate venison and talked of many things other than my audition. It was late, and I was exhausted, having sung the Count in *Figaro* in Edinburgh barely twenty-four hours earlier.

I retired to my austere room at the Bayrischer Hof, too tired to care whether I had made a good impression. At seven the next morning I was awakened by Wieland who was in the lobby asking if I would breakfast with him. Over rolls and coffee he said, 'Mr. London, I must tell you I haven't slept all night. I have searched all over Europe in vain, and I want you to sing the Wotan at the festival next year'.

I was deeply moved, utterly disarmed. Yet I knew that I had neither adequate time to prepare such a gigantic assignment nor the vocal maturity to assume such demanding roles. I told him so and hoped he would not consider me ungrateful. 'You are a phenomenon,' he said. 'You are the only singer I have ever known to refuse a part.' We settled on my singing Amfortas in Parsifal, which was to be the premiere of the 1951 festival. Wieland later drove me to the station, and I felt we had, in a short time, established a warm relationship. Indeed this ripened into a friendship which I cherished over the years we worked together.

George did not mention that 1951 was the first time the

festival would take place since it had been closed by the Allies after the war. Winifred Wagner, the widow of Richard Wagner's only son, Siegfried, had been the director of the festival during the war. She was a supporter and great admirer of Adolf Hitler, and Bayreuth had been considered a Nazi stronghold. Winifred was banished immediately after the war, the Opera House was closed and she had to give up the direction of the Wagner Festival. Six years later, her sons Wolfgang and Wieland were finally allowed to reopen the opera house.

Prior to the opening, London climbed the hill to the festival house every day for rehearsals. Although he had a car by then, he lived nearby and thought the walk would be good for his health. He enjoyed the well-kept gardens that led to the theater, built according to Richard Wagner's instructions and kept up to perfection

As usual, George prepared himself fully for the role of Amfortas. The part is not very long, but it is central to the plot and includes two lengthy outbursts that are very difficult and in which the voice is very exposed. He was particularly eager to fulfill the conductor's expectations. He sensed Knapperbusch's support from the pit and was thrilled by the sounds coming from the orchestra, particularly during the introduction to Amfortas's complaint.

During the rehearsal period, Wieland received several threatening phone calls because George London was Jewish. He paid no attention. The day before the first performance he was warned that the Holy Grail, which George would hold up in his hands during the first act, would not light up as directed in the score. Wieland again ignored the warnings and told everyone that the show would go on. George was aware of the threats; they added an extra dimension of tension to the first night, and when the moment came to hold up the Grail, he raised his arms with some trepidation. Wieland and the electricians were standing in the wings. There was a moment of suspense, then little by little the Grail lit up, and the performance continued without incident.

The performance was a tremendous success. Wieland's staging was a landmark in the development of his craft, and his *Parsifal* production was given in Bayreuth for nearly twenty years with minor modifications. George had a huge personal success and owned this role in Bayreuth over the next decade. *Parsifal* was recorded five times with George as Amfortas (1951-1963) showing the "almost intolerable intensity" (as one critic put it) of his interpretation.

After a *Parsifal* performance in 1961, he wrote to his parents: "I feel that I am able to reach people in a human way that evades most of my colleagues. It is a great satisfaction, and the people let me know that they have gotten the message."

It seemed almost prophetic that London could feel so close to this operatic character who suffered a "wound that would not heal." At the end of his life, during his final illness, he would identify with Amfortas and his impassioned plea for death and redemption.

Parsifal was given every year during the Bayreuth Festival, while other Wagner operas rotated during different summers. George returned to Bayreuth to sing Amfortas nearly every summer until 1964. In 1956, 1959, and 1961, he also performed the title role in *The Flying Dutchman*. Each appearance in the summer festival included a long rehearsal period and a commitment to a number of performances.

Even after George London's huge popularity in Vienna and the exciting success of his Bayreuth performance, the long-awaited debut at the Metropolitan Opera was not an anti-climax. Though George knew the intoxicating feeling of applause from an enthusiastic audience, for an American singer, recognition at home remains the most important.

The 1951 season's opening of a new production of *Aida* took place in the revered, old opera house on 39th Street. It was the second season of Rudolf Bing's 22 year reign as director. The house was packed. The Golden Horseshoe boxes filled with the crème of New York society, and expectations were high since the performance was marking the return of the celebrated soprano Zinka Milanov. The title role marked the debut of a most promising young tenor, Mario del Monaco, as Radames, and it was the debut of the American bass-baritone as Amonasro. London prepared perfectly for the role and used outstanding make-up and royal deportment to conquer the public at once. The next day, the critic and composer Virgil Thomson hailed George "the greatest singing actor of our times." He had become an undisputed opera star. He was just over thirty-one-years-old.

Yet most of all, George needed the approval of his parents, and this performance at the Met provided the occasion. They knew of his triumph in Vienna, and that he had a great success in Bayreuth, but those were remote places of which they had only a vague notion. Now he made sure that they would see their son with their own eyes on the stage of the most famous opera house in the United States, and not just in a small part, but in a starring role.

He arranged for his parents' trip to New York for the opening on November 13, 1951, and a picture of the three was taken after the performance. London stood, clearly elated, towering over the older couple, who were dressed in stylish new clothes. His mother was wearing a corsage of orchids, the final proof of affluence. George was no longer the lanky youth of earlier photos, but a handsome, broad-shouldered young man, obviously at ease in his well-cut tuxedo, and eager to show his good fortune to the world.

At last he had shown his parents that the long years of work and deprivation were not in vain, and that his confidence in his own abilities was more than youthful dreams. Now he would be able to support his parents in style. It was certainly a special moment of bliss for him.

He was also surrounded by many faithful friends who had come from California to witness his success. There was his first teacher, Nate Stewart and his wife Doris, Lloyd Rigler, and Larry Deutsch, who had encouraged him in the early days. And most importantly, he was supported with fierce loyalty by his new voice teacher Paola Novikova. London had met her the previous year, and she had helped him to prepare for the Amfortas role. She was a Russian refugee who taught in her studio on west 72nd Street during the winter, and migrated to Vienna in spring and summer to follow her most famous student performers like Nicolai Gedda and Irmgard Seefried among others. She had studied with the legendary baritone Batistini in her youth and had an uncanny ear, as well as a perfect knowledge of style. London took lessons with her regularly throughout the remaining years of his career.

He continued to be driven by the same competitive spirit that had gotten him this far. He took an apartment for the duration of his Met engagement, and between performances he proceeded to work daily with Novikova to prepare for forthcoming recitals and for the parts he was to sing in New York the following years: Don Giovanni, Boris Godunov, the Count in *The Marriage of Figaro*, and Scarpia in *Tosca*.

He signed his first recording contract with Columbia Records and made his first solo recording, always a great event for a young artist. And he signed an agreement with an artists' public relations management firm, a step considered essential to keep the name of George London in the news as much as possible.

During the next few years he performed all his favorite roles at the Metropolitan Opera in New York, as well as on the Met tour, and he became one of the leading bass-baritones in the company.

Chapter 5
Courtship

1954 was a year of great change in George London's life and mine as well. I came to the United States as a teenager from France during World War II with my mother and uncle. We settled in New York. My parents were Russian; I was born in Berlin, and grew up in Paris where I spent all my school years. With my multilingual background, I felt very comfortable as a refugee in cosmopolitan New York. At 19, I married a French-Russian refugee and had two sons within a few years. However this union did not last, and by 1953 we had separated. In 1954, I was 30 years old, living a very comfortable but dreary life with my little boys, a Swiss nanny, and an Irish setter.

As one of the Met's regular subscribers, I was one of many fans to hear George London in *Don Giovanni*, *Aida*, and *Tosca*. Each time I was bewitched by the velvet voice with the seemingly boundless power, and I was impressed by his forceful acting.

It never occurred to me that I would meet him. In spite of my interest in opera and my mother's close friendship with Chaliapin (the famous Russian basso) and his family, I did not know any of the current opera stars and was content to admire them from afar.

We met one Sunday evening, April 24, 1954. I had actually spent the bulk of that day lying in bed, feeling sorry for myself. I was determined to stay home with *The New York Times* and my setter Banco at my feet. My mother, who lived just a block away, arrived in a chic black suit and bright blue hat. She was perfectly groomed as always and determined to force me to get up.

"How come you're still in bed? You know you're going to Lydia Chaliapin's Easter party with me." When I answered that I did not feel like going, she became upset. "You never want to go anywhere with me, but you always tell me that you like Lydia so much. We never miss her Russian Easter party. She makes beautiful colored eggs and great *kulitsch* (a Russian cake). My friends will be there, and also Lydia's young students (she was a voice teacher). I understand that Leo Taubman, the pianist, has promised to bring George London."

It was difficult to resist my mother's arguments. She had an imperial bearing and a matching temperament, and in a clash of our personalities, she always won. We were very close, and I adored her. However, I made most major decisions without consulting her because I knew that if she disagreed, I would have a terrible time convincing her that I was right. I avoided discussing my marital problems with her, for I did not want to upset her. In fact, there was nothing she could say to relieve my anguish, and so I decided to keep silent. I was not going to fight about an ordinary Sunday afternoon party, and, after all, maybe she was right. I should go out and meet new people.

I dressed quickly in an elegant outfit that I had brought back from Paris. I remember it exactly: it was a black sheath with a white satin bolero, knotted tight under the chest, which showed off my small waist. It was a beautiful day, and we had no trouble getting a taxi which took us from my Park Avenue apartment to Lydia's at Seventh Avenue and Fifty-Fifth Street, one block from Carnegie Hall. At the entrance, Lydia greeted me affectionately and said at once: "Norechka, you must meet George London!" She took my arm and directed me toward the dining room.

At the same moment Leo Taubman, who was George's accompanist and Martin Taubman's brother, turned to

George, who was eating a succession of caviar sandwiches, and said, "There's a girl, quite a dish, who just arrived. You have to meet her."

As I walked through the crowded living room, I could see George standing in the next room. His ebullient personality seemed to fill the room. He was wearing a light-gray suit, a blue shirt, and a rather wild tie. His hair was black, very shiny, and slightly wavy. He was smooth-shaven, his skin slightly tanned (he later joked that it was from the floodlights!). As I entered we stared at each other. I caught a look of admiration in his dark-brown eyes and for a fleeting moment I felt captivated by his radiance.

We were introduced, and I remember complimenting him on a wonderful performance of his I had seen recently. He seemed pleased, and we exchanged a number of pleasant remarks. I was enchanted by his speaking voice, which did not have the booming low sound that was typical of bass singers, but had more of a caressing baritone quality, as if each word invited you to a dance. I tore myself away, thinking that I should not monopolize this important guest, and drifted toward the living room to greet friends. All of the young hopeful singers present were dying to speak to the successful star; perhaps some advice, some special touch would rub off.

I noticed that George spoke very kindly to everyone, but within minutes he was again at my side and did not leave me for the rest of his stay at the party. He sat next to me while we were eating, both of us having piled our plates full from the lavish buffet. I don't remember what we talked about. In the end he told me that, unfortunately, he had to leave early because he was going to join the Met tour and perform *Don Giovanni* the next night. But he hoped to see me again upon his return to New York.

After his departure, Lydia told me that everyone had noticed that George was attracted to me. I, too, had noticed and felt very flattered, but I dismissed any expectations, thinking that such a handsome man was bound to be a flirt and nothing more would happen, even though, with my failing marriage, I was ready for an adventure. Two days later, my maid announced that I had a call from Atlanta. I said, "I don't know anybody in Atlanta," but she said the party at the other end insisted on speaking to me. It was George. He said he wanted to see me; he would be in New York that weekend. Could I have dinner with him? I agreed, and on Friday I was waiting for him to pick me up, getting quite excited at the prospect of our date.

When I opened the door for him, he looked at me with delight. I was wearing high heels, but even at five-foot-five I had to look up into his shining eyes. We decided to have dinner at Quo Vadis, a popular restaurant on East Sixty-Third Street. For years afterward we went back there to celebrate the anniversaries of our first evening together.

It was an excellent restaurant with red-covered banquettes around the main room with beautiful flower arrangements, and a large display of tempting desserts. We were seated at the right of the entrance and ordered our meal and some red wine. And after that I don't remember anything except that George, looking straight into my eyes with great intensity, spoke on and on. He talked about himself, how had now reached a comfortable stage in his career but he did not feel happy alone. He was ready to make a permanent commitment. The woman he would marry would have to be attractive. She would have to be a lady and know how to get along in the world. She would have to love and understand music and opera, and she would have to love children. In return, he would love and worship her and give her everything he possibly could every day of his life.

I thought that either he was the greatest master of courtship since Casanova, or perhaps, just perhaps, the most extraordinary person I had ever met. My experience with postwar society, to say nothing of my ex-husband, made me skeptical, and I laughed when he told me that he had thought of me constantly since our meeting that Sunday.

I was quite ready to consent to a flirtation, but I certainly had not thought of anything more serious. Here was this man, immensely attractive and persuasive, who was already proposing to spend the rest of his life with me. I felt as if I had had too much to drink.

Still, we enjoyed each other's company so much that we did not feel like going home after dinner. He suggested we go to Upstairs at the Downstairs, a nightclub in fashion at the time. This turned out to be the only time we ever went to a nightclub together in our life! We sat in a crowded room in total darkness, listening to performers singing love songs or reciting poetry. George took my hand and, at the touch of his incredibly soft skin, I was lost. We held hands for a long, long time.

Still we could not part. He took me home to my Park Avenue apartment, and I suggested he wait for me. I would get my setter Banco, and we could walk the dog together. We walked around the block again and again. It was my turn to talk. He knew from Leo Taubman that I was separated but not divorced. I told him about my life and my two precious little boys. He was a good, supportive listener. Suddenly, it was nearly three o'clock, and reluctantly we said good-bye in front of the apartment house.

I went back home in a daze. What had happened to the down-to-earth, unemotional person I had been just the day before? I was bewitched. In one evening, George had unlocked a flow of emotions that I had carefully buried in my subconscious. Although I was profoundly moved, I thought it was still time to push these feelings back where they belonged and prevent my life from becoming incredibly complicated.

After that evening, George confided to a friend that he was crazy about a girl he had just met, that he was possessed and dreamed about her all the time. He was desperate, for he was travelling all the time and was about to leave for Vienna for many upcoming performances. He wanted to see me once

45

more before leaving and called me from Boston. "My last performance is in *Tosca*," he told me. "This is a great opera for me. Scarpia is a wonderful role; he dies at the end of the second act, so I'll be free early. It's our only chance to see each other again. The next day I have to leave for Europe." In spite of my misgivings, I did not hesitate to meet him. I was starved for attention, flattered by the urgency in his voice. After all, I reasoned, nothing had happened; furthermore, he was leaving, so that would be the end of it.

It was a short date, but long enough for us to find out how much we meant to each other after only two evenings together. In spite of the explosive character of our first date, I had concluded that it might have been a one-time event. I had little confidence in men's sincerity. I was not prepared for the wave of feelings that engulfed both of us when we met after *Tosca*. We promised to write and hoped to meet in Europe, for I was going to France in June. I planned to go to Paris first and then go on to a rented villa in Deauville for the summer. We parted with a passionate kiss full of promises and many questions.

We started a correspondence. He wrote beautifully, in a large, artistic handwriting with every letter well-formed, typical of his outgoing and generous nature. His letters told of his performances, his life in Vienna, his friends over there, and his desire to show all of this to me. I had to tear the letters up, for I did not want to leave them around, although, since we were separated, my husband was mostly absent and seemed to be relieved whenever I was busy. Otherwise I did not feel particularly guilty about my romance. Rather I felt somewhat proud that I had a distant admirer and was carrying on an illicit correspondence with him.

In June, the household left for Paris; my boys were now nine and seven, and we had to wait for the end of the school year. We had rented a summer house at the French beach resort, Deauville, and after two weeks in Paris, we moved there with Sasha, our maid, and the faithful Banco. My husband suddenly had "urgent business" in New York.

I received George's letters in a P.O. Box at the post office. He wrote that he would have some free time in August and wanted to visit me. I answered that it would be fine since I was alone, but that I could not meet him in Deauville where I knew too many people. However, there was an adjoining resort on the Normandy coast called Trouville-sur-Mer where I could reserve a room for him in a good hotel. He agreed to my suggestions—we were going to see each other again after three months of separation.

I became very agitated at the idea of seeing him again. How would it be; how would I feel? In New York we were clearly infatuated with each other. I wondered if it was love or just a passing romance, and if it would deepen when we met in France. Perhaps we would wonder why we had been attracted to each other. Three months is a long time, and in the interim we had each gone about our lives as if nothing had happened. The letters had woven a tenuous thread between us.

So I drove to Trouville full of apprehension. He had come all the way from Austria to see me. Would the passion still be there? Would he still like me? As I walked into the hotel lobby, he looked at me. The piercing black eyes became soft, light brown, and joy was dancing in them. I knew that he was thrilled to see me, and for him, at that moment, I was the most beautiful woman in the world. He had the ability to make me feel that way all the years we were together.

I was smitten all over again, and each day I waited impatiently for the time when I could be with him. We went to many restaurants along the coast and walked along the old port of Honfleur at sunset, which so many French impressionists have painted. Every hour we spent together seemed enchanted to both of us. But each time I had to go back to my household and the children, and therefore I was unable to spend as much time with him as he wanted. He begged me to come to Switzerland and spend a week with him at a resort called Arosa at the end of August.

I was terribly tempted, but hesitated. First, it was difficult for me to get away without telling anyone; but above all, I was afraid. Obviously I was in love with him, but I felt this was still just an affair that I could forget someday. If I took this trip and lived with him, there might be no way back. I knew that I was not an adventuress looking for cheap thrills. My love for George was already much more than a mutual sexual attraction. I admired his generous spirit, his zest for life, his strength mixed with gentleness, and I was in awe of his single-minded drive for perfection in his art. It was clear to me that with such a man, one did not have a "fling;" but I also wondered if I was ready to take the risks and make the sacrifices that a commitment would require.

Before George left Trouville, I told him that I would try to come to Switzerland three weeks later. I booked a plane flight to Zurich. Twice every day I would change my mind about going or not going and wrote wavering letters to George. Finally the day came, and of course I went. I was extremely nervous and yet full of wild anticipation.

The plane landed in Zurich after a short, uneventful flight. Zurich was a busy airport. The passengers were herded into a huge baggage claim area, which was separated from the public room where friends and relatives wait for them behind a large glass wall. As I was waiting for my suitcase, I could see a very tall, dark-haired man in a navy trench coat with epaulettes on his broad shoulders pacing back and forth in frenzied agitation. Apparently George was not sure I would come and was so worried that at first he did not see me. I waved and waved, and finally he recognized me. A huge smile transformed his brooding face. Again the black eyes turned light brown.

He took my luggage and escorted me to his sports car, an Austin-Healey convertible, which fortunately had the top up. It was pouring rain, and I looked in vain for windows to roll up. This particular model had plastic windows that could be attached in case of need, but George did not think the weather warranted being closed in. I settled down in the seat next to him, and we left for the hour-long drive up the mountains to Arosa. He drove like a lunatic, and I was speechless with fear at every curve. He turned to me and said: "You like *Boris Godunov*, don't you? I will sing the part of Boris for you," and proceeded to do so.

There I was, being driven at one hundred miles an hour in a downpour, getting wet and cold and being serenaded with an entire opera by a world-renowned singer who was probably catching pneumonia along with me. I thought I must have been crazy to come. I was tempted to jump out at the next stop sign, but he never slowed down. At last we were in Arosa, and we soon arrived at the hotel, where I warmed up and ate a delicious meal that lifted my spirits.

Since late August was the end of the season, we were almost alone in the hotel, and I did not feel too conspicuous. After the initial uneasiness, our week together was a time of bliss. I discovered the meaning of love and affection and trust. I began to appreciate even more the many qualities of George's character: his generosity, his absolute honesty, his sensitivity, his sense of humor, and the extraordinary vitality that he injected into everything around him.

We took long walks in the mountains, and the breathtaking sights seemed in harmony with our happiness. We talked about his life and his plans for the future. George could never make small talk; rather, he spoke about feelings, about convictions, about disappointments. He believed in what he said and was prepared to go to great lengths, if necessary, to support his beliefs.

I became acquainted with his extraordinary self-discipline. Everyday he set aside several hours to study his role in *Arabella* by Richard Strauss, which he was due to sing at the Metropolitan the following February and later record in Vienna. He was to be the male protagonist, Mandryka, a rural nobleman who falls in love with the heroine. It is musically very difficult, and he repeated one particularly difficult phrase endlessly. "Every word, every note has to be second nature to me before I can think of going on stage in a new part," he said. Years later, at the annual opening ceremonies of the Moscow Conservatory, I understood all too well when the director told the new students: "Starting a career as a singer is like entering into religion."

As our euphoric week in Arosa drew to its end, George began to tell me about the torments that assailed him. He seemed so sure of himself, but inside there were always doubts about the next role, and worries about "the voice," although he felt sure of his technique; and there was the self-inflicted torture from his quest for perfection. I discovered his addiction for late-night discourses about everything that was wrong in the world and about his personal torments, which he would completely forget the next morning when I got up greatly concerned about what he had said. I found that he wanted my complete approval, as well as my enthusiasm for anything and everything, from selecting his ties to the gifts that he bought for me. He was convinced that if he liked something, I would like it, too, as a matter of course.

During that week, he proposed to me and brushed aside my arguments about difficulties and about the children. Knowing the condition of my marriage, he did not consider divorce an insurmountable obstacle.

George told me over and over that I would be the perfect wife for him. I warned him against idealizing me and feared I could not measure up to his expectations, but he reassured me constantly. We talked about music and art, literature and politics, and found that we were stimulated by our conversations, but we could also sit together in silence enjoying each other's presence. I realized that because he expected it, he brought out the best in me. How could I not rise to the challenge of a man who treated me with such adoration and respect?

Life with him would not always be simple. Perhaps his

dedication to his career would be greater still than his love for me, but I could not refuse the extraordinary offering of living with a man of such caliber. When George asked me to become his wife, I answered, "Yes, I will with all my heart and soul."

The week in the mountains remained in our memories like a dream, but another year full of problems and turbulence would pass before marriage became a possibility. The same George London who was so disciplined and wise about his career was passionate and impulsive in private life, a typical Gemini. He convinced himself that his wishes could be fulfilled easily by day, but wrestled with his demons at night.

He believed that the two most important women in his life could not fail to like each other. He was devoted to his mother who had always encouraged him and made many sacrifices for him, particularly during the lean years in California. He was her only child and now that he was successful, she wanted to be involved constantly and often interfered in his private life and career. When he was in Europe, he felt free to do what he pleased, but during the Met season she came to New York and insisted on visiting him every day.

However, he could not imagine that she would disagree with him when he described to her all the virtues of his intended, and so he told her all about me. She was violently opposed to this marriage. All she could see was the fact that the woman was already married, had two children whom one day he might have to support, and on top of all that, she argued, the woman was probably not even Jewish.

He could set her right about the last objection, but he was dumbfounded by her reaction. He was sure that when he came to her with news of his great love she would be delighted. If he remembered her opposition to his former relationships, he dismissed it, thinking that they had not been serious, and that perhaps she had sensed that fact.

During that autumn of 1954, we saw each other only a few times, for he was on a concert tour in and out of New

York. Whenever he came to town, he stayed in the same suite at the Alden Hotel on Central Park West. He looked forward to our meetings with tremendous anticipation, but the perfect harmony of the time in Arosa was gone. My divorce was difficult and took many months. He was shattered by his mother's opposition to his marriage. He had always thought so highly of her, of her sacrifices for him during his adolescence, and he was always persuaded that when he finally chose a wife she would approve his decision without reservation. He became increasingly somber and tormented.

I could understand her objections; after all, it would be normal for her to have preferred a young girl without children for her precious son. His attitude toward me seemed to change. We could not spend much time together in order to talk and straighten things out between us, for he was always leaving for another recital. Knowing that it was difficult for him to function in an atmosphere of strife, I tried not to upset him even more. I did not press him for decisive statements and promises. He told me how much he loved me, but I wondered how strong his mother's influence would be.

George hoped to improve the situation by arranging a meeting between his mother and me. He thought she would be won over by my personality. He was scheduled to sing a performance of *Aida*, and his mother and I were to sit together in the orchestra. We met at the stage door. George introduced us, and she greeted me pleasantly. She was barely five-feet-two-inches and very slender with a good figure and shapely legs. She had dark hair and brown eyes and, in spite of her youthful figure, seemed older than her sixty-four years. There was clearly a family resemblance between her and George, except that it was hard to believe that he could be the son of such a small woman.

We went into the auditorium. To my relief, the opera started almost immediately so there was little time for small talk. George was superb in the role of Amonasro; I was totally engrossed in his performance, his great voice and perfect phrasing. But his mother looked at her watch to see how soon the opera would be over. I thought, "How can I ever get along with her?" Obviously this feeling was mutual and I certainly did not charm her in the least. We had little to say to each other during the intermissions and parted politely without much warmth on either side.

George was terribly torn and depressed. I was becoming more and more doubtful about our future. Nevertheless, I intended to go through with the divorce. I was glad to have gotten the courage to break away and leave a useless, stagnant life. By the end of November, I left for Las Vegas, Nevada.

I did not want to be away from my sons at Christmas, and so I obtained a special dispensation from the court: I could go back to New York for a week, but then would have to stay an extra week to complete the total six week stay required for a divorce.

I took a room with kitchenette in a motor inn just outside town. It was cheap—which was important as I did not have much money except for a forty-dollar daily allowance from my husband before the divorce—but at least I could take long rides in the desert behind my bungalow. At that time Las Vegas was nothing like the resort town it is today. There were some casinos where you could gamble, which I did not do, and get a very lavish and cheap buffet lunch, which I did. I economized on everything, including meals, to bring back Christmas presents for everyone. Besides riding, there was nothing to do. There was no television then, and I could not get any classical music on the radio, only country music, which I did not like. I was terribly lonely and missed my sons, Andy and Philip, acutely. I had never been separated from them for such a long time.

I spent hours exploring the shops in Las Vegas to find gifts for George and for the children. There was little choice, and my budget was limited. I had to settle for identical toy cars in different colors for the boys and a special tie case for George. I thought it was rather appropriate, as he had such a weakness for beautiful ties and traveled so much. I wished I could give him a more important present, but I simply did not have much money.

The days seemed endless until December 23 finally arrived, and the plane took me back to New York and everything I loved. Christmas with the children was wonderful. Their father was skiing in Switzerland for the holidays and would not interfere. They were delighted with their toys and many other gifts they received from my mother and other members of the family. As usual we had a beautiful tree and spent a cozy evening with much hugging, simply happy to be together.

On Christmas Day I met George. He had called me often while I was away, and we had many good conversations. We were very excited to see each other after being apart for so long.

Years later, after over twenty years of marriage, I still felt that extraordinary anticipation whenever I was to meet him after a separation. He would stride toward me on his long legs with an expression of love and admiration on his face that always made my heart beat faster.

That Christmas Day he was obviously delighted to see me and immediately handed me a little box. It contained a blue enamel locket on a chain, which he declared fitted me perfectly. In turn, he seemed very pleased with my gift. We had a short but harmonious visit, and we promised to see each other at length the next day.

When I met him the following evening, I sensed at once that there was something wrong. He was unhappy and distant. I questioned him repeatedly until he finally admitted that he had had another discussion with his mother. She thought our relationship had no future, and that I obviously did not truly care for him. We decided to put aside the heavy decision about marriage for a time and proceeded to enjoy the happiness we felt in each other's company.

George decided that I had to meet Paola Novikova. By

then she had been George's singing teacher for the past four years. The relationship between a voice teacher and his or her pupil is often very close. Singers feel a greater dependency upon their teachers than do instrumentalists because a singer carries his instrument within himself. He cannot hear himself objectively and depends on someone else's advice more than any other musician. Also, the voice changes as it develops and as the singer grows older. Therefore, most opera singers continue to take lessons throughout their careers, even when they are already well-established. The voice teacher develops a strong bond with the pupil, a bond that often becomes very personal.

Paola was informed of all the offers for new roles that George received. He was expected to discuss with her if the role was suitable for his voice and if she thought it was right for him at that current stage in his career. Since he would be studying the music with her, her approval was essential. George told me that if she did not approve, she could undermine the learning process and make it virtually impossible for him to give a good vocal rendition of the part.

With this kind of control over the career of their pupils, many teachers, including Paola, are tempted to assume control over their pupils' private lives. They reason that the singers' activities in addition to their lessons and performances will influence the quality of their work. Paola was certainly most critical about George's female interests, which she felt had to be on a special level worthy of her star pupil.

Therefore, George introduced me to her with some trepidation. The week after Christmas, he took me along to one of his lessons. He had told Paola all about me, and I knew pretty much what to expect. She was Russian, a roly-poly person with dyed red hair, white skin, and big brown eyes. She had a regal air in spite of her short size, for she had been a performer when she was young. She had tremendous musical knowledge and was without doubt one of the best teachers around. She adored George, admired his talent, and wantcd the best for him. This was so evident that I immediately liked her in spite of her theatrical greeting. Soon we chatted away in Russian. Then I sat down silently while he vocalized, and she made comments. I admired her perfect ear and her suggestions and his uncanny ability to implement immediately what she advised.

From time to time she turned to me before playing the next exercise on the piano and said with finality in Russian, "George is a genius." I nodded my approval and smiled. When we left she kissed me affectionately, and I knew she approved of me: I was the right one for him.

I was much relieved. I don't think I could have maintained a relationship with George if Paola had also been against me. George was delighted. There would be no jarring criticism from her. In fact, we were both invited to her New Year's party.

We were in a great mood that evening. We made a handsome couple, dark and fair. I was thrilled to hold his arm as we entered Paola's apartment. Evidently we were expected with a good deal of curiosity. Everyone wondered "Who is the girl George London is bringing into the inner sanctum?"

It was an international crowd, about thirty people, including several well-known singers, musicians, and accompanists (Werner Singer, Paola's husband, being one). The talk was mostly about music and opera, primarily who was singing which role during the Met season. I was well informed about those subjects and managed to talk with different groups sometimes in Russian or French when necessary. Everyone treated me with kindness and seemed to like me. George was radiant; he felt confirmed in his conviction that I was perfect for him. But we did not talk about the future; we were basking in our love for each other.

I could not help wondering what the year 1955 would bring. The next day I returned to my exile in Las Vegas in much better spirits than when I had left. Another four weeks lay ahead of me, and the time went by slowly. Finally the day came. I went to court and the divorce decree was issued. It took a little over ten minutes to erase the past years. I was once again a free woman.

Chapter 6
Marriage

"One must, in this world, love many things
To know finally what one loves best."
ISAK DINESEN

Flying back from Las Vegas, I realized that I wanted to make up the time that I had been away from my sons, and compensate for my relative neglect during the last few months. We would be together. I would love them better than ever. I had to face the fact that we had to leave the ten-room Park Avenue apartment and give notice to the governess that I could no longer afford. I was fortunate to find an apartment just two blocks away on Eighty-Fourth Street, between Park and Lexington Avenues. It was far different from what I had before. There were three tiny bedrooms and a large living-dining room, but it was in the same neighborhood, important because the boys would not have to change schools. I was delighted with our new quarters.

Now that I was divorced, I wanted to be settled in my own place with the children and not give George the feeling of being pressured into marriage. In fact, even if it had been possible, I did not think it wise to marry again immediately. After all the turmoil of the past year, I needed some time to myself to reorganize my life, and I thought that too many sudden changes would be overly stressful for Andy and Philip.

For the present I was content with loving George and being able to go out with him openly. At the time of my return from Las Vegas, he had a very busy schedule at the Metropolitan, and I was busy with moving and spending time with the children. We could not be together as much as we wanted

Unbeknownst to me, while I was in Las Vegas, George, too, had his share of aggravation. In November 1954, he wrote to his parents and specifically to his father, for his mother knew already, "about my big and serious romance." George wrote, "Nora and I were drawn to each other enormously from the moment we first met. . ." He explained that I was about to divorce, and that he had seen me over the past year. The letter continues:

> The time we spent together proved to me that I had met the woman whom I felt as destined to be my wife. As mother will confirm, she is very attractive, fairly tall, and slim, with beautiful green eyes, a wonderful smile and a luxuriant crop of dark blonde hair. She is of Russian-Jewish stock. Mother thought she was White Russian (she looks like it), but both her parents were Jewish. . . . She has had a wonderful education and a wonderful upbringing. Yet, there is absolutely nothing snobbish about her. She is completely natural and unspoiled and completely sincere. She is warm and kind and has the most serene disposition I have ever encountered. She is highly intelligent. She is tender and understanding. And in a crisis (she) has character and strength. Above all, she loves me with all her heart and wants to be for me a help and a support, a source of inspiration and strength, a refuge of tranquility and peace, and, indeed, she is all of these.

He added, "I know that you will find it an objection that she has two children. Indeed, I admit it would be more ideal if she did not, although her boys are adorable, charming and affectionate. But you see, I love Nora, and she is the woman I have been waiting for all my life, though I confess I never expected ever to meet anyone as wonderful as she." In the last paragraph he wrote, "I want my dear parents' understanding and love and support in what I am planning..." I read this letter for the first time over thirty years later.

Evidently, even though he pleaded his case so eloquently, he did not get a favorable response, for in another letter some weeks later, he tried again: "Right now she is the woman I love, the inspiration I have been so sorely needing, and I feel she is indispensable to my future happiness. If we are worthy of it, God will bless our union..."

But it seemed that nothing he said would convince his parents. When I saw him again, he was in a somber mood, and soon he told me that he was terribly tormented. His mother, whom he had always worshiped, was constantly talking against me and opposed his marriage vehemently. He could not sleep, and it was affecting his work. His mother had come to New York from their home in California and was staying at the same hotel where he was living. She would visit him in the morning at breakfast and upset him for the rest of the day with her negative attitude.

He begged me to talk to her, hoping I could change her mind about me. At first I refused, but he seemed so dejected that I agreed. I could not bear to see him so unhappy.

It was a most awkward meeting. I had not seen her since the night of *Aida*, before my divorce. Evidently I was more threatening than ever, as I was a free woman now. Our conversation was labored. When she objected to the fact that I had children, I replied that I could understand her feelings, but that if George and I married they would not be a financial burden to George for they were well provided for. I told her that, furthermore, we had not set any time for a marriage and that there were still a number of obstacles. Nothing I said seemed to have any impact on her. Finally she said, 'When you marry George you will possess him." I answered: "No one possesses another human being. I could never feel that way, and I certainly would never interfere with George's career." She remained unconvinced and I left, feeling that my visit had been futile.

On my way home I felt sorry for her in spite of my anger. There she was, sure that she was losing her only son, her famous son, because of me. She did not realize that he had grown away from her because of his fame, his talent, his travels, his taste for culture and beauty. He had changed, and she could no longer understand him, even though George took great pains to appear steadfast in his feelings toward her. In spite of everything, he remained attached to her and continued to write to her every week.

I wondered if his father was as difficult as George had warned me. I did not meet him until the following winter, and eventually we got along quite well. In spite of himself, he rather liked me and enjoyed talking with me, although our conversations were laborious because he was quite deaf and refused to wear a hearing aid. With George's mother, I eventually achieved an uneasy peace. He realized that his desire to get his parents' approval, which he had wanted so much, would remain unfulfilled. Some weeks later his mother returned to California, and his decision would be made without her.

Now the major obstacle to our wedding plans was the fact that George and the children did not know each other. Once, when I first met him, he saw the boys from a distance in the park. He said the boys were wearing identical gray flannel pants "looking very French."

During the many months of our courtship I had purposely avoided any meetings between George and the children. As long as this was just an affair, no matter how serious, I felt that it was not proper to expose the children to it.

It was spring, and George was about to leave for Vienna once again. He wanted to get married and was pressing me to set a date for the wedding. Now it was my turn to waver, and although I loved him as much as ever, I told him that I could not marry him unless I was sure that he and the boys would like each other. If there was too much friction between George and the children, life together would be impossible.

The summer provided a perfect time for a meeting. As

soon as school was over, I went to Europe with the boys as usual and spent a few weeks at my mother's house in Paris. Then George and I both made reservations at the Hotel du Lac in Brissago on Lake Maggiore in Switzerland. I traveled by train with Andy and Philip, then aged 10 and 8 respectively, and we arrived first. The hotel was beautifully located, and from the balcony of my room I looked at the glistening lake and the breathtaking landscape beyond. I was nervous; another very important step in our lives was about to take place. The perfect atmosphere of the hotel and the beauty of the site seemed to be a good omen.

George arrived by car some hours later. This time, our reunion was wonderful. There was no discord between us, and we felt immediately totally in tune with each other. He felt supremely confident, and I felt optimistic. He met Andy and Philip in the garden of the hotel and set out to charm them. He did not even have to make an effort for he truly loved children and naturally appealed to young people, but most of all he was everything they wanted. They were ready for him.

Here were two boys in need of fathering, two little New Yorkers who had been surrounded by a European family. As they told me years later, "He was filling a gap in a welcome way. We thought he was very American, that was very exciting. He talked about baseball, he understood us, which was great stuff, we liked that and we called him Tex!" I need not have worried. I watched with deep pleasure as they built up an easy friendship that would grow into lifelong ties.

One day George sat patiently on the pier with Andy, who was an ardent fisherman; another day he persuaded Philip, who was rather shy, to go into the water and try swimming. We went on excursions around the lake and visited my uncle Senia who was vacationing in nearby Locarno. My uncle and I had remained very close since we left France together in 1940, and I was devoted to him. He liked George, understood immediately what he meant to me, and gave us his blessing.

Soon our two weeks were up. Our stay was a total success, and I knew George would be the kind of father I wished for my children, these two and any others to come. Now it was only a question of deciding where we would get married. George had taken the summer off, but he needed to do some work with a coach in Salzburg so we thought that would be the perfect place. He went ahead to prepare matters. I brought the boys to Geneva where they met their father with whom they spent a week before going to summer camp in Switzerland.

George met me at the airport in Munich and surprised me with a brand-new Mercedes sports car, white with beige leather seats. He was immensely proud of his purchase, and I admired it enthusiastically. He drove the short distance to Salzburg, faster than ever. We stayed at the Hotel Zistelalm, which is just outside of the town and up on a mountain with a beautiful view.

The location was idyllic, we thought, perfect for a wedding, but we now encountered some unexpected difficulties. An Austrian law required a period of ten months between a person's divorce and remarriage. So in my case, we had to apply for a special dispensation, and we were not sure when this would come through.

George was getting nervous, for he would have to leave for Vienna soon. He much preferred getting married in the intimacy of a small town where we could avoid the press. The Salzburg festival was over, and there were not many tourists. I met an acquaintance on the street who tried to pry some news from me, mentioning that he had heard rumors about our marriage. I flatly denied anything of the kind.

Because neither of our families was present, we wanted the event to be kept private, and, in fact, we did not know ourselves when it would take place.

George wrote to his parents later:

On the morning of the 30th of August, 1955, I received

a call to the effect that everything was in order, but that I had to go to Linz, 75 miles away, where the courthouse for that district is, in order to get an official seal. I was back from Linz at three, and at five we were all in one of the beautiful rooms of the Mirabell Palace, which must certainly be the most beautiful setting for a civil ceremony in the world.

We met George's friends Henry and Ginny Pleasants, then at the American Embassy in Bern; Franz Spelman, music correspondent for *Newsweek*; and Erik Werba, George's accompanist, in front of Salzburg's City Hall, located in the Mirabell Palace, which was once the sumptuous residence of Salzburg's mighty cardinal-archbishop.

George had been in such a rush that he had to ask Henry Pleasants and Franz Spelman to get flowers on their way. He gave me a bouquet of sweet tea roses. I was wearing a white linen suit, and George wore a grey suit with silk shirt and pale-blue tie, looking unusually conservative and serious.

We climbed the majestic stairway to the first floor inside the palace, and our small party was directed to one of the main halls. Evidently, in spite of the sudden decision, the authorities had been warned in advance and wanted to do things right for the wedding of George London.

We entered a huge room with marble floors and pink marble columns, which was the cardinal-archbishop's reception room once upon a time. The room was almost empty except for a long table covered with green cloth in the center where the *Standesbeamter*, the Austrian justice of the peace, was sitting flanked by a clerk and a secretary. He looked solemn, and we took our assigned places silently. Henry, Ginny, Franz, and Erik sat together on a bench. George and I stood in front of the table.

A flood of sunlight coming through the tall windows illuminated our group, and I glanced outside for a second at the glorious French garden bursting with flowers in bloom, all in my honor. George and I were holding hands. He was squeezing mine so hard I thought it would break. We were profoundly moved, and I was afraid I would start crying.

The judge got up, and the tension was broken. He spoke in such a strange Austrian dialect that we could barely understand his little speech, and suddenly we both could hardly refrain from laughing.

The judge called the witnesses, Franz Spelman and Erik Werba, and we tried to regain our composure. Behind us, Ginny was crying, and we were overcome with emotion. George put the ring on my finger, and we took our vows with great solemnity.

After we were pronounced man and wife, a little old man suddenly hobbled in and sat at an organ on the far side of the hall. He proceeded to play with great fervor, ending with Mendelssohn's wedding march. The music resounded in the great empty hall, and we all had tears in our eyes. We walked out dreamily to have pictures taken in the palace garden. For years afterward George regretted that, owing to his excitement, he did not give a good tip to the musician who had given us such a unique pleasure.

In the evening, we had a small candlelight dinner party at our hotel for the few people who had been at the wedding. We were glad that these devoted friends were sensitive to our feelings and left shortly after the meal. We felt our tremendous dedication to each other so intensely that we wanted to be alone to start our new life.

He loved me all the years of our marriage. Every day he found time to tell me how beautiful I was. He had so many gifts; he gave so generously of himself to his public, to his friends, to anyone who needed him. He was loved by so many, yet he never took anything for granted.

Thinking back, I am in awe of his achievements and his humanity. I often wonder if I made him happy, and for my answer I will have to be content with a few lines George wrote to me for our twentieth anniversary on August 30, 1975:

My darling, —I thank you with all my heart for all the happiness you have given me these past twenty years. And I am so grateful for the boundless and unfailing support you have given me through good times and less good ones.

You're the best woman I've ever known, and I love you very dearly. Your George.

Chapter 7
Vienna

Three days after the wedding, on September 2, 1955, George sang the four villain roles in *The Tales of Hoffmann*. We had piled our luggage into the trunk of the white Mercedes and driven to Vienna. George had rented a furnished apartment in a handsome old building at Schubertring 4. It was within walking distance of the opera, near the concert hall, and came complete with a maid named Gretl, who had blond hair and a white apron and a white lace cap just as if she had just stepped out of a Viennese operetta.

She opened the door, curtsied, congratulated us, and we entered a room filled with flowers. The news of our marriage had spread quickly. The wire services had picked up the story, and there had been a mention in the papers, not just in Austria but all over the world. George had sent a telegram to his parents, but the wedding notice appeared in the *Los Angeles Times* before they received it. A friend had called his mother and broken the news to her. It was a shock for her, really not what George had planned, and did not make things easier for us in the future.

I had the good fortune to reach my mother by phone in Montecatini, a resort in Italy, where she was vacationing. After my announcement to her, there was a moment of silence and I said, "Maman, aren't you going to say something?" "Yes, yes, I wish you great happiness," she squeezed out at last. Later she came to love and admire George and once remarked to me, "George is the favorite of my four sons-in-law" (my sister having married for a second time as well).

These shaky beginnings in our family relations no longer affected us. We adapted to our married life without any effort, as if we had always lived together. The apartment was very comfortable. It had a large living room, with dining area and a balcony and a handsome bedroom with a beautiful porcelain chimney. Oddly the bathroom was at the end of a long hall, unheated in the winter, and when the weather was cold, we had to sprint from bed to bath if we wanted to avoid freezing on the way. I was thrilled to be with George. There seemed to be a shining light around him, and I was now a part of his luminous orbit. I adapted carefully to his ways, for I knew how important it was for his work.

The *Tales of Hoffmann* was given at the Theater-an-der-Wien. By now George had become a seasoned member of the famous Vienna ensemble. The performers were attractive, talented, dedicated, with beautiful voices, and the artistic level was always high. The same singers performed together again and again; they enjoyed their work. No one was in a hurry to take the next plane to another opera house at that time.

George was accepted by the close-knit ensemble as one of their own, and he loved to sing in Vienna. He told me later that in those days, performing several times a week with the same colleagues was such a joy; he would have done it for nothing. He was proud to be part of this famous group and at the same time enjoyed his personal popularity. He spent long periods of time in Vienna and sang a total of one hundred-forty performances between 1949 and 1955 at the Theater-an-der-Wien. He sang *Don Giovanni*, thirty times; the four villains in *The Tales of Hoffmann*, nineteen times; *Eugene Onegin*, thirteen times; and the Speaker in *The Magic Flute*, which is a cameo part usually given to an important star, thirteen times. In this role, he was part of the cast in the last performance of the Vienna State Opera at the Theater-an-der-Wien on October 2, 1955.

The Viennese public was knowledgeable and rewarded artists with enthusiastic applause and the kind of adoration reserved for pop singers in the United States. The fans loved the young American baritone with the dashing figure and romantic dark looks.

After the *Hoffmann* performance, I was introduced to the fan phenomenon. As George emerged from the stage door he was besieged by hundreds of ardent admirers, mostly young females begging for autographs. This scene was repeated after every performance, and it took George an hour of signing and answering questions before he could leave the theater. Some of the fans who came backstage became true friends. I liked them at once, and they in turn approved of me.

It must have been difficult for those of his friends who had appropriated him as "their" star to accept that he now had a permanent mate. Edith and Gottfried Kraus, two of George's best friends, were present after each performance, and they propelled me through the crowd and kept me company for as long as it took George to get out. They obviously adored George in a knowing and perceptive way, and their friendship helped me to endure the waits. I was never jealous of the fans; that was part of his life. I accepted their adulation like everything else, but it would have been difficult for me to stand there alone next to a crowd that ignored me.

Before our marriage, George had become known as a ladies' man in Vienna, where he drove around in a succession of sports cars. As Joseph Wechsberg wrote in his *New Yorker* profile about him in 1957:

> ...somehow an alluring young lady seemed to be a built-in accessory of each of these cars; at least, the idea was current in Vienna that when London traded in a car the young lady went with it and he got another with the new one. . . When he was billed at the Theater-an-der-Wien, a special 'London audience' would show up, con-

sisting of attractive postgraduate bobby soxers. But women of all ages were drawn to him, and while the younger ones carried on about 'Georgie,' the older ones sent him yards of still warm Apfelstrudel, a delicacy that, in a thoughtless moment, he had publicly announced he was fond of.

After our marriage, prophets predicted that the fans would abandon their idol. But it made no difference to them. They were there in growing numbers, as we were able to see after the first post-marriage performance of the *Tales of Hoffmann*. They just made believe that I did not exist. Later, when George sang at the big opera house, they migrated there and, taking their cue, I would wait with our friends across the street, as inconspicuous as possible until he was free and could join us for supper.

I understood very soon that this adulation, this signing of autographs, was part of the performance for George and the other artists. The approval of public and fans is essential to the singer who puts his artistry up for examination at each performance. In fact, is there ever enough applause to compensate for such a trial?

On October 2, the Theater-an-der-Wien closed with *The Magic Flute*. The entire company was preparing for the move back to the rebuilt Staatsoper. For a month, George's time was spent in rehearsals and preparations for the opening. On November 6, he was to sing the title role in *Don Giovanni* and on November 11, Amonasro in *Aida*. George told me that, "the four months I'm giving the Vienna Opera this fall is a must. It is the climax of my career here, where my important career started."

I understood perfectly what this meant to him. I also knew well before our marriage that there was a good deal more to him than the dashing, gregarious façade. He was a true Gemini, endowed with a dual personality. For every joke that he told with such mastery there was doubt and torment about the next performance, the next concert, the next note, and there was a supersensitive ego wounded at the slightest provocation.

He never went out on the evening before a performance, so we spent much time together. I served somehow like a captive but sympathetic audience to whom he could externalize his constant worries about his interpretations, his career, his next engagement, his finances, his rapport or lack thereof with his friends, colleagues, and conductors. Often he was theatrical, sometimes repetitive, but always sincere. He needed to talk about these self-doubts in order to present the assured extroverted persona to the outside world.

If he tried my patience, he sensed it and would make up for it a hundred times by his constant proof of love and affection. In his effort to make me understand and share his love for Shakespeare, Shaw, and Sean O'Casey, he would read to me long passages from their works. With his voice and emotional interpretation, the obsure text became clear to me, and he was childishly pleased with my approval.

I was living in a state of bliss and was more determined than ever to make his life as easy and harmonious as possible. It seems that I succeeded, since he wrote to his parents in December: "Nora's never-failing good humor provides an ideal atmosphere of tranquility for me which I need for the rigors of work and contact with the evil world. She is a wife and companion in the truest sense of the words."

The apartment was very cozy. Gretl curtsied whenever we spoke to her, and in spite of her Viennese dialect, I soon managed to understand her. I enjoyed marketing in the open-air stands, and, thanks to Gretl's cooking, we were provided with many pleasant meals. We settled into a happy domestic routine, which we unwisely disturbed by acquiring a wire-haired dachshund called Daisy, the first in a series of dachshunds. I have two to this day.

I took Daisy with me everywhere. This is possible in Austria, where dogs are allowed even in restaurants. On days when he was not singing, George and I took Daisy for a walk, which invariably led to Demel. George loved sweets, and in the 1950's Demel was the most famous pastry shop in Vienna. The waitresses were draconian, old maids who melted with love when George appeared. They couldn't do enough to please him, and he had barely sat down at his favorite table when a piece of fresh apple strudel was put in front of him. This would be followed by a serious discussion about the best dessert of the day, and then, almost as an afterthought, I was allowed to order, too. The preferential treatment George was given by the waitresses was so obvious that George and I laughed about it, and I admitted magnanimously that he was surely their best customer.

Immediately after his last performance at the Theater-an-der-Wien, George started rehearsing at the big opera house. The inside was not completely finished; there were workmen everywhere, carpeting the stairs and painting the ceilings. It was chaotic, but rehearsals had to go on. Under the circumstances, I thought I could take my dog to a rehearsal, so I sneaked Daisy into the theater. She liked music, I guess, and stayed quietly under the seat where no one could see her. But when I walked through the foyer, one of the workmen exclaimed in horror, "What? A dog in the emperor's opera house!" I felt terribly guilty until a few days later when I met Hans Hopf, a famous tenor, backstage with his huge German shepherd.

After rehearsal, George often went to the workshop of the opera for fittings, and he insisted that I come with him. The head of the costume department and his staff hovered around George and did their utmost to satisfy him. They kept addressing him with his title, "Herr Kammersänger" (court singer), which the Austrian government had bestowed on him in 1954. He was the first American to receive this honor. In an excess of zeal, they even addressed me as Frau Kammersängerin, for in Austria everyone must have a title. The first time this happened, I turned around to find out to whom they were speaking.

George was very demanding and wanted everything to be perfect. For *Don Giovanni* the costumes were made of the finest silks and softest leathers. In the first act, he wore a trim red suede jacket, very flattering for his slim waist. For the famous Champagne Aria, the traditional white silk costume had very big puffed sleeves, and the breeches were to be as short as possible to show off his shapely long legs. In spite of everyone's efforts, it seemed impossible to find a pair of white tights long enough to accommodate those legs. This created a crisis; the head of the department was summoned and swore that there would be tights for the general rehearsal. There was a similar costume in black for the second act, thus another problem finding the correct black tights.

When the tailor was finished, George had to try the shoes, white pumps with a large buckle for the white costume, the same in black, and high gray suede boots for the first scene. There was a new crisis, for nothing fit even though the shoes were made to order. Only Americans could have such long narrow feet!

Again there were many "Herr Kammersängers" and promises that all would be well before the first run through, which no one, including George, believed for a moment. He returned many times to make sure that everything would actually be ready in time. Eventually the costumes turned out beautifully and enhanced his performance.

Although George was working, these first weeks in Vienna were our honeymoon. We were together constantly, and yet we never got tired of each other. We always had so much to talk about: music, arts, politics. Sometimes we went to museums where George wanted to show me his favorites, Brueghel and Dürer, or we just walked through the winding streets admiring the Baroque buildings or window-shopped at night in the Kärntnerstrasse, a favorite occupation for George who did not like to go to bed early after dinner.

George was elated when we found out that I was going to

have a child the following spring. He wanted a family of his own and welcomed the new responsibilities he would have to face. He felt earnestly that it would give new meaning to his work.

I had to go back to New York to take care of the boys, and during my absence George missed me a great deal. He complained about Daisy. "This dog roams around so sadly, looks for you everywhere—it is so depressing that I am ready to give her away if you don't come back soon." I answered in jest, "If Daisy is gone, then I won't come back." I realized how much my presence meant to him after such a short time, and knowing that Andy and Philip were in good hands with their nanny, I hurried back to Vienna.

George had invited his mother to come to Vienna for the reopening of the opera house. His father was too frail and not interested, but his mother had been eager to go to Europe for years. He wanted her to have this long-awaited trip, and even though he was afraid of the tensions it would provoke now that we were married, he did not have the heart to cancel it. She arrived while I was in New York, and George installed her in the Pension Schneider where he had often stayed. Everybody knew him there and promised to take good care of his mother, as she did not understand German. George also mobilized our English-speaking Viennese friends to entertain her, as he was increasingly busy with preparations at the opera house. She was delighted with Vienna and duly impressed by her son's popularity. There were many articles in the papers, and his picture was prominently exhibited in the record shops all over town.

George was waiting for me at the airport when I returned, as always pacing back and forth until he saw me. We had lived together only a short time, but we had grown very close, and we felt an intense joy at being together again. During the drive home, however, I felt that he was tense. He confessed that he was nervous and that the forthcoming opening of the opera house was terribly important for his career. He was determined to give his best in this city where he was so popular.

Simon Bourgin, special correspondent for *Time Magazine*, wrote about the opening:

> With the Great Day only one week off, Vienna's 'opera fever' is at full height. The Viennese, who recognize their helplessness under this affliction, have resigned themselves to thinking and talking little but opera until the house's opening.
>
> In effect November 5 begins a kind of 'Coronation Week' for the Viennese. They are treating the return of their opera house as a royal event, giving it the gilt and glory that they might otherwise reserve for a crowning.
>
> The center of anticipation is naturally the opera house itself. For the first time in ten years the high wired fences surrounding it are removed. The Viennese have been walking through the newly opened sidewalk arcades of the opera house as if they were on hallowed ground. The opera crossing, where the Kaerntnerstrasse (Vienna's Fifth Avenue) and the Ringstrasse intersect, is the busiest in Vienna.
>
> For the rest, Vienna is putting on a house cleaning that is almost changing its face. The streets around the Opera House have been widened and installed with giant arc lamps. On the public squares and street corners over most of downtown Vienna neat square flower pots have been set. The Josefsplatz, which the Viennese like to call the most beautiful baroque square in the world, has had a complete new face cleaning. The Spanish horses have been returned to their Josefsplatz riding hall even before their stables were ready – so they could perform simultaneously with the Opera opening. Even the shabby Mozart café, not a palace at all, is getting its front refurbished.
>
> In the windows of Demel's, Vienna's great confectionary shop, the golden days of the Vienna opera between the two wars have been revived. Maria Jeritza as Tosca,

Lotte Lehmann as Marschallin, Vera Schwarz as Rosenkavalier, and Rosette Anday as Carmen are in the window, all made of a special sugar mixture.

The opening will be covered by 300 foreign journalists and photo reporters. NBC has a complete film staff in Vienna shooting a 90-minute full-length TV feature, called 'Rebirth of Freedom.' The unique thing about this opening is that the Vienna Opera (finished in 1869) was the only building destroyed in Vienna during World War II and almost at the very end.

On March 12, 1945, just a few days before the Red Army took Vienna, American bombers attacked. Five bombs hit the opera stage and fire broke out. Two huge reservoirs storing 300,000 gallons of water had been built in large concrete basins before the house for just such an occasion. But when the fire came there were almost no engines and 300 other Vienna buildings were burning too. For two days the Viennese watched in the streets and wept as their precious opera house burned. Only the facade on the Ringstrasse with the loggia, the foyer and the grand staircase remained.

Other post-war opera houses have reopened as in Berlin and Hamburg this year. But only the Vienna opera re-opening is a world event. This is because the Vienna opera alone is supra-national. For a century, Vienna has created an operatic tradition that all Western peoples have shared. For the Viennese, music is a religion, and the State Opera House, the most prominent building in downtown Vienna, a high temple of worship. The Viennese regard their music with the seriousness that other people reserve for crises of state.

What makes Vienna what it was, is and could be? The public. There is no other public in the world which has not only an instinctive sense for what is good and what is bad, but also knows how to distinguish between mediocre, good, and excellent.

George rehearsed with great enthusiasm. He was delighted to learn that his picture would be on the cover of *Newsweek* on October 31, 1955, with a story about him and the opening of the Vienna State Opera written by his friend Franz Spelman. *Newsweek* printed a handsome picture of George as Don Giovanni, holding the curtain of the rebuilt opera house and the caption "Baritone George London—Rebirth of Vienna State Opera." He was very pleased; for it was the first time he received such important publicity in the United States.

Don Giovanni and *Aida* were to be given five days apart during the gala premiere week, both with totally new productions. Thus George was involved in numerous rehearsals. I went with him most of the time, and he introduced me to his colleagues, the conductor, his dresser, and all of the people backstage. He was convinced that my presence was necessary to his well being, and that I was the right person in the right place. I felt perfectly at ease, as if I had been attending his rehearsals all my life. He had the ability to make me feel like I belonged. Little by little I ceased to be shy and became the supportive partner he needed. I never thought about this; it just happened.

When I was not in the theatre with George, I did the errands for the household. I returned to the open-air markets where I enjoyed walking between the stands choosing cauliflower in one, salad and carrots in another. I always went to the same butcher near our house who gave me the kind of steaks we liked, somewhat different from the Austrian taste. The butcher knew my name, and we exchanged brief greetings at each visit. But on the day of the *Don Giovanni* performance, as soon as he saw me among the crowd of customers he yelled to his aide: "And the best steak in the house for Kammersanger George London, who will sing *Don Giovanni* for us tonight." Every Viennese felt a real involvement in these performances. If they could not be inside the house, they would still listen to every note broadcast by loudspeakers in front of the opera.

Finally it was the night of the dress rehearsal. The theater was filled with an audience of state officials and invited guests. Sometimes, when the show is not ready, dress rehearsals are still tentative, and the rehearsal is closed with no spectators allowed. Then the singers will just mark some arias by singing half-voice to preserve their voices. But this one was just like a performance, and it went splendidly. The audience was enthusiastic; George was pleased. "If I sing as well at the performance, I'll be satisfied," he said.

On November 6, George followed his established routine for performance days. I kept out of his way, for I knew that he did not want to talk much. I answered the phone for him and transmitted nothing but good wishes and good news, insuring a peaceful atmosphere around him. He went over the entire score once more, looking specifically at new stage instructions. As it was rather cold, he decided against a walk and did his usual exercise program in the bedroom. At 5:00 P.M., he went to the opera house. This routine seemed to soothe his nerves and prepared him so well that he felt calm and sure of himself when the performance started.

I followed him backstage an hour later and walked into his dressing room in my new dress, looking as good as possible in my pregnant condition. George, who was sitting in front of the mirror, interrupted his makeup and complimented me on the dress and the hairdo. Then he went back to his task, applying the moustache and pointed beard, which he trimmed carefully. Slowly he *became* Don Giovanni. He was already in costume and stood up to vocalize. I could tell that he was in great voice and told him so. He cleared his throat several times and sang another arpeggio. Then, evidently satisfied with my verdict and pleased as well, he smiled and joked that I'd better go in if I didn't want to miss the first act. I wished him the customary *merde* and left. His mother and Paola Novikova, who had come to Vienna for these special performances, had visited him earlier for a few minutes. I was the last to go; he was in a good mood, relaxed and confident in his own ability.

I sat down in the red velvet seat, way in front toward the right. There was a hush; the lights went out. Karl Bohm, the conductor, started the overture. I was breathless and prayed that George would be in great form. I knew that he was secure both vocally and dramatically. He had performed this part many times around the world and polished every note, every gesture. On this evening, all of his experience came together for a unique performance. It was the same for the other artists, his friends who had sung with him so often at the Theater-an-der-Wien. There was Irmgard Seefried, an unforgettable Zerlina; Lisa Della Casa, a strikingly beautiful Donna Anna; Sena Jurinac, the perfect Donna Elvira; Anton Dermota, a stylish Don Ottavio; and Erich Kunz, a typically Viennese Leporello. In their new sumptuous costumes, they all looked attractive, acted with flair, and brought to life the perfection of Mozart's masterpiece.

Si Bourgin described the performance in *Time Magazine:*

In this *Don Giovanni*, the sets are scarcely noticed for the singers. It's a dream cast and this will surely go down as an ideal performance. George London is suave, sinister and elegant as the Don. Erich Kunz is the finest Leporello of his time, and Ludwig Weber is regarded as the finest Commendatore singing today. The three women, Lisa della Casa as Donna Anna, Sena Jurinac as Donna Elvira, and Irmgard Seefried as Zerlina being beautiful as well as great artists compete for honor with such restraint and art that Vienna will remember their contest for a long time.
The audience was carried away into a world where voices, music, and theater merged to enchant the senses, transplanted into the eighteenth century, where beautiful people, dressed in shimmering silks, moved with elegance, where passion and humor were intertwined in an eternally stimulating plot, where the music was enthralling and deeply moving in a perfect combination of voice and orchestra.

After the Champagne Aria, Don Giovanni's showpiece, which London sang at great speed, the audience went wild. The bobby soxers in the gallery and the standees screamed and stamped their feet, asking for at least a bow; but Don Giovanni runs out at the end of his aria and the conductor went on as required. At the end of the opera the applause was tremendous and the public stood up in an ovation for the singers, the conductor, the orchestra, the staging, and no doubt the genius of Mozart.

George was fulfilled. This particular evening was the crowning of his Vienna years, and he had given his best to the knowing public that had made him a star.

The critic Karl Lobl wrote:

The tall, slender, dazzling-looking and utterly charming London has no competitors in this difficult role. His Don Giovanni is in Mozart's spirit. He succeeds in making the difficult transition from the subtly humorous and delicately erotic to the demonic personality driven by destiny.

Thirty-five years later I heard, for the first time, a CD of this performance. I listened with some trepidation. Was it going to be as good as I remembered, or had I been intoxicated by the excitement of the moment? It was great; it was wonderful, even better than I remembered. It filled me with extraordinary emotion to hear his familiar voice preserved here in his prime.

That night in November 1955 when I went backstage after the performance, George was radiant. Still in costume and makeup, his eyes sparkling, almost out of breath with exultation, he was devastatingly handsome. He kissed me lightly, to prevent his makeup from soiling me, and I thought how fortunate I was to be loved by this man.

The dressing room was full of flowers (in Austria and Germany it is customary to give flowers to male as well as female singers). Everywhere there were telegrams of congratulations, chocolates— and the inevitable apple strudels. Our friends helped to carry most of this back to our house while I waited patiently across the street from the artists' entrance in front of the Hotel Sacher.

Finally George appeared, smiling and holding more flowers. He was mobbed by his admirers. He signed autographs and found a kind word for many whom he recognized. At last they let him go, and we met his mother, Paola, and some friends at the Sacher, where a table was reserved for us.

Other members of the cast also went there for supper. The food was excellent; it was the place to go after the opera. The restaurant was crowded, and as each singer arrived the diners applauded. The management shrewdly gave prominent tables to the biggest stars. George was still under the spell of his performance and for a few hours he ate and drank and joked with his friends.

When we got home at last, he said. "I'm so happy that you could be with me on this special evening. I'm very grateful. Yet we must not take anything for granted." He repeated this phrase often with real sincerity. It was this side of his character that prevented him from becoming arrogant in the face of his enormous success.

During the opening week on the nights when he was not singing, we went to the opera to hear *Der Rosenkavalier* and *Die Frau ohne Schatten*, both Richard Strauss operas that George loved. He could be terribly critical when the singing was not up to his standards, but he enjoyed these performances and admired his colleagues.

Five days after *Don Giovanni*, he sang Amonasro. He had a special love for this part, and sang it often in Vienna and at the Metropolitan in New York. He always enjoyed transforming himself into a wild-looking, bellicose, patriotic African king. It is a relatively short part, requiring little more than twenty minutes of singing, but again his success was tremendous.

By contrast, recitals require nearly two hours of uninterrupted singing with only piano accompaniment and no costumes or theatrical effects to help the artist. London, however, loved giving recitals, and he had a unique rapport with
the concert audience in Vienna.

In the beginning of December, he gave a recital in the big
Musikverein Hall, which has beautiful wood carvings and
fabulous acoustics. The hall was packed. London sang a program composed of Handel arias, Schubert Lieder, opera arias,
and some Negro spirituals, which were loved in Vienna but
could not be performed by a white man in the United States.
His humanity and generous spirit was communicated to each
member of the audience through voice and artistry. He said,
"They spend their hard-earned money to hear me, and I have
to give them the best of me."

The people felt his dedication and gave him an ovation at
the end. He was glowing with their appreciation and the feeling of great accomplishment of his art. During his singing
years after performances, he was joyous, almost intoxicated
with his success, yet never arrogant.

Soon after this concert I left Vienna and went back to
New York to prepare for Christmas. George came a few weeks
later, and we had our first family reunion, and he assumed
gallantly the responsibility of head of a household with children and a dog. After the Holidays he had a series of performances at the Met followed by a concert tour in the spring.

In May, George returned to Vienna for the Festwochen,
or festival weeks, which lasted through June. He had given
up the apartment in Vienna, and he decided to stay at the
Imperial Hotel, which was close to the opera house and the
Musikverein concert hall.

He was given a huge room facing the front on the second
floor. In the morning an old waiter brought his breakfast and
asked, "Did Herr Kammersänger sleep well?" Upon George's
affirmative answer, the waiter added, "Yes, this is the room
where der Führer always slept." At which point George

jumped out of bed and asked to change rooms.

Gottfried Kraus commented:

> The re-opening of the Big Opera House was a turning point in the history of the Vienna Opera, the meaning of which we understood only later. Not all the performances which we had loved in the intimate Theater-an-der-Wien, particularly the Mozart operas, could be transferred to the big house without problems. Above all, the magnificent Opera House led to a desire to emulate other international opera houses. When Herbert von Karajan became the Director in 1956 and instituted a sort of international stagione system instead of the repertory system, he gave up the unique Vienna ensemble.
>
> Similarly, the singers of the Vienna Opera began to follow the general trend and seized every opportunity to perform in opera houses in the old and the new world.

This trend had already started in the Theater-an-der-Wien. Rudolf Bing engaged the most important singers for the Metropolitan Opera. Ljuba Welitsch, Lisa della Casa, Hilde Guden, Leonie Rysanek, Paul Schoffler, and Han Hotter left for many weeks to perform in New York and other important opera houses.

George London's international career also curtailed his presence in Vienna. Whereas in the beginning he had spent five months in Vienna, he now came only for short periods in September, October, and during the spring festival weeks. He added only a few new parts to his Vienna repertoire: Scarpia in *Tosca* in June 1953 and Wolfram in *Tannhauser* at the Volksoper (the smaller popular opera house). He sang *Don Giovanni* and the Count in *The Marriage of Figaro*, *Scarpia* with Renata Tebaldi, and *Escamillo* with Karajan conducting, but his performances in Vienna became less frequent.

However, in May 1961 the Viennese public witnissed a concert performance of the original score of *Boris Godunov* in the "Konzert Hall." It was obvious that London's interpretation, his voice, his expression, his economical gestures were incomparable. This Boris was not a mere opera figure, but a human being surrounded by an aura of greatness, loneliness, and sorrow.

He returned also once again to the Theater-an-der-Wien. The beloved house, empty since 1955, reopened after renovation for the Vienna Festival weeks in June 1963. George London was welcomed with love and endless jubilation by the public in the place where his career had started.

The 1963 return to the Theater-an-der-Wien where he had sung his very first performance in Vienna was an emotional event. The house has only eight hundred seats, and the rapport between the singer and the audience is very intimate. During this concert, London sang Brahms's *Four Serious Songs*. At the end there was a moment of silence, then a tremendous burst of applause. The audience understood the message of the composer and the accomplishment of the artist. George gave his best to the Viennese who loved him and gave him some of the happiest moments of his career. He remained deeply attached to the city and the people of his first success and returned faithfully to Vienna every year to perform his repertoire at the Staatsoper

Chapter 8
New York and the Metropolitan Opera

After the excitement and adulation of Vienna, New York was somewhat of a letdown for George London. The Metropolitan does not occupy in New York the importance that the Staatsoper holds in Vienna. At the Metropolitan, even though he was recognized as a star, George did not receive the same kind of adoration; it simply did not exist. Nevertheless, he was greatly appreciated and respected. He had a fan club and a large and devoted following, and he enjoyed singing in the old opera house at Broadway and Fortieth Street, which, he said, had wonderful acoustics. It was a thrill for him to stand on that stage and look out into the Golden Horseshoe, the row of boxes that was always occupied by America's most prominent families. Although Canadian born, George had become a patriotic American and was proud to be on the stage of his country's foremost theater. In the 1950's and 1960's, the Metropolitan was the most famous opera house in the world, and he felt privileged to be a part of it. Yet it did not add up to the exultation of Vienna. While in New York, he took lessons with Paola every day and met with his manager, Bill Judd, who was vice-president in the Arthur Judson division of Columbia Artists Management at that time. He also took advantage of his free time to learn new music and rehearse his concert material with one of his accompanists, Leo Taubman or Werner Singer, Paola's husband.

After his first appearance in *Aida*, London had sung many

roles at the Met. His greatest success was *Boris Godunov*, which was given in English in a new translation. He also performed leading roles in *Faust, Tosca, Tannhäsuer, The Marrige of Figaro, Carmen,* and *Parsifal.*

In February 1955, he sang the premiere of *Arabella*, which he had been studying for many months. This was a new production of the opera starring Lisa della Casa, the greatest Arabella of her time, in the title role and George as Mandryka, her suitor. Both were perfect in their parts, and for the first time in the Met's history, this opera became a success. George interpreted the role of a provincial nobleman arriving in Vienna in search of a wife. In Vienna he had worked with Alfred Jerger, who had created the part under Strauss's own direction. At the general rehearsal at the Met everyone admired the result of these efforts. Dragan Debeljevic, Lisa's husband, who had come with their little girl, Vesna, thought that George and Lisa made an extremely handsome couple, both singing and acting. It was so perfect that their onstge relationship seemed believable. The two had sung together often in Vienna and enjoyed each other's performance.

At the end of the opera when George (Mandryka) was about to kiss Lisa (Arabella), little Vesna ran toward the stage and screamed, "I don't want this man to kiss my mommy!" Dragan was a most handsome man, and since George and Lisa sang often together, our two real life couples became great friends.

Lisa Della Casa writes now:

Fifty years have passed since we first met, and yet my memories of this wonderful man, extraordinary artist, and lovable colleague remain absolutely vivid and strong. And now as I think back about him in total silence, I still don't know what I appreciated or admired most in this fascinating being: the intelligence, the seriousness, the discipline, the empathy, the charm, the humor or the fairness; and then also, in spite of his success, the genuine modesty. During our work together, I could observe that he always strove seriously for perfection as a singer and performer.

In the role of Arabella I experienced at least fifteen different Mandrykas. In my opinion and conviction, George was the greatest and most believable. He had everything that this difficult part required from a singer and actor: the voice, the looks, the charisma, and the right interpretation.

I remember vividly our appearance in Berlin with an audience of thousands. At the announcement that we would sing the great duet from *Arabella*, there was an ovation, and at the end the public literally went wild.

My husband and I had the opportunity to know George amidst his beloved family. He exuded true warmth, love, tenderness, and bliss. His untimely death was an irreplaceable loss.

George London had great success as Mandryka in *Arabella*, which he considered one of the most difficult roles in his repertoire musically; for it lies both very high and low for the voice, and it starts off with a long aria at his entrance. Erich Leinsdorf, who conducted the opera at the time and with whom George enjoyed working for many years, recalled, "When George made his entrance in the first act wearing a brown suit and matching fur coat, he looked so fabulous that he had conquered the audience before opening his mouth."

In 1956, George started his Met season as Count Almaviva in *The Marriage of Figaro* in a new staging for Mozart's bicentennial. He wanted his return in *Figaro* to be special. Although he had sung the role many times before, he gave it special care for this new staging. During the preceding autumn he made a short trip to Paris to catch a performance of the play *Le Mariage de Fiqaro* by Beaumarchais at the Comédie Française. Twenty years later, he recalled:

I was particularly interested in the part of the Count,

which I was preparing for a new production at the Metropolitan. The cast included two of the most distinguished actors in France: Julien Berteau, who played the Count and Robert Hirsch as Figaro.

These two provided an exquisite intellectual duo armed by the mordant words of Beaumarchais. I watched Berteau like a hawk and was busy taking notes during the entire performance. I sketched his costume and paid special attention to his stunning white wig and his beautiful high buckled boots. I was impressed by the economy and the elegance of his gestures and his attitude. The Count is often portrayed as a blustering boor, a sort of addled aristocrat. But Berteau obviously had quite different ideas and played him as a vital, intelligent and dangerous opponent. The struggle between the two men was not merely one of who should get Susanna first, but was rather an ideological confrontation between established authority and the aggressiveness of the rising bourgeoisie which presaged the French Revolution.

When I soon afterwards played the Count, I did not slavishly imitate Berteau who was a much smaller man with quite a different personality, but I implemented many aspects of his characterization, and I did shamelessly copy that wonderful wig and those marvelous boots; as a matter of fact, I went the very next day to the Comedic Française and persuaded them to execute these for me.

Certainly the characterization, the wig, the boots, and for good measure the perfect Mozart style he had acquired in Vienna all contributed to London's success in the 1956 production. He tossed off the fiendishly difficult music of the Count's great aria "Vedro mentr'io sospiro" without effort. George sang this role many times at the Met as well as on the tour, mostly with Lisa della Casa, who was an enchanting Countess; with Cesare Siepi, a superb Figaro; and with Erich Leinsdorf as conductor.

The Marriage of Figaro, one of the greatest operas ever

composed, has always been one of my favorites. It is also one of the longest, and George is in it to the very end. By the time we got to bed after unwinding and supper, it was close to two o'clock. After the performance on the evening of March 30, we had supper at home with George's old friend from California days, Max Lipin. The two men kept trading jokes. George was a famous raconteur. He could imitate every accent, and we all laughed for hours. Finally we separated when it was nearly three o'clock.

At six in the morning, I woke George to tell him that it was time to go to the hospital. My labor pains had started. Disbelieving, he mumbled that he had just gone to sleep and could not possibly get up. I was well aware of George's inability to get up early in the morning. Although he clearly took command of our household's outside contacts, he let me control the comings and goings at our home. One of my sacred duties was to guard his rest, above all his morning sleep time.

He had constant arguments with conductors who wanted to rehearse at nine o'clock in the morning. George asserted that he could not possibly sing a note before noon. The conductors liked his musicianship and total dedication and usually compromised on eleven o'clock. Even that time was a hardship for him; in order to get his voice going he had to get up three hours earlier. He used to say that when he got out of bed, he sounded like a cracked basso. He admired Birgit Nilsson even more when he discovered that she could get up and sing Brunnhilde's taxing solos before breakfast, as she proved in London during the Walküre recordings. George even had trouble coping with life's ordinary chores early in the morning. If he had to take a plane at 9:00 a.m., he would talk about it for days in advance, then set his alarm for 7:00 and tell everybody in the family to make sure that he was awake. I knew all this, but, of course, in this case I could not spare him.

I had already called the doctor, who told me to go to the

hospital. I decided to fortify George with some coffee and toast. Suddenly he was wide-awake and got dressed in no time flat. Now he behaved like any other father-to-be: he was a nervous wreck, much more agitated than I. It was his first child, while I had been through all this before. When we got to the hospital, last night's aristocratic Count could not find his insurance card and could barely remember his name. It took such a long time to do the paperwork that our daughter was nearly born in the entrance hall of Mount Sinai Hospital.

But all went well. We were both enchanted with our little girl and called her Marina, after the Polish princess in *Boris Godunov*.

The hospital room was bursting with flowers, which overflowed into the hall already lined with flowers from an adjoining room where Paul Newman and Joanne Woodward had a baby the same week. The two fathers admired their respective newborns through the glass window like all the fathers in the world. George's happiness was touching. I was very pleased to have a girl now after two boys. George did not care about the sex of the baby; he felt a religious awe and love for this tiny human being for which he was responsible.

"My life has now taken on even more meaning," he wrote to his parents, "and I feel that a solid foundation has been built where my life and my career can grow towards heights that I fancied I might one day achieve. God has been very good to me, and I am not too proud to humbly acknowledge how very grateful I am for all of the blessings which have been bestowed upon me."

From the sublime to the ridiculous, on the evening following Marina's birth, Daisy, our dachshund, probably looking for attention, proceeded to have an attack of epilepsy. Poor George, who had been up since dawn, spent the evening in search of a veterinarian working on a Saturday night with the help of my thirteen-year-old nephew Patrick. The following day he was afraid to tell me that the dog was sick. I was irritated because he yawned constantly, and I kept asking him what he had done the preceding night. He answered that he went to a movie, but he was such a poor liar that I did not believe him for a second and wormed the truth out of him. Daisy recovered and never had another attack. I guess she felt that she had made her point.

Shortly after my return from the hospital, George had to leave for a long concert tour. The parting was difficult for him. Like all his emotions, his paternal feelings were extremely strong from the first day and grew even deeper with time. From then on the separations, which were a way of life for him, became more and more difficult. But there was no other way; the career for which he had made so many sacrifices demanded yet more of him. In the end, it mattered more even than his family.

In the course of the trip, he wrote with satisfaction to his parents on April 7: "I am in wonderful condition. I am singing better than ever. I have developed a security and an assurance which I never knew before and am thus able to maintain a consistently high standard."

After the concert tour was the Met tour, and then George was off to Europe. Our small apartment was cheap, and we could save money by staying there. I had decided to follow George to Europe as soon as the boys' vacation started, and we knew that the family's travels would be very costly.

From the very beginning, we decided that we would take the children wherever he was singing for any length of time. We reasoned that if we did not do this, he would hardly ever see them and would miss these early years of togetherness. I would plan and implement our summer trips.

It was not always easy to be together but, looking back, I am glad we managed it. George enjoyed spending his free time with Marina and later with our son Marc and became close to them. It was important for me as well to be surrounded by my family, and yet to be able to go to George's rehearsals and performances.

After the summer of 1956, we went to Buenos Aires, where London was to perform *Don Giovanni* and *The Marriage of Figaro* during an engagement at the magnificent Teatro Colon. We were there together with Lisa della Casa, her husband Dragan, and Birgit Nilsson. At that time Buenos Aires was a handsome and prosperous city. Between performances, all the artists did a lot of shopping since the exchange rate was favorable. The performances were very glamorous and the artists were feted lavishly by Buenos Aires opera lovers. When we returned to New York we had to find a new place to live. At first, nothing materialized, then I suddenly found a place. George was in the midst of a rehearsal at the Met when I called him. "I know I'm not supposed to disturb you, but it's absolutely essential that you come and see this apartment immediately, otherwise someone else will get it. I think it is ideal for us, but I can't decide without you." He agreed. "I'll meet you at the address in half an hour."

He came, loved the apartment, signed the lease, and returned to the rehearsal. We had some misgivings, since $500 a month was more than we expected to spend. This apartment fetches $30,000 per month today. Some weeks later we moved into a penthouse at 262 Central Park West, a wonderful apartment with three large bedrooms, a library, and huge living and dining room. All of this was surrounded by a wide terrace with a magnificent view of Central Park.

Eventually we all settled into our respective rooms, a big improvement over our previous cramped quarters. The large entrance hall, which had black and white vinyl tiles, led to the children's bedrooms, and the master bedroom was down another hall. This room was large enough for George's desk since he preferred to study and work in his room away from the bustle of the household. This is where he learned new music and reviewed older scores, rarely going to the piano except when working with an accompanist. He spent most of his time in his room.

Our growing collection of paintings decorated the walls

of the living room. There were a number of paintings by the French painter Maclet representing scenes from Paris, and George soon bought some Chagall lithographs, an Italian sculpture representing Don Quixote, and a Chinese bronze Kuan-Yin. George loved art. Wherever he performed, his time was divided between the hotel, the theater, and the museum, if there was one. He always preferred the more dramatic subjects and spent a long time observing period costumes and manners. He stared at his favorites, talking about how much he would love to have this or that painting in his home. Sometimes I looked around, fearful that a guard would overhear and become suspicious of his intentions. I would quickly say, "Darling, you can't have this, it belongs to the museum."

At times his desire was so strong that he bought large reproductions of his favorites (a Leonardo, a Durer, and a Murillo), and then admitted that they were not good enough to hang in the living room. But everywhere he went he bought art: German expressionists, Japanese prints, more sculptures. The walls of the apartment were soon filled. However, George did not want any pictures of himself. "I know what I look like, and my friends can see me in the theater," he said. Later, he did accept a painting of himself as Boris Godunov, commemorating his performance at the Bolshoi.

The years from 1957 to 1964, which we spent in the apartment on Central Park West, spanned the most successful years of George's singing career internationally, and above all, at the Metropolitan. The best measure of an artist's success in New York is whether he sings at the opening of the season. George sang at the opening of the Met season in both 1957 and 1958. Other coveted performances are new productions and the Saturday afternoon broadcasts, which are heard all over the United States and Canada (at that time there were no telecasts). Over the years, London sang in twelve new productions and twenty-five broadcast matinees. At one time, it was also considered an advantage to sing on Monday nights, the so-called society nights, but their appeal was already fading during the 1950's. The artists felt that on society nights the people came mostly to look at each other, not to listen to the singers, and therefore there was little applause. A regular weeknight audience was much more enthusiastic and more knowledgeable, and this was more satisfying for the cast. Of course, every major artist wanted to sing in the openings, the broadcasts, and the new productions. They also wanted an increase in their fees. In the 1950's and 1960's, the Metropolitan Opera was the best theater in the world. It paid less than other houses, yet it could attract the most famous artists because it was prestigious to appear there.

By the mid-1950's, George was paid twenty-five-hundred dollars a performance, the equivalent of over $25,000 by today's standards. However, contracts are still negotiated the same way today, as they were then. Solo contracts were signed two or three years in advance, and in most cases the artist' managers did the bargaining. London felt that his manager did not get the right kind of contract for him and believed he did better negotiating directly with Rudolf Bing, the general manager of the Met. He felt that if Mr. Bing promised certain conditions, he always kept his word. On the other hand, George was an important artist, much needed in a specific repertoire. He was always on time, perfectly prepared, and not given to capricious behavior. No doubt all this weighed heavily in his favor at contract time. In some of his roles, such as the Flying Dutchman, he has not been matched to this day, fifty years later.

Therefore, in the late 1950's and early 1960's, George went to see Rudolf Bing to discuss plans for the following seasons. He realized that the opera house needed to give some performances to those who covered his roles, in case he had to cancel, as well as offer important opportunities to other baritones, but he knew exactly what he wanted to sing and how long he wanted to be in New York (usually not too long). The Met was prestigious, but George made more money on concert tours and guest appearances. The open and frank conversations usually ended to George's satisfaction. He criticized some of Bing's repertory decisions, but not Bing's business practice. Once an agreement was reached, London's manager took care of the details and exact dates.

Eventually George found that he was better off negotiating for himself at all houses and did most of the negotiating for Bayreuth and the Vienna State Opera as well. His European manager, Martin Taubman, took care of details there. George negotiated repertoire and dates; however, he always left the bargaining about fees to his managers. He did not feel that it was good for him to argue about money.

On October 28, 1957, George London opened the Metropolitan Opera season in the title role of *Eugene Onegin*. It was a new production, and his co-stars were Lucine Amara and Richard Tucker. The hero's part, a brooding and Byronesque character, suited George extremely well, he had sung it many times with great success in Vienna.

Paola Novikova went to all the rehearsals and supervised every nuance of his interpretation and every detail of his costume and makeup. Although George had to look pale and bored, a deathly pallor was unbecoming on stage. Obviously he had to accept the instructions of the stage director, but sometimes Paola would tell George that he was too far back on the stage for the best effect during an aria. He always listened to her and at the next rehearsal, he compromised and stepped forward toward the audience without losing contact with the other singers on stage.

At the beginning of November 1957, there was a "close-up" feature about George London in *Life* magazine. The article was titled, "I Prefer Villains and the Sinners" and showed George in various character make ups from *Faust* and *The Tales of Hoffmann*. There were pictures of him jogging in Central Park, lifting weights, taking a lesson with Paola, and at home, with his family. Much love and intimacy was captured by the famous photographer Gordon Parks.

London was extremely pleased with the article. He could

not ask for better publicity, for at the time *Life* was one of the most widely read magazines in the world. These were good years. George could do no wrong in his career, and his family was flourishing. Indeed, these were good years for many Americans. During the later part of the 1950's everything seemed possible. The economy was thriving, and the world was at peace. The world of opera was enjoying a golden age with great voices capable of filling roles in any repertoire.

George's only complaint was that he was not doing enough recordings, but eventually he recorded all his roles, except Amonasro, which he always regretted. Today there is an important collection of compact disks of all his roles in several versions (even pirated copies of *Aida*), many more then he could have imagined since he did not live to see the advent of the compact disk.

In October 1958, George London sang at the Met opening again, this time as Scarpia, with Renata Tebaldi - his favorite Tosca. Eventually he sang Scarpia with most of the famous Toscas of his time, including Birgit Nilsson, Licia Albanese, and Maria Callas. Tebaldi liked performing with him and said "he was so handsome and taller than I." He was Scarpia for Callas's debut in the role, when she returned to the Met in 1956. On the night of the premiere, he went over to her dressing room to wish her "in boca lupo," the traditional good luck operatic saying. She was very impressed and told him that no other colleague had ever done that. During that season they appeared together on television in a rare *Tosca* second act performance for the Ed Sullivan show. After this, they remained friends and would see each other whenever she came to New York. The last time was for lunch at the Plaza Hotel, just a few months before her death in 1977. She was lonely and depressed. She asked him to stay for dinner, but he was living in Washington and had to go back. He was troubled by her sadness and shocked when she died soon afterwards.

He enjoyed playing the role of Scarpia, not only because

he was killed during the second act and could go home early, but because he loved Puccini's music and relished portraying the arrogant and ruthless Roman chief of police. He said, "Scarpia is not only a vicious and brutal executioner, he is also a grand seigneur in love with the most beautiful woman in Rome, and he has to have her." Sometimes during *Tosca*, as he was leaving the theater, he would go back toward the wings when the third act started. He wanted to hear the tenor sing his big aria that night or listen again to the soprano. He never ceased to be interested in other singers and loved all the music in the operas, not just what had been written for bass-baritones. He would stand backstage and watch the performance with the technicians and supporting members of the cast. When I was there with him, George had his arm on my shoulder and if he was pleased he murmured, "Isn't it beautiful?" as if it was his first night at the opera. He admired many of the singers with whom he performed, particularly Renata Tebaldi, Lisa Della Casa, Birgit Nilsson, Guilietta Simionato, Leonie Rysanek, Mario del Monaco, and Nicolai Gedda. He did his best work in their company.

During the following years, he repeated in New York the huge success he had in Bayreuth as the hero in Wagner's *Flying Dutchman*. At the premiere, George as the Dutchman and Leonie Rysanek as Senta generated such radiance and intensity that there were twenty-three curtain calls after the second act. The audience applauded right through the intermission. George wrote about this in a letter to his parents on January 14, 1960:

> The reception which Leonie Rysanek and I received at the Met last night following our big second act duet was the greatest I have ever experienced there. I had felt that there was a special atmosphere that we had created, and we were both in excellent voice, but we were quite unprepared for the way the house came down when we took our first bow together. As we stood before the cur-

tain she turned to me; tears came into her eyes, and she
threw her arms around me and embraced me before the
whole audience. It was so touching and so spontaneous,
I was deeply moved and the audience, too. There were
over 20 curtains after the second act and about the same
at the end. This was one of the most wonderful experiences of my career—one of those evenings that make up
for so much of the stupidity, common-place, and ups and
downs of this profession. I shall never forget it. Of course
Paola and Nora were in seventh heaven.

Obviously after such emotionally charged performances
we could not simply go home and go to bed. It took a long
time for George to "simmer down," as he put it. This was a
good excuse for having parties at our house after the opera.

I became very adept at organizing such late suppers, which
would be prepared during the day so that I could go to the
performance without worry. Everything was ready for our
friends and there was plenty of food, particularly for the singers, who were always hungry after a performance. There were
stories circulating about singers arriving at post-opera parties being served some cookies and soda by well- meaning
but ignorant hostesses, obviously unaware that many artists
do not eat before a performance. George was determined that
no such thing would happen in his house, and the buffet was
loaded with a variety of dishes for his guests.

On party nights I went straight home from the opera instead of going backstage. This way I was there to greet our
friends. On different occasions, they included his colleagues
Renata Tebaldi, Maria Callas, Leonie Rysanek, Birgit Nilsson,
Richard Tucker, Giorgio Tozzi, and Nicolai Gedda. Also in
later years the Russians, soprano Galina Vishnevskaya and
the baritone Pavel Lisitsian, whom we first met in Moscow,
would come after their first performances in New York. We
also invited conductors like Erich Leinsdorf, Dimitri
Mitropoulos, Karl Bohm, and the composer Gian Carlo

Menotti, in whose opera (*The Last Savage*) George starred. After the premiere of *The Tales of Hoffmann*, George reported to his parents on November 2, 1958:

> Following the opening we had an elaborate party which was intended as a celebration. Among our guests were Senator and Mrs. Javits, who are old friends of Nora's, Sidney Lumet the brilliant young movie and TV director and his wife, Gloria Vanderbilt, Mr. and Mrs. Billy Rose, Mr. and Mrs. Skitch Henderson, Steve Allen, Van Cliburn, the Soviet conductor Kiril Kondrashin, my colleagues Cesare Siepi and Roberta Peters, and the writer Joseph Wechsberg, and, of course, Bill Judd and Miss O'Neill of Columbia [Artists Management]. The party was really a great success with a relaxed atmosphere and excellent food. Everyone was delighted.

Many of his friends were journalists who came to visit when they were in town. He became close friends with RCA director George Marek, whom he met while doing a recording for RCA. In turn, at the Mareks' George met Harry Belafonte, and they spent many evenings together. Harry and George would often entertain the guests with a succession of anecdotes told with ever-increasing detail, getting raunchier and raunchier as the evening wore on. This friendly competition could go on until three o'clock in the morning, leaving the other guests exhausted from too much laughter.

After a performance, George was always in high spirits. In those days there were no bad performances for him. Some were greater than others; he was not a machine, but he was completely secure technically. He loved to be surrounded by friends, show off his beautiful home, and make sure that everyone was provided with ample food and drink. He would remember that one singer drank only beer after performances, another only white wine, and another a special mineral water.

He also took care of entertaining the guests. Not afraid to

use his voice since the next performance that was three or four days away, he talked at length. He delighted everyone with the latest jokes, doing his imitations of Italian, Jewish, Russian, or German accents. He expected his friends to stay until the early-morning hours, forgetting that some people had to get up the next morning to go to work.

The day after a performance George slept late. He used earplugs and heard nothing. The household was kept as quiet as possible.

In the summer of 1958, the family went to Vancouver where George sang *Don Giovanni* for the festival in a staging by Gunther Rennert, a director he admired a great deal. There was an excellent cast that included the Canadian debut of a young singer who overwhelmed George with the beauty of her voice and the ease with which she sang the incredibly difficult arias of Donna Anna. Her name was Joan Sutherland. George was so enthusiastic that he arranged an audition at the Met for her. Rudolf Bing was not present as he was on summer vacation in Europe, but his assistants who heard Joan did not engage her. However, she did not need any help from them. The following winter she had a huge success in *Lucia di Lammermoor* at Covent Garden. George cut out the reviews from the *London Times* and the *Manchester Guardian* and showed them to Mr. Bing. "This is the soprano I recommended last summer," he said. Joan made a triumphant debut at the Met the following year.

When Marina was two years old, we wanted to have another child. There was too much of an age difference between her and the older boys, therefore she was like an only child. I became pregnant during our stay in Vancouver. Therefore, I was unable to accompany George on a tour of Israel the following spring. He was fascinated to discover Israel during this trip, and while there, he performed excerpts from *Boris Godunov* with the Israel Philharmonic, conducted by Josef Krips.

George was home by the middle of March and sang *Don*

Giovanni, *Boris Godunov*, *Tosca*, and *Eugene Onegin* at the Met. I attended all of these, and trekked backstage at each intermission, but found the steep stairs to the dressing rooms in the old opera house increasingly difficult to climb.

Onegin is a long opera. The third act has two scenes, and the hero is in both. That evening it was very late by the time we got home; there was no question of company, for I was too tired. We nearly had a repeat of Marina's arrival. Again I had to wake up George in the early morning hours. This time he was not half as nervous, but just as sleepy. However, I was in a greater hurry; there was no time for breakfast. The streets were deserted Sunday morning, April 5, 1959, as the taxi rushed us to Mount Sinai Hospital. Later we had the great joy of welcoming a healthy baby, this time a boy we named Marc.

After the birth, George had to leave for a concert tour and wrote from Dartmouth College, New Hampshire: "I am grateful and happy and pray that my son will grow up in a peaceful world. That is all I have to yearn for. I have just about everything else."

The penthouse, which seemed so roomy at first, was slowly filling up. Daisy had gone back to her ancestors and was replaced with a playful beagle. He had a sad and wise expression and was aptly named Socrates. Then my nephew Patrick enrolled at Riverdale Country School where Andy and Philip were also going and came to live with us. He occupied one of the maid's rooms with a separate entrance at the back, an arrangement that suited him perfectly. He was almost grown up; Andy and Philip, too, were becoming teenagers, and the back entrance was convenient for letting girlfriends in and out of the house. The three boys also took advantage of the apartment to give their own parties with loud music and dancing. When things got out of hand, they enlisted George's help as bouncer. Whenever undesirable youths tried to crash the party, the boys called George, who, incensed by such behavior, put on his most menacing expression. He threw the unwelcome guests out bodily with a thunderous "Don't you dare come back here!" The doorman overheard one of the outcasts saying on his way out: "Boy, they have a giant there who gets rid of people."

George, always sensitive and considerate, wondered how I could cope with the small fry, the teenagers, and a husband who worried about rehearsals, recordings, and performances all at once. "I love everything about my life and about you," I answered. "It's like being on stage every day in my favorite play."

Chapter 9
Life in Bayreuth and the Ring in Köln

George spoke very often about his performances at the Bayreuth festival and his special working relationship with Wieland Wagner. There were many weeks of rehearsals in preparation of the scheduled performances, so I decided to come to Germany with the family to avoid months of separation and to provide a stable home life for George.

He had described repeatedly the high level of the performances and the special atmosphere in and around the Festspielhaus. My turn to experience the spiritual impact of Wagner's shrine took place at a rehearsal of *Parsifal* soon after my arrival in Bayreuth. Not surprisingly, I was very much in awe. I had met Wieland Wagner the preceding summer at the Vierjahreszeiten, a famous hotel and restaurant in Munich. We had dinner with Wieland and Hans Knappertsbusch; the next table was occupied by the Duke and Duchess of Windsor and a large party. The conversation at our table was entirely in German, which at that point I had hardly spoken in twelve years. Although I understood everything, I had trouble finding my words and said little the whole evening. I explained my silence to George later. "They must have thought that I am a moron," I said. "Nonsense," he answered, laughing. "They enjoyed the food and thought you were a beautiful and perfect wife who knows better than to interrupt an interesting conversation."

I was tremendously impressed by Wieland. He was of average height, with prematurely graying hair, and bore a strong resemblance to pictures of his grandfather. He exuded strength and assurance, which came from his encyclopedic knowledge of all kinds of subjects, from Greek mythology to Germanic legends. He commented with scorn about his youthful experiences in Hitler's time. He proclaimed himself to be liberal and to have an innate distrust of heroes, the police, and the military. Recently Wieland Wagner has been accused of pro-Nazi activities during the war as well as anti-Semitism, but at that time George was not aware of this. He admired Wieland's talent, whose major interests were the festival and his own stagings.

In an afterword to Victor Gollancz's book *The Ring at Bayreuth*, written in 1966, Wieland wrote,

> We are no longer prepared to accept the aesthetic theories either of Richard Wagner or of his immediate successors as sacrosanct in relation to his works. My generation has been, and still is, concerned not to luxuriate in aesthetic conceptions as if these were defined immutably for all time but to seek out the inner laws inherent in a work of genius and to interpret it uncompromisingly, as we find it mirrored in our souls.

In answer to this search, Wieland produced a succession of provocative, not always successful, but always fascinating stagings for Wagner's operas.

George wrote in *The Saturday Review*:

> When I first met Wieland Wagner [in 1950] he was thirty-three years old. He died on October 19, 1966, at the age of forty-nine. His entire career covered a brief span of fifteen years. Yet in this period he completely revolutionized the staging of Wagner operas and profoundly influenced the style in which many contemporary operas are produced.

No wonder George found Wieland "the most fascinating

individual I ever met."

Wieland had the reputation of being difficult and abrupt if he did not like you. For instance, when George introduced to him a young soprano with a beautiful voice but who was not overly bright, he commented, "What is this voice doing in this woman?" and dismissed her summarily.

It was difficult to get close to him. However, he was always very courteous to me, no doubt a reflection of the respect and feelings of friendship he felt for George. As I entered the auditorium for the *Parsifal* rehearsal, I felt intimidated. I was about to sit down somewhere toward the back when Wieland spotted me. "Frau London, come and sit here," he said, pointing to the seat next to him. This was unusually friendly on his part for I knew he did not like people in the halls during rehearsals and George had to ask for permission to bring me.

There were at most ten people in the audience when the lights went out. I had the impression that the performance was given just for me, like for the king of Bavaria who demanded a private performances of Richard Wagner's works.

Soon I was surrounded by the music, which I had never heard played quite like this. George wrote for *The Saturday Review:* "The entrance of the Knights of the Grail is unforgettable: From the deepest recesses of the vast stage, seemingly from infinity, an army of swaying men moves closer as the music grows in almost unbearable intensity until they have assumed their places around a huge circular table in the center." Then the Knights of the Grail intoned the Grail motif. The voices, chosen from Germany's best choruses, seemed to come from heaven. Then Amfortas was carried onstage on a litter. Instinctively I clutched my hands in a tight grip. Soon George's voice rose strong and moving, in his long "complaint." I was close to tears and shattered by emotion.

When the lights went on at intermission, I could not say a word. Wieland, perhaps aware of my feelings, turned to me and said: "Grandfather could not have visualized anyone

greater than George London." He always spoke of Richard
Wagner as if he were in the next room and would come over
at any moment to give his opinion.

This rehearsal remains in my memory as one of the greatest musical and theatrical experiences of my life. I returned to
Parsifal each time George sang it and every performance had
a degree of excitement and fervor I found nowhere else. For
an artist in the 1950s, being part of the festival was like entering a religious shrine. The singer felt part of an elite that
performed artistic feats worthy of the heroic figures he im-
personated. The Wagner family reinforced this impression.

It was impermissible for an artist involved in any of the
operas to behave obnoxiously in public. For example, after it
was reported that a soprano had been seen drunk at the Eule,
the artists' favorite restaurant, Wieland declared, "The
Bayreuth Isolde cannot be an alcoholic," and she was not re-
engaged.

I felt privileged to be a part of this special world. Although
I wondered why Richard Wagner had picked so drab and
undistinguished a town for his Festspielhaus, I accepted the
uncomfortable housing and rainy climate.

George loved to work there. The artistic level was high
and he enjoyed the weeks of rehearsal that built up to challenging performances. During these weeks there were many
meals taken together with other artists. Everyone relaxed,
ate large quantities of heavy German food, and swapped
outrageous jokes. As soon as the festival began, the town
was invaded by tourists, the restaurants became crowded,
and we no longer went out.

Because the artists expected to stay for a long time, most
of them came with their families. We often visited each other
and also entertained friends coming from nearby Munich.
The first summer, in 1956, George invited all his colleagues
to come over and admire his four-month-old daughter. The
tenor Ramón Vinay, who was performing the role of Parsifal,
came with his camera and captured Marina's big brown eyes

and long eyelashes. George was bursting with pride.

The weeks of preparation went by too quickly and soon the festival began. Every performance started at four o'clock, and the crowd milled around the opera house in evening dress and tuxedos in the early-afternoon sunshine. After each act there was an hour-long intermission, which allowed everyone to build up their endurance by fortifying themselves at the adjoining Festspielhaus restaurant.

Because of this custom, George was faced with a dilemma during *Parsifal* performances. He appeared in the first and the third act but not at all in the second. This act lasted one hour, the two intermissions took another two hours. So there was an interval of three hours between his appearances on the stage. He tried to sit around in his dressing room and have dinner brought to him, but the food was cold and distasteful. He reviewed the score one more time, then paced around the hallway visiting with friends and other singers, generally not knowing what to do with himself and, as he said, "losing the concentration." Finally he found a solution. As soon as the first act was finished, he removed costume and makeup. I drove him home where he had a good hot meal, then a quiet nap for an hour. Then I drove him back to the theater where he still had an hour to put on a fresh makeup, vocalize briefly, and put on his costume. Now he was rested and full of energy for the last act. I returned the car to the parking lot and rushed back to the opera house just as the crowd was coming in. For this reason, I almost never saw the second act of *Parsifal*.

The first year George encouraged me to see as many of the operas as possible, for he wanted me to experience the entire magic of Bayreuth, not only his performances. This was a period of many great Wagnerian singers and it was a privilege to be there. Unfortunately, George could not go with me too often as he was especially busy that summer.

He was to sing the role of the Flying Dutchman for the first time in a staging by Wolfgang Wagner. Wolfgang, co-

director of the festival with Wieland, was very knowledgeable as well, and there was a great rivalry between the brothers. Presently Wolfgang is the sole director of the Bayreuth
Festival. George spent long hours working with Paola
Novikova, who came to stay with us to prepare him for this
role, which he termed "terribly demanding, vocally covering
the widest scope of dramatic and lyrical singing." The great
American soprano Astrid Varnay sang the role of Senta in
this production and she writes about her work with George.

As a young girl in New York City, I was enormously
impressed by Ezio Pinza. But, in time I became aware of
the fact that Mr. Pinza was passing the high crest of his
career and wondered if anyone would ever come along
to take his place for my generation. And then it happened!
A singer by the name of George London appeared, and
there seemed to be very little in his voice category that
George London *couldn't* do. A Mozart singer of style
and grace, he also had all that it took for the standard
French and Italian repertoire, and, in a day and age when
no singer not born to that language ever tried to sing in
Russian, he was invited to do Boris at the Bolshoi, the
first American singer ever honored with a role in that
repertoire.
He proved himself to have all the phenomenal vocal,
theatrical and stylistic attributes that make for a definitive Wagnerian. In so many ways, George London was
larger than life.
At rehearsals he was all business, totally immersed in
the intellectual, emotional, musical and dramatic demands of whatever he was interpreting, adjusting like a
finely calibrated machine to the impulses coming to him
from conductors, directors and his colleagues on the
stage, plus responding to the impulses of his own noble
convictions. But – when the rehearsal ended, or the curtain came down on a performance, he quite unexpect-
edly became a wise-cracker, who could have a whole

group of friends and colleagues convulsed with laughter in whatever language happened to be going at the time. He had a working knowledge of them all.

Most regrettably, destiny only allowed me to participate in one portion of his career, sharing the stage with him in the Wagnerian repertoire, although this was not our first collaboration. He joined my husband conductor Hermann Weigert and myself in a Munich recording studio in 1953 for a smashing rendition of the Aida-Amonasro duet, which had me regretting for years that we never got to sing the whole opera together in the theatre. We then met again in Bayreuth in a 1956 production of *Der Fliegende Holländer*, which I described in my memoirs, but apparently George London knew about me even before we first met. As a matter of fact, in early 1951, when the Wagner brothers were about to raise the phoenix of the Wagner Festival from the ashes of World War II, they seriously considered engaging a relatively "unknown quantity" by the name of Astrid Varnay. Scheduling being what it is in our business, I was unable to make it to Bayreuth to audition for them. So they went out and asked a collection of conductors, singers and other colleagues what they thought of my work, and, as Wolfgang Wagner later told me, one of the people who sang my praises was George London, who must have heard me somewhere, but whom I had never actually met face-to-face at that time.

When you come to think about it, George London, who was known for the kindness and encouragement he gave young artists was already doing kindnesses for qualified colleagues in the early springtime of his own career.

There are many times when I have reflected how much George might have contributed to the art and craft we share if he had been spared to this world longer – I am convinced he would have been a manager who could and would have changed the face of opera. This was tragically not meant to be, but I am convinced he has given us a shining example of what magic can happen when art and craft come together on the highest possible level. I sure miss him.

The premiere was a tremendous success, George wrote to his parents: "I felt that I had done, vocally and dramatically, a first-rate job. This role really suits me, and I feel in time that I can become especially identified with it." The Flying Dutchman became one of his most favorite roles. In 1960 he repeated his success in an inspired new staging by Wieland Wagner. In the *Saturday Review* article of 1967 George described as unforgettable,

> ...the entrance of the Hollander's ship; a vast blood-red sail descends from the heights of the stage to meet a gigantic prow which rises from the floor, giving the impression that the ship, in its hugeness is bursting into the auditorium; the Hollander, himself, during his entire monologue, crucified on the prow of the doomed vessel, arms outstretched, motionless throughout the scene, only his face bathed in a ghostly light revealing his torment and his tragedy.

Although George preferred the role of Boris Godunov, the Flying Dutchman became my favorite part for him. Perhaps he was more handsome as Don Giovanni or more dramatic as Boris; but I felt that he identified most completely with the Dutchman who was condemned to roam the seas like a wandering Jew. The role suited him vocally, covering exactly the range of his voice and showing it off at its best. In the Bayreuth production, he wore a black leather costume, high boots, and a long cape made of netting, which made him appear even taller. He was made up to look older than he was, with a gray wig, a gray beard, and lines in his face. He looked extremely handsome. The critic Martin Bernheimer feels his was "an unequalled definite interpretation."

After this premiere, which opened the festival, there was a reception at the city hall given by the Wagners for the principal stars and specially invited guests, including the German head of state, ministers, and some well-known international figures. The city hall was the former castle of the margraves (German nobility), and the supper took place in a long dining room by candlelight with a waiter in livery standing behind each of the high-backed tapestry-covered chairs. It was a fairyland evening enhanced by all the compliments that George received. I felt elated, happy for him and for myself to have the good fortune to share these hours with him.

Winifred Wagner (Wieland and Wolfgang's mother), who had been banished from Bayreuth because of her relationship with Hitler, was eventually allowed back with the provision that she would not interfere in the management of the Festival. She occupied an apartment in a wing of Haus Wahnfried, the palatial villa Richard Wagner built for his family. She took a fancy to George London and invited us for tea. Several times he was able to get out of it, but finally we could no longer decline. We entered the house through a huge hall filled with pictures of Wagner and his family and were led upstairs to a separate, cozy apartment. Winifred greeted us, clearly pleased by our visit. As we sat balancing delicate china cups on our laps and chatted amiably with this pleasant old lady, I could not help thinking that less than twenty years earlier, she had been sitting this way with Adolf Hitler. She was tall, with white hair pulled back in a chignon, and had white skin with handsome features. We spoke German, for she had been so completely assimilated into German culture that she rarely used her native English tongue. We talked mostly about opera and past interpreters of the great Wagner roles. She was obviously knowledgeable and opinionated, she had been the wife of Richard Wagner's son, Siegfried, and had also known Cosima Wagner, Richard's wife. Thus she was a direct link to the nineteenth century. Although the subject was never alluded to, it became clear in the course of the conversation that her political opinions had not changed over the years and that she still revered the Nazi past. George felt that if we had met her then, and he had not been a singer she admired, she would not have hesitated to send him to the gas chamber. When we left we breathed in the cool summer air and knew we would never visit her again.

In 1961, George sang again in Wieland's staging of *The Flying Dutchman* in Venice at the Teatro La Fenice. This lovely baroque auditorium, heavily decorated with gilded carvings, had extraordinary acoustics.

The engagement was in May and for three weeks we lived in the Grand Hotel overlooking the Grand Canal in an apartment furnished with precious antique furniture. The rehearsal schedule was light, the weather was mild, and we took long walks in the narrow alleys of Venice.

One night after a performance, we were walking back to the hotel, and, as usual, the gondoliers were trying to attract customers by shouting "Gondola, gondola, Signore." Suddenly one of them, recognizing George, called out to him, "But you, sir, you don't need any boat, you already have your own ship even if it is a ghostly one."

Every summer when he arrived in Bayreuth, Wieland Wagner sent over a score of *Die Meistersinger von Nürnberg,* with a note hoping George would consider the part of Hans Sachs. Each year George replied that he did not see himself as the benign, poetic German shoemaker. But George was already learning the role of Wotan for *The Ring of the Nibelungen,* to prepare for a new staging of the *Ring,* which was to be shown in Bayreuth in 1965. Wieland Wagner decided that there would be tryout periods for the productions in the Cologne Opera House during successive years. Rheingold opened on May 22, 1962, Berndt Wessling, in his biography "Wieland Wagner, der Enkel" the grandson writes:

The Wotan of George London dominated the scene. His powerful, moving, imperious voice drowns out the busy Sawallisch Orchestra. A star among stars in Cologne this led to a fiasco when other, rather provincial substi-

tutes took his place in later revivals of the Tetralogy.
They did not come close by far to the level of probably
the most important Heldenbaryton of his time

The premiere of the second opera in Cologne, Walküre
took place on May 26, 1963. Wessling writes: " Anja Slije
was the youthful, engaging Brunhilde and Hildegard
Hillebricht the Sieglinde and Sawallisch conducted a trans-
parent, perfect performance. "

Thus Cologne became an extension of Bayreuth with the
same conductor, Wolfgang Sawallisch, and many of the same
performers who were supposed to take part in Wieland
Wagner's 1965 new *Ring* in Bayreuth.

The third opera staged in Köln was *Siegfried*, opening on
October 13, 1963. For each opera there were nearly three
weeks of rehearsal and George missed the children acutely
during his travels. When he did not see them he mentioned
his longing in every letter.

His friend, the bass Mark Elyn remembers this period:

When George arrived in Cologne to rehearse for the coming "Rheingold" and subsequently the entire "Ring." I
had already been in Cologne for a season and had sung
a number of roles and felt somewhat at home there. I
went up to George soon after his arrival and greeted
him and he remembered me from Los Angeles and seemed
happy to see a friendly face. We had lunch together
that day and talked about music and singing and all the
things that singers and friends talk about. The next day,
with no rehearsal of my own to attend, I went to the
stage to watch Wieland Wagner direct George and the
others in "Rheingold". Right before the lunch break,
Oskar Fritz Schuh, the Generalintendant (the director)
of the theater came to greet and welcome George to
Cologne. They had known each other from working
together in Vienna in the past and Schuh, who was not
noted for being the warmest or most caring individual in

the world, thought that it would be polite to welcome a famous guest star. Schuh asked George if there was anything he needed or if there was anything he could do to be of assistance, while never for a moment (being Schuh) thinking that George would actually make any request of him. George said "Yes, There is something. "The kantine (cafeteria) in this theater is simply a disgrace. The artists at rehearsal or during a performance need to be able to eat something beside a Brotchen with Wurst" (roll with sausage.) Schuh, though taken aback, sort of recovered and said that it was very good of George to bring this problem to his personal attention and that he would see that something was done to remedy this situation. Schuh, of course, had never set foot in the cafeteria and did not, in all probability even know where it was and never intended to find out. George knew all of this but really felt that he was in a position to say something to try at least to better the conditions for his fellow artists. We laughed hard about the incident later but I think it was most impressive and illustrates another facet of George and his character and personality." Elyn continues: "My wife, Jackie and I had a small apartment in a rather nice building, half a block from the theater, but on the fourth floor and with no lift. I asked George if he would like to brave the stairs and come for dinner and he said he would be happy to do so. He came again very often and after sampling some of the Cologne restaurants that were not wonderful at that time, we all decided that at least on performance days, he should eat with us. He used to come early and the menu never varied. Jackie used to make us all a filet steak, boiled rice, and a tossed salad and we always had cooked fruit for dessert. That was, he decided, the best thing for his digestion and his taste buds. He was happy and we were happy to have him with us. After dinner we would have tea and he would vocalize a little and go off to the theater, probably around 6:00. I learned a great deal from his vocalizing and often he would explain to me what he was trying to accomplish with this or that exercise. On some occasions, he would ask me to sing some of these vocalizes and he would offer suggestions and give me some tips or criticism. He was always eager, from the start, to help every young artist, even when he had a performance of his own coming up in a few hours. In this way and other ways, he was the most generous singer I have ever known.

Mark Elyn continues his recollections:

These performances of the "Ring" operas were a huge milestone not only in the history of Wagner performances but of opera performances in general. And at the center of this great Ring cycle stood George London. I recall one occasion when I had a rehearsal with a conductor and wonderful coach called Fritz Lehan. He was a leading conductor at the Cologne Opera. The easiest route to his studio was to cross the stage which we did. On stage, Wieland Wagner was directing the cast of "Das Rheingold" and nearly every cast member was on stage. Lehan and I stopped for a few minutes to watch the rehearsal. They were rehearsing one of Loge's scenes and Wieland directed the singer to be very active running around all over the place etc...George was in the scene, standing there with his great spear and looking very noble. We watched for a while and Lehan remarked to me: "Mark, look at this scene: there is Loge running around and jumping all over the place and there is George London, just standing there and he is able to draw your eye and is ten times more interesting." Of course, he was absolutely right. This role of Wotan was tailor made for George or perhaps more accurately, George was born to play that role. In this Wieland Wagner production he achieved something that few other singing artists ever achieve.

Since George was lonely during these long periods, I came to Cologne with Marina, Marc and their nanny for the period of rehearsals and performances of *Siegfried*. During our stay the weather was miserable, cold with icy rain nearly every day. After a visit to the cathedral and shopping in the many toy stores, there was not much to do.

I decided to take Marina and Marc, only seven and four years old then, to part of a rehearsal, so they could see the dragon in *Siegfried*. They had a great time and shrieked with fear and delight. I related their reaction to Wieland Wagner with some hesitation, for he could be quite forbidding, but he was extremely pleased. "Yes, that is what I want; after all, it is also a fairy tale," he said.

This was the period of the closest collaboration between Wieland and George. They never tired of the rehearsals and went on discussing the operas at lunch and dinner in a small Italian restaurant, called Salvatore, which they had discovered. Wieland went into detailed psychological analysis of each character in the *Ring* and wanted to stress the subconscious impulses of good and evil in his new production. George found him fascinating, brilliant, continually inventive, and later wished he had been able to record everything he said.

He wrote in his article for the *Saturday Review:* "My personal debt to Wieland Wagner cannot be overstressed. He opened up for me a world of insight into dramatic characterization. His ideas about Amfortas, the Hollander, and the three Wotans, all of which I sang under his direction, were endlessly fascinating."

After the opening performance in Cologne of *Walküre* on May 26, 1963, which happened to be four days after the composer's birthday, George commented in a letter to his parents: "Last night was vocally and artistically one of the most perfect performances of my career." Wieland wrote to him the next day: "I must congratulate you for your extraordinary achievement on Sunday. You have fulfilled completely my expectations for your Wotan, yes, even surpassed them. I am very happy and I thank you. That was a really worthy birthday celebration for Richard Wagner. Stay the way you are and remain faithful to me."

The Ring of the Nibelungen was given in its entirety in Cologne in the autumn of 1963. George London sang the three Wotans for the first time in the same week. There were some cuts in the *Siegfried* Wotan but no one seemed to object. It was a major achievement for George and all the new stagings were a great success, promising even greater achievements for the festival production of 1965. George and Wieland, who came from such different backgrounds, were linked by a common devotion to their art. But their precious friendship lasted only another three years. George was unaware that Wieland Wagner had been diagnosed with lung cancer as early as 1962. He died in 1966, and George never sang in Bayreuth again.

Chapter 10
Caring for the voice

During the years 1956 to 1962 London's career as a singer was at its apex. He was offered more engagements than he could accept for the most interesting roles and productions in the greatest opera houses in the world. His appearances were greeted with enthusiastic applause from thousands of admiring people, and on any given night after the performance, he was usually elated and well pleased with himself.

It was late at night or the next day that he started to question and doubt. Deep inside he knew his worth, yet he felt that to sustain his position he had to get still better. To this end he devised a series of routines that would ensure constant improvement.

He was very health conscious and every morning, without fail, he did his physical exercises. These included a series of breathing exercises with weights if he was home, a series of sit-ups, and an awesome number of push-ups, which he did with his feet up on a chest of drawers. After showering he examined his physique, then went on to look at his face with evident disapproval. He disliked his eyes, which were set too close for him; his nose, which he dubbed too small for his face; and most of all his "fleshy jowls." He was difficult to photograph and often complained that if he had been more photogenic he would have been able to make a career in the movies or in television. If he had had perfect features in addition to all his gifts he might have been too full of himself. But he wanted to be handsome, not out of vanity, but because it would promote his career to greater heights.

His appetite was commensurate with his six-foot two-frame. He ate a copious breakfast while listening to records, usually baroque music. He read *The New York Times* thoroughly whenever available and complained that there was no news in regional papers when he was on tour. He always completed the Times crossword puzzle in record time, writing all of the answers in ink, with a fountain pen.

When he was in New York, he went to Paola Novikova's apartment for a singing lesson almost every day. He would sing scales and arpeggios and other musical patterns, repeating them over and over to build the right physical position out of which the perfect sound could be produced. He sang arpeggios on the vowel *A* up through the *passaggio*, or passage tones, to the top of his range darkening the vowel as he proceeded higher. He perfected sustained notes on the I *(ee)* vowel until the legato flow of the breath met with Paola's approval. He made sure that he had perfect support of the breath, which was always necessary but particularly so for the long phrases of Wagner's music.

After the vocal exercises, which lasted about half an hour, Paola's husband, Werner Singer, came in for an hour. He often traveled with George as his accompanist and mostly played during the lessons. During this part of the lesson, they rehearsed new material or went over some Schubert or Brahms songs for the hundredth time until every intonation and every piece's phrasing passed Paola's criticism. George also practiced new roles with her and wrote to his parents, after the premiere of *The Flying Dutchman*: "To Paola, I owe a great deal, because her insight into the vocal and interpretive aspects of the part were of incalculable help to me." Her knowledge in matters of voice and music was endless.

George had introduced his friend, the tenor Nicolai Gedda to Paola and he too started working with her. Gedda wrote in his memoirs that thanks to her lessons "my voice became more flexible and equalized...one should not be able to detect any differences between the various registers; the sound should be the same all the times...The real difficulty for a singer is that the quality, strength, and positioning has to be just as good on the high notes as on the low ones."

George London, like Nicolai Gedda and many others of their colleagues knew that frequent lessons were essential to keeping the voice in the best possible condition.

After his lesson, if he did not have a performance the next day, George would loaf a bit, do some window-shopping, and have a late, late lunch because it was well past two o'clock by then.

In New York, he loved to go to the Russian Tea Room on 57th street where he was pretty sure to meet an acquaintance. After lunch he only had to cross the street to have a quick chat with his manager or check up with the patient Mary Crennon, who booked all the artists' travels, and make sure that he was not leaving anywhere "at the crack of dawn," as he said, which meant anytime before eleven the day before a performance. By four o'clock George wanted to be home to have time to study. He preferred to have a year's time to learn a new part and explained how he went about it in a speech to a young audience:

> I developed a system to prepare an operatic role which thereafter served me quite well. The first step was to master the text of a new role. If the language of the opera was one that I only partially understood (I didn't have too great a problem because I learned to speak French and German fluently and Italian serviceably; I am thinking in my own case of Russian), I wrote in the score above each foreign word the exact English equivalent so that while I was studying the part every time I went through the score with my pianist, the words were imprinting themselves in my mind and a time came when I knew what every word meant and thereby I could give the infinite colorings and the nuances to my interpretation.

The thing that makes an artist interesting is the fact that he *can* give colorings and nuances, and if you don't know what the words mean or only have a general idea you cannot do this.

Having memorized the words, your next problem is to work on the pronunciation of those words. If there was a recording of the role sung by artists native to the part, I would study those recordings very carefully, listen for the genuine authentic inflection.

George was fanatical about diction.

"In English, we have *tee* and *dee* sounds and we don't roll our *rs*. These are built-in handicaps in singing foreign languages." Further describing his methods for study, he added:

Having mastered the text, I was ready for the musical coaching of the role. If, in studying a worthwhile piece of music, you are scrupulously faithful to the printed direction and dynamic markings of the composer, you will as a result already have seventy-five percent of your interpretation. The interpretation basically and fundamentally comes from the music, and if you have paid attention to the sixteenth note, the staccato markings, the portamento, the contrast in dynamics that are written in the score, you will have gone a long, long way to having developed the style and the interpretation of the role.

George explained his good relationship with conductors as follows:

An outstanding conductor will take up your role where the coach has left off. He will have his own strong ideas about the character and at this point your advance preparation musically and dramatically will serve you well. You will be able to fight with conviction for certain things that you feel strongly about. The conductor may not always agree with you and in that case you must learn to compromise. I could usually find a *modus vivendi*.

London always tried to find a well-known performer of the part he was preparing and then persuade him to work with him. They were mostly retired singers who were flattered and pleased to transmit their knowledge and their artistry:

In my career, I was fortunate to find some truly outstanding people with whom I studied privately my important roles. Before I went to Europe in 1949, I sought out a Russian bass-baritone by the name of George Dubrovsky. He was a younger colleague of Chaliapin and he was a product of a school of acting which was typical of the Russian lyric theater and also of the Moscow Art Theater. From Dubrovsky I was able to learn an entire style of operatic acting, gestures and attitudes such as only one of his background could show me. It was Dubrovsky to whom I went to study *Boris Godunov* (a part with which I became somehow identified) and which I was privileged to sing in all parts of the world in later years. Dubrovsky had sung the part of Boris over five hundred times and he passed on to me all the treasures of his accumulated experience in the role. He taught me not only the details of my own part but particularly of the characters with whom I would work. He made of me a stage director should it have become necessary. He taught me the role of my son, the Tsarevich, and of Shuisky, people with whom I worked very closely.

He showed me how the boyars should bow, how the people should properly cross themselves in the Orthodox fashion, how the archbishop should bless mc (how the archbishop blesses you is different than when your mother blesses you in Russia) and a myriad of such details. He assumed that the stage director would not know these details and experience proved that he was correct. With Dubrovsky, I studied *Boris Godunov*, I studied

Scarpia in *Tosca* and also Mephistopheles in *Faust*, and I worked with him every movement, every gesture and I knew exactly what the people working with me were going to do. I was ready in those parts.

During the years in Vienna, I studied several of my important roles with a man named Alfred Jerger. He was a great singing actor at the Vienna Opera and in leading German theaters from the twenties to the forties. He had a demonic personality, reminiscent of the young Tibbett though he was not as fine a singer. Jerger was a Viennese, and he trained me for the role of Don Giovanni in the elegant tradition which had been typical of the administration of Richard Strauss, and this tradition was carried over into the postwar ensemble of the Vienna Opera. He saw Don Giovanni as a Renaissance man, a powerful, elegant and fearless person, and he helped me build a characterization which over the years I was to alter little.

For the role of Eugene Onegin, I also went to Jerger although it might have been more ideal to study with a Russian, but I never could find one who had actually sung it in performance. Onegin is a highly problematical figure and difficult to portray. I heard the opera when I was in Russia, both in Moscow and in Leningrad, and I was as dissatisfied with the two Russian Onegins I heard as I was with my own. I never really felt happy with my performance of Eugene Onegin although the critics thought that I was a good Onegin. I was somehow always frustrated about my Onegin and in spite of the diligent work that I did with Jerger on this role I was not prepared for the events of the opening night performance at the Met of *Eugene Onegin* in 1957.

During the rehearsals, I had been warned. . . There is a famous duel scene which takes place on the outskirts of Petersburg in the winter. Through an unfortunate, stupid set of circumstances, Onegin is about to fight a duel with his best friend, the young poet Lenski. It is a desolate scene, snow on the ground, and the stage director made a special point of telling me: "Now look, before you move into position for this duel, you must cock the pistol because if you don't cock the pistol it will not go off. Therefore you will have trouble killing Lenski."

So during all of the rehearsals I cocked the pistol and I walked back and I turned and I held the pistol and the music built up in crescendo and I lowered the pistol and pointed it at Lenski's heart and I pulled the trigger and it exploded and everything went fine. For the contingency that I should forget to cock the pistol, a stagehand had been placed in the wings also with a pistol and therefore should my pistol not fire, one could expect that his pistol would fire and give the same illusion.

Well, it was the excitement of opening night, I took the pistol, I walked into position, I raised the pistol, the music started building up to the crescendo, I started to walk towards Lenski, and I realized that I had not cocked the pistol, and so when I brought the pistol down and pulled the trigger nothing was going to happen and I was praying that my savior in the wings would be on the ball. I lowered the pistol, it was pointed directly at Lenski's heart. I pulled the trigger and of course nothing happened.

But nothing happened backstage either. Our stagehand friend was off having a smoke, I assume, or perhaps a drink; in any case he wasn't there. Now, I held this pistol in this position for a long, long time. It probably was only five seconds but it seemed like five hours, an eternity. The tenor, Richard Tucker, couldn't take it, he couldn't stand the tension, there was no reason for him to collapse on the stage, nothing had happened, but he started to sink to the ground and the second he hit the floor the pistol went off, offstage. I rushed forward as I am supposed to. The only other person on the stage was Lenski's second, a character called Zaretski, and I said to Zaretski "Dead!" Lenski, of course, was lying there, Zaretski was kneeling next to him and Zaretski turned to me and as was also in the score he said: "Dead" and then under his breath, so that only I could hear it: "of a heart attack."

Mandryka in *Arabella* was another role that George London studied with Alfred Jerger, who had been the very first Mandryka under the baton and direction of the composer, Richard Strauss. When he was preparing the part of Golaud in *Pelléas et Mélisande*, London worked with Carlton Gould who had sung the role in Paris with Mary Garden, the first Melisande. The he consulted Lawrence Tibbett, who had preceded him in the role. He was very gracious and gave George his own costume for his performances at the Met.

George was aware that people of different nationalities and different backgrounds moved in different ways, and he tried to implement this in his acting.

"The theater has its own rules and verities," he said.

> One can borrow from and be influenced by life but should never try to substitute human for dramatic behavior. The performer who is moved to real tears by a scene he is playing succeeds only in troubling and embarrassing the audience. Between human and theatrical emotion there is a fine dividing line, and one may never cross it.

All together, George had a thorough musical and dramatic knowledge of his role by the time rehearsals started at the opera house. These took place in various rehearsal rooms a week or so before the performance and on the stage if it was a new production or a first for the season. (If an artist was not singing the first performance, there were hardly any rehearsals, just a short practice session with piano, possibly with some of the other principals.)

George insisted that by the time he went on stage the role had to be "like second nature to me." He preferred trying new parts in small theaters in Europe, but sometimes this was not possible and so he did his first Scarpia at the Met and his first Flying Dutchman in Bayreuth.

Because of his intense preparation preceding his performances, he was able to go on stage with a great deal of assurance. He did not endure the agonies that plagued some of his colleagues. It is said that soprano Lily Pons was sick before every performance. Another soprano prayed fervently in her dressing room before her entrance on stage, and a famous tenor held hands with his wife in the wings until the last second.

George did not indulge in such practices; however, on the day of a performance he followed a special routine, always the same, which provided him with special security, possibly it was his way of being superstitious "if it worked last time it will work again."

He got up around ten-thirty and, after exercising, had his usual breakfast of coffee, one egg, toast, and salad. He believed implicitly that he would become ill if he did not eat salad twice a day. While eating, he listened to a favorite piece of music, Monteverdi or Vivaldi, or Schubert quartets, or a Mozart symphony; never vocal music on such days. Then he vocalized for about fifteen to twenty minutes. This took place either in the bedroom or more often in the bathroom with the water running. I once asked him why he sang in the bathroom, and he said, "In the beginning I always lived in hotel rooms and I was afraid to disturb the neighbors. So I ran the shower thinking the noise would cover my voice. Anyway, it *sounds* better in the bathroom."

When Marina was in nursery school, all the children were asked what their fathers did for a living and she answered, "My Daddy sings in the shower."

Although we had a piano at home, George preferred a pitch pipe and went through a series of scales, arpeggios, also making crescendos and decrescendos using different vowel sounds and taking his voice slowly to the highest notes of his range.

If he was satisfied with what he heard, he stopped soon, all was well; if he felt that he was not in good voice, he kept on trying more exercises. I listened and came in to tell him that I thought that he sounded wonderful. To which he replied each time, "Do you really think so?" To be convinced that he was in good voice was a large part of the battle.

He used to say that a singer's misfortune was that he could not really hear himself because he carried his instrument within himself. On the day of a performance George did not answer the telephone. He liked to be left alone as much as possible. If the weather was nice, he went for a walk with the dog or enjoyed a short solitary stroll. By early afternoon he took a nap and after that he shaved, late in the day, since he had a very thick beard and wanted his skin to be perfectly smooth before applying his stage makeup.

At five o'clock he had dinner, the same menu each time, consisting of rare steak, baked potato, the inevitable salad, and very light tea.

Just before dinner he once again went over the score of the opera he was singing that night, at least for the thirtieth time. This was another ritual that gave him a feeling of ultimate security and started the slow transformation of George London into the character he was going to be on stage that night.

He left for the opera house immediately after dinner. Exactly two hours before the beginning of the performance, he was in his dressing room, in front of the mirror, starting to do his makeup. Usually he did this himself; sometimes he enlisted the help of the makeup artist of the house if he thought he or she was talented.

Actually he loved to do his own makeup and engineer the changes of his eyes, eyebrows and cheekbones. He said his own features were too weak, thus an ideal canvas for stage makeup, which can be very heavy because the actor is far away from the audience. Most of the parts he played required a moustache and a beard, which were pasted on very securely with spirit gum. For Mephisto or the villains in *The Tales of Hoffmann*, he pasted fake bumps on his nose to make it larger and stronger. He insisted that the smallest detail was crucial in giving him the character he wanted. When he was finally satisfied with his work, he called for the person in charge of wigs.

Of course, the look of a singer's wig is of the greatest importance, but it is also important that he feels comfortable in it. London hated to have anything cover his ears, even partially, because it made it difficult for him to hear himself. Almost all the roles he sang required a wig; some he owned himself, like the beautiful white wig for the Count in *The Marriage of Figaro*, acquired in Paris, or his Boris wig; but mostly they belonged to the theater where he sang, in order to match others in the production.

The wig was combed and dressed freshly for each performance and pasted on with great care. For *Don Giovanni*, George kept his own black hair, penciled in to make his forehead somewhat lower, and wore a moustache and a small black beard. In later years, when his hair receded too much, he had to accept the fact that he needed a wig even for this role. "When you finally understand the role of Don Giovanni you are too old to play it," he said ruefully.

Once the wig was in place, there was a last check of the face, a line added on the forehead or a few hairs from the moustache cut off so they would not interfere with the movement of his lips. Then he would call the dresser to help him put on the costume, which sometimes was terribly heavy. Boris's coronation cloak, richly embroidered with stones, weighed nearly fifty pounds. He fiddled for a while with hooks, with belts, with the perfect angle of a sword, the ideal way of wearing a necklace. Suddenly he stood up very straight. He was ready; any trace of hesitation, anything tentative was gone—he *was* the character.

He started to vocalize again but not too much. It was said that some singers left their best notes in the dressing room because they vocalized too long—George sang only a few phrases from the text. By then I had arrived in his dressing room. I did not want to come at the last minute for fear he would worry about my absence. I wanted to be present when he vocalized to assure him once again that he sounded great.

However, he was already in his own world. He smiled at me absently, never forgot to tell me that I looked beautiful, and then sent me off with "I think you should go into the house." I wished him luck or rather "merde" as was the custom and left. He examined himself in the mirror once more; his gestures were the gestures of his character. The loudspeaker announced five minutes to curtain time and if he appeared right at the beginning, he walked slowly to the stage, clearing his throat one last time just before going on.

At intermission, I went backstage and reported that the performance was going wonderfully, that he was in great form, and that the public loved it. I did not go into details about the other singers' performance, for if they were not good, he was irritated anyway, but if they were great he knew and was elated.

He took off the costume, which usually had to be changed for the next act, and cooled off. He rested for a while or had a sandwich if it was a very taxing role, for he used an enormous amount of energy and was always hungry. If he was satisfied with his performance so far, he was notably more relaxed and exchanged some gossip with me. He wanted to know which friends or well-known personalities were in the audience. Once, during the intermission of *The Tales of Hoffmann* Sir Laurence Olivier and Noel Coward came to congratulate him. He was thrilled. "My God, both of you!" he exclaimed.

I usually came back at every intermission, unless I had special friends with me, in which case I warned him in advance so that he did not expect me. If someone he knew to be in the theater did not come back to greet him after the performance, George was deeply offended or he wondered if perhaps "he or she did not like the performance" or "did not think I was good tonight." Years later when George London was director of the Kennedy Center, he noticed that some of the world's greatest classical artists reacted the same way.

After the performance, except when we had a party at our house, I rushed backstage. I wanted to be the first to congratulate him and be with him as soon as possible after the last bow in front of the audience. He radiated strength and joy, never fatigue, no matter how long the part. He was jubilant. This was a high for him, the moment of achievement. As soon as he started to take off the costume and remove the makeup, the euphoria would dissipate.

But London was still elated and smiling when he greeted the friends and admirers who came to his dressing room. By then he had changed except if it was a complicated makeup that took a long time to remove. After many compliments and small talk for close to an hour, he was ready to leave.

If there was no party or no date with friends at a restaurant, he went home where a supper was ready. He ate lightly and drank some wine and enjoyed the supper, for he was very hungry after a performance. Almost all his roles were dramatic and required strong, often tortured interpretations. These suited his personality but they were very taxing—they took a great deal out of him.

When he relaxed at last, it was time to go to bed. While he was undressing he invariably started to ask me questions about the performance. He put me through the third degree: how was this particular tone in the big aria; how was this gesture in one scene; did I notice the change in his position at such and such a place? I had learned to observe the smallest detail, to hear the slightest nuance so that I could answer all his questions. He reviewed his whole performance again trying to pinpoint any possible flaws. He analyzed the character he had played in the most minute detail and gained new insights into his behavior. This self-examination could go on for hours unless I managed to put a stop to it by begging him to go to sleep, assuring him over and over that he had been outstanding. He trained me to be so critical that I became a most discriminating and exacting audience. He often discussed the performances of the other members of the cast, explaining in detail the reasons for their success or failure in their roles or singing technique.

I could not just sit there and enjoy his performances. I had to be alert to any fault he might ask about later on. In those years I saw George - and no one else - perform Don Giovanni, Scarpia, the Flying Dutchman, Amfortas, Amonasro, Onegin, and Boris Godunov. Now that I have seen different artists, sometimes very good ones, in these roles, I realize only fully what an extraordinary performer George London was. I understand that his interpretations had an added dimension born of sheer intensity, perfect timing, and inborn charisma in addition to his voice, which had a unique recognizable quality.

London's quest for perfection was at its height during recording sessions. The best live performance leaves cherished memories but can never be re-created. Therefore the only permanent legacy of a singer is his recordings. George was aware of this and was eager to record the complete operas of all the parts for which he was known, as well as a number of solo disks. He had contracts successively with different companies: Columbia Records, London Records, and RCA. Then he ended up freelancing. For each recording a separate contract was drawn, sometimes for a flat fee, sometimes for royalties. When George was asked to do the Wotan for the London recording of Wagner's *Das Rheingold*, he opted for a flat fee of two thousand dollars. He thought, "After all, how many people are going to buy a complete recording of a Wagner opera?" What he did not know was that this was one of the first complete opera recordings in stereo. The sound effects and the all-around quality of this set were so new and outstanding that it became one of the all-time best sellers in the classical catalogue and was recently reissued as a compact disc after nearly forty years. George used to laugh it off. "This was my worst business decision," he said.

There was always a difference between live and studio recordings. Occasionally a company decided to record a performance in the theater while it was taking place. Usually they spliced together parts from several performances to ensure perfect quality. In such a case, the singers received an additional fee as well as their fee for the performances, but there were no retakes and no control over the end product. Still the live CD issues of the performances of *Parsifal* and *The Flying Dutchman* in Bayreuth are the best because they have an extra spontaneity and dramatic impact.

Most musicians prefer studio recordings, where they have the last say about each take. For years, the conductor Bruno Walter did not permit the release of the Brahms *Requiem* with George London and Irmgard Seefried because one phrase of the chorus did not sound right. Finally, after Walter's death, George persuaded his daughter to give permission for this outstanding recording to be released.

London was not as fanatical as Bruno Walter about his solo recordings, but of course he cared very much and listened highly critically. After each take, which usually covered one scene or one aria, everyone involved went into a room where the technicians replayed what had just been recorded. Then the singer and the conductor decided if it was good enough for posterity or had to be done over again because it was either too slow or too fast, or the high note was not good or the orchestra and singers were not together.

Many of the recording sessions took place in London, Vienna, or Rome and afforded an occasion for a trip to these great cities. A special camaraderie developed between the artists during the long hours of rehearsals and takes. Sometimes there were big scandals: one famous Italian tenor beat the walls with his fists because a session was scheduled on his birthday; another time the whole cast threatened to walk out because the recording company unfairly wanted to replace one mezzo with another during a *Walküre* recording.

In Vienna you could sit on a balcony overlooking the hall where orchestra, conductor, and singers were working and watch the members of the orchestra doing crossword puzzles between takes. They were bored by all the repetitions; they had played these pieces hundreds of times with a long list of equally exacting conductors, slower or faster, louder or softer. It was quite a change for them when George London did an all-Wagner recording with the famous Wagnerian conductor Hans Knappertsbusch. Kna, as he was called by his friends, was known to hate rehearsals. When he walked in, he said, speaking of *The Flying Dutchman*, "Gentlemen, you know it, I know it. Georgie! Let's start." And they proceeded to record the twelve-minute long aria in one take. It was perfect. After they listened to it the technicians begged for another take for security, which was done. Then they went on to record the other Wagner arias planned for this recording.

After the session, which lasted all afternoon, singer and conductor had dinner at the Sacher and drank a lot of white wine, Kna's favorite, to celebrate the happy occasion. To this day this recording remains one of London's best, for he sounds fresh and enthusiastic, not tired out by endless repeats.

George also liked it, although like most artists, he listened to his recordings once when he received them, decided that he could have done better, and put them away on the shelf forever.

However some years later, at the request of some friends, he played the great Wagner monologues and a scene from *Boris Godunov*, listening intently. When the music ended, he said, "You know, it was not bad." Most of all it mattered to him "to leave my mark," as he said.

Chapter 11
Russia and Boris Godunov

On September 17, 1960, *The New York Times's* front page carried the following headline: "George London Sings Boris Role in Moscow and Wins an Ovation." The article went on:

> MOSCOW, Sept. 16—The American baritone George London received a standing ovation at the Bolshoi Theater tonight for his performance in Russia's greatest national opera, Boris Godunov.
>
> It was the first time that an American had been starred in an opera on the stage of Moscow's large opera. Mr. London sang the dramatic role of the medieval Czar Boris in Russian.
>
> At the end of the third act of the Mussorgsky opera when Boris dies, the audience of more than 2,000 persons rose and applauded the forty-year-old singer for eight curtain calls. Even the remainder of the all-Soviet cast that filled the stage joined in the accolade to Mr. London's stirring performance.
>
> "This is the climax of a life's dream," said Mr. London in his dressing room after the opera. "It is like Mohammed going to Mecca. I have played Boris many times and it is one of my favorite roles. It is a great honor at last to be able to play it here in Moscow—in its original setting."

He was not immediately aware that the story made front-page news, though he was jubilant that night and the glow

1. George age 5

2. George age 16,
   ready to graduate
   Hollywood High School

3. Ali Ben Ali in *The Desert Song*, 1945

4. Announcement of the
Bel Canto Trio, 1946

5. As Coppelius in
   The Tales of Hoffman,
   1949

6. As Dr. Miracle in
   The Tales of Hoffman,
   1949

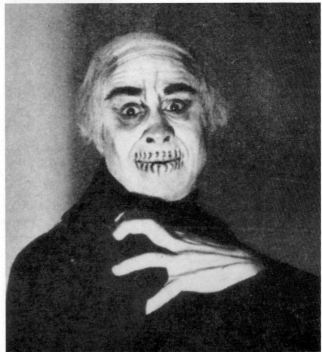

7. Portrait, 1949

8. As Eugene Onegin,
Vienna, 1950

9. As Eugene Onegin with
   Ljuba Welitsch, 1950

10. Stage Door, 1950,
    with Ursel, Edith and
    Gottfried Kraus

11. An interview with the Vienna Newspaper *Kurier*, 1950.
     No. 1 "How do you like the Viennese women?"
     No. 2 "How were you received by your colleagues at the Opera?"

12. Escamillo in *Carmen*
    with Dusolina Giannini,
    1950

13. Amfortas in *Parsifal*,
    Bayreuth, 1951

14. Amonasro in
    Aida, 1951

15. George London
Vienna, 1955

16. Studying *Parsifal* with Weiland Wagner, Bayreuth 1951

17. With his
    singing teacher
    Paola Novikova,
    1952

18. *Don Giovanni*, 1953

19. Wolfram in
Tannhauser,
1953

20. *Don Giovanni,* 1953

DAS
BUNDESMINISTERIUM
FÜR UNTERRICHT
BEURKUNDET HIERMIT/DASS
DER BUNDESPRÄSIDENT
HERRN

GEORGE LONDON

MIT ENTSCHLIESSUNG VOM
14·DEZEMBER 1954 DEN TITEL

KAMMERSÄNGER

VERLIEHEN HAT

WIEN/AM 1·JUNI 1957

DER BUNDESMINISTER FÜR UNTERRICHT:

21. Announcement of the Title of
"Kammersanger"
given by the President of Austria, 1954

22. As Don Giovanni with
    Irmgard Seefried, 1955

23. Mandryka in *Arabella*,
    1955

24. With Roberta Peters
in *Arabella* rehearsals,
1955

25. Count Almaviva in
The Marriage of Figaro,
1956

26. *Boris Godunov,*
    Bolshoi Theatre,
    Moscow, 1960

27. George, Nora, Marina
    on terrace of the
    apartment, 1957

CREDIT: GORDON PARKS

28. George and Nora
 with his parents,
 1958

29. Rehearsing for
 The Flying Dutchman
 with Wieland Wagner,
 1959

30 Golaud in
   Pelleas et Melisande,
   1959

31. Scarpia in *Tosca,* 1959

32. Cast of *Boris Godunov* backstage at Bolshoi Theatre, Moscow, 1960

33. In the dressing room of the Bolshoi Theatre, 1960

34. *Boris Godunov*,
courtesy of the
Metropolitan Opera
Archives

35. With Nora, Baritone Pavel Lisitsian and make-up artist, Bolshoi Theatre 1960

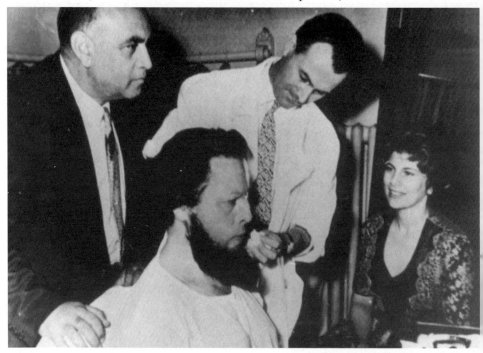

36. Wotan in
Das Rheingold,
1961

37. George with
his children
Marina and
Marc

38. With conductor Hans Knappertsbusch and Weiland Wagner, Bayreuth 1961

39. Headshot, 1962

DECCA **GEORGE LONDON**

ZUR VEROFFENTLICHUNG FREI! FOTO: TELDEC / BILDARCHIV
NACH VEROFFENTLICHUNG BELEGEXEMPLAR ERBETEN

40. George and Nora with Richard Leach, President of the Metropolitan
Opera Guild, 1962

41. Abdul in
The Last Savage
by Menotti, 1964

42. President Lyndon Johnson and Mrs. Johnson greeting George London and Nora London, White House, 1968

43. Receiving Mozart Medal from Austrian Minister, 1971

44. George with
    Senator Charles Percy
    1973

45. Teaching Master Class, 1976   CREDIT: HENRY GROSSMAN

46. George, Julis
Rudel and the
Honorable Willian
McCormick Blair,
dedication of the
John F. Kennedy
Center

47. George with Roger Stevens, Founder and President of the John F. Kennedy Cent

remained with him for a long time. Alone in the audience in the crowds of Russians, I kept thinking, "He did it, he did it, now no matter what happens, his wish has been fulfilled." Once he had told me, "I will sing Wagner in Germany, Faust in Paris, and *Boris Godunov* in Moscow." I thought the first two projects were very likely but was doubtful about the third. The Russians, at that time the Soviets, were proprietary about their opera, and it was extremely difficult to get an engagement there for a foreigner, let alone a singer wanting to perform their own favorite by a Russian composer.

George's friend and manager at Columbia Artists Management, Herbert Fox, knew how much George wanted to perform in Russia. Herb was a man who did not take no for an answer. While he was in Moscow negotiating for Columbia Artists to get the Red Army Chorus to do a tour of the United States, he told the negotiator from Gosconcert, the agency in charge of all the productions and concerts in the Soviet Union, "Mr. Supagin, you know that every manager has a favorite artist for whom he wishes a special engagement. I have a favorite bass-baritone, an American named George London, and I would like him to do some guest appearances in the Soviet Union. His greatest ambition is to sing Boris Godunov at the Bolshoi." "Dear Mr. Fox," replied Supagin, "I also have a favorite artist, an American, a bass-baritone called George London." And to Herb's amazement, Supagin proceeded to tell him that while stationed in Vienna during the Soviet occupation, he had heard George perform the role of Boris Godunov on Christmas night, 1949.

Supagin agreed that London should come to the Soviet Union and sing the role of Boris in Moscow. This being exactly what Herb wanted, they drew up a contract for a number of opera and concert appearances in Moscow, Leningrad, Riga, and Kiev, a tour that would take about four weeks.

In a return gesture, Columbia Artists engaged a well-known Russian baritone, Pavel Lisitsian, for performances at the Metropolitan Opera and a tour of recitals.

At the beginning of September 1960, we packed for a month-long trip to the Soviet Union and said long and tender good-byes to the children. The younger ones were left in the charge of nanny Marie Claire. Andy and Philip, now fifteen and thirteen years old, went to Riverdale Country School on the school bus and could be trusted to behave under Marie Claire's benign supervision.

I was warned to take winter clothes and bought a gray suit with a long fur-lined jacket, which would keep me warm without being too conspicuous and which turned out to be perfect most of the time. In preparation for the long waits for transportation and many evenings in hotel rooms, Paola persuaded us to learn a card game, which proved very useful when we became too bored. We played constantly in Moscow, in other towns, in airports, and never played again in our lives. I don't even remember the name of the game. We took powdered coffee, tea, soups, and the indispensable immersion heater, which George took everywhere so that he could have a hot drink late at night in hotel rooms after performances. He was always thirsty and did not want to drink anything cold after singing, as he believed this was bad for the throat.

After the long trip we arrived in Moscow, the first leg of the Russian trip. We were greeted by our specially assigned guide from Gosconcert, which was government-owned and had total control over everything and everyone connected with the arts in the Soviet Union. Olga, our guide (or private spy, as we called her), turned out to be quite nice, spoke astonishingly good English, and followed us everywhere during our stay. We were able to get rid of her only now and then, by visiting our embassy or our American friends, or in our hotel rooms.

We were struck by the drabness of the airport, the city streets, and the hotel; everything was gray. Even the hotel suite adorned with welcoming flowers was depressing.

We were booked at the Hotel National, which was the

best in Moscow at the time and was considered the most comfortable. We were given a large suite with a huge bathroom containing an old-fashioned bathtub standing on four legs. We had been warned that every room was bugged and started out the first evening whispering our first impressions to each other.

We continued whispering when we went to bed. Suddenly, in the dark, George shouted, "To hell with it, they can listen if they want. I'm not going to whisper for a whole month." That was the end of that and he spoke freely for the rest of the trip.

He was so outspoken and so loud that one day, while visiting Israel Shenker, one of our journalist friends in Moscow, and exchanging political opinions, our friend raised his voice and addressed the suspected microphones: "This last opinion was expressed by George London, visiting here, and not by myself."

Everybody believed that the only places safe for conversation were in cars or on the streets. Relatives of friends whom we were asked to see would not come to the hotel but met us on the street in front of the post office. The streets were extremely crowded, with throngs of people rushing in all directions. There were hardly any cars on the broad avenues at that time. Everyone stood on line for food and for almost all other goods, yet the theaters and the concerts were packed. The price of tickets was cheap and the entertainments provided a much-needed relaxation for these people whose life was difficult and constrained.

I was excited to be in Russia, about which I had heard since my childhood from my mother. Also, I spoke the language sufficiently well to converse about any subject I wanted; but it was immediately evident that I was a foreigner, for I had a strong accent. I wondered whether I would feel some real bonds with these people or if whatever Russia had been like in the past had disappeared completely.

I found that the people we met were friendly, outgoing,

eager to share a good meal and whatever they had. But it must be said that we met only other musicians or artists, well-educated people who had relatively privileged positions in society. The people in the streets and the crowded shops were rude and boorish. They shouted insults at each other, pushed and shoved, but were always relatively polite to me, for they knew immediately that I was a foreigner from the look of my clothes.

Even my most ordinary outfit was much better than what they had, and I found myself giving away whatever I could spare. Even our incorruptible Olga accepted my hairbrush and stockings when we left.

In 1960 Russia was still suffering from terrible shortages of every kind. This improved on subsequent visits. In Leningrad, the people still talked about the war and how terribly they had suffered from hunger during the siege of the city. The gray clothes and the short gray days made you forget that the war had been over for fifteen years.

The day following our arrival in Moscow, George went to the Bolshoi Theater for the first rehearsal. I went along, and so did the inevitable Olga. The opera house was a short walk from the hotel. We went in through the small artist's entrance and were immediately introduced to some singers waiting there. Then we went to a rehearsal room where the conductor, Melik Pashaev, was waiting with the stage director. Both greeted us cordially.

The rehearsal began and as usual the director made several suggestions. Some George accepted, but he expressed reservations about others. Olga interpreted dryly: "He does not want to do that." I saw immediate hostility spreading over the gathering and, though I had first kept silent, I decided to interfere. I explained in Russian to the director that George thought that his ideas were excellent, that only in one or two places he was used to making different gestures, and that if he, the director, did not mind, George would like to act the way he was used to.

Everybody smiled again and, from then on, I did all the translating, avoided hurting anybody's feelings, and conveyed George's diplomatic utterances to the Russians. I thought if the translators were as clumsy in affairs of state as they were with us, it is no wonder people never get along with each other. Anyway, we parted great friends, with everyone looking forward to the next rehearsal.

George remembered this rehearsal in a 1968 speech:

I went to my first musical rehearsal with the conductor. He did not speak English—we conversed in German—and he paid me the very great compliment that I sang in the Russian style. And then there was a staging rehearsal that same day with the stage director, a little man by the name of Baratov. Mr. Baratov had been in America, had done a tour with the fabulous Moscow Art Theater in the U.S. in the 1920s. We sat there with my wife sitting between us acting as interpreter, and he told us all about his tour in America: "Oh!" he said. "I played New York, Chicago! Terrible! Gangsters! Boom, boom!—Gollywood [the Russians have no *H,* so every *H* becomes a *G*] John Barrymore! John Barrymore, wonderful actor! played every night for six months in *Gamlet.*
He was an amusing little man and he had some ideas about *Boris Godunov* that were very helpful to me, not much, just a couple of really important tips and suggestions that helped to strengthen the character. He pointed out to me that in a few places I was being too self-pitying, that I should be more aggressively bitter, and this helped strengthen those scenes.
Baratov had just restaged *Boris* in Leningrad and described with pride some new pieces of business he had introduced. For example, when Boris enters for his scene with the Fool in front of St. Basil's, the hungry populace implores him for bread. Baratov had the Czar's retinue toss coins to the people, which they were to pick up and angrily hurl back. No doubt this was intended to endow the people with socialist dignity in a pre-socialist era. I

told him, tactfully, that I did not feel it was true to life. Although he disagreed, he left this out of the Bolshoi production.

The dress rehearsal was onstage the next day. George had been told not to bring his Boris costume: they had their own, which conformed to their staging. He tried the costumes, which had been made for a Russian bass and they fitted him almost perfectly. I stayed with him until I was sure that he no longer needed an interpreter. Then I walked across the stage to go to the auditorium. The stage was immense, the deepest I had ever seen.

George was rehearsing the scene in which Boris first appears, on his coronation day. According to the stage direction, Boris walks slowly from the very back of the stage to the front accompanied by the music and the sound of church bells. As George recounted in his speech:

This was the dress rehearsal of all dress rehearsals because I came out in the coronation scene and that was my first contact to the greatest star of the Bolshoi Theater and the star of this opera, and that is the chorus. It is the greatest chorus I have ever heard, it is overwhelming. I finished the coronation scene and then I came out for my big scenes in the second act, and as I looked out into the theater, it was packed. As I later learned, it was filled with practically every singer, actor, dancer, theater person in Moscow. Most of these people didn't have tickets for the performance; that was mainly for the fat cats and it was generally hard to get in. I went through these scenes in Russian at the Bolshoi, in Moscow, in a kind of a trance, and when I finished the scene on my knees, the house came down. It was an ovation, at the dress rehearsal. I got up feeling embarrassed and a little foolish and I found myself taking bows as if it had been a performance. It was very thrilling and very exciting and I was superstitious about it, lest it be too wonderful, lest the performance be not as good.

I rushed backstage, for I knew everyone would speak to him in Russian, persuaded that he understood. They congratulated him and embraced him in the effusive Russian way. Even the conductor came to praise his performance. George asked me to speak to the young woman who played Fedya, the Czar's son. There are two scenes in the opera where the Czar is very close to his son and the singer was wearing such a heavy perfume that George could hardly breathe and had a terrible urge to sneeze. I went over to her dressing room and explained George's allergy and she immediately promised not to wear any perfume on the night of the performance.

London was moved by the approval of his peers: they were his colleagues and they knew best. If they thought he was good, he would surely win the approval of the Russian audience.

Still, he faced the next evening with some trepidation. This was it—the big night he had anticipated for so many years.

We walked to the opera house together, two and a half hours before the performance. I went backstage with him, as he needed me as an interpreter. He had discussed the makeup the day before and decided to let the makeup man help him, for he seemed extraordinarily capable. The result was remarkable indeed. George added a line here, a shadow there, and had a picture taken on stage during intermission—his best Boris picture ever. He posed also with baritone Pavel Lisitsian, who visited him in the dressing room. He was satisfied with what he saw in the mirror and he felt in good voice. He did not need me anymore and I went to my seat.

I felt terribly alone in the huge auditorium. The curtain rose and soon there he was, walking slowly upstage in his splendid golden costume, holding the scepter against a background picturing the beautiful Archangelski and Uspenski cathedrals with their colored domes, and the Kremlin walls. He was doing something extremely difficult in a foreign environment.

In his 1968 speech, George described his feelings about

the performance:

> If my reception at the dress rehearsal augured well for the performance, it did not succeed in stilling the nervousness that assailed me. I felt that this was the supreme test of my artistry to date.
>
> I made that first long, long walk to center stage where I sing my first aria. The stage of the Bolshoi is enormously deep. When you start out for the entrance of the coronation scene, you start at the very back of the theater. It is like sitting at a baseball game and looking out at center field, it is just about that far. There is a little peasant woman up in the flies and she is running back and forth and is ringing two cathedral bells that are part of the permanent equipment of the Bolshoi. They don't have some poor desperate assistant conductor hitting some chimes as they do in most theaters. These are cathedral bells, which is a fantastic effect except when you are standing back there ready to go on, it just about takes your head off.
>
> As I slowly came into view of the audience, I was greeted by waves of applause and suddenly all nervousness vanished. From that moment until the end of the performance I was in a state of complete euphoria. At the final curtain I received a standing ovation. Huge baskets of chrysanthemums were brought up on the stage. My colleagues applauded and some embraced me. Even Mrs. Khrushchev stood up. Her husband wasn't there, he was at the U.N. endearing himself to everybody by pounding on the table with his shoe. My dear friends, the baritone Lisitsian and the conductor Kondrashin and their wives, came backstage to compliment me, as did Ambassador and Mrs. Thompson and the entire American press corps. The soprano Galina Vishnevskaya (the wife of Mstislav Rostropovich), whom I had never met, rushed over, threw her arms around me, gave me a resounding kiss, and just as abruptly left. And then it was over. I was quite in a daze. Having finally divested myself of costume and makeup, I walked slowly with my wife back to the Ho-

tel National where we celebrated quietly on caviar and sweet champagne and went to bed.

I was awakened about five o'clock in the morning by a cable saying that the story had hit the wires in the States, that there was a big headline story on the front page of *The New York Times* with a profile about myself inside, and I guess this was just about the happiest moment of my life.

Two Americans traveling in Russia attended this performance and noted that the audience of more than two thousand people rose and applauded the forty-year-old singer for eight curtain calls. Even the remainder of the all Russian cast "joined" in the accolade to Mr. London's starring performance.

We walked back to the National arm in arm, an anonymous couple among late pedestrians in a Moscow street, we were thousands of miles away from California, where George first dreamed of performing Boris. We did not speak a word until we reached the hotel.

The following week, he was again greeted with ecstatic applause at a sold-out recital in the concert hall of the conservatory. The audience was clearly knowledgeable. He later found out that Russian audiences did not applaud without discrimination, but if they approved, they were enthusiastic and affectionate. George's accompanist, Leo Taubman, had arrived from the States to play for him during this concert tour. In each recital, George sang a group of Mussorgsky songs or an aria by Borodin in Russian.

After the first concert, I was accosted by a Russian journalist who told me he did not believe that George could not speak Russian, that he was just pretending. I was annoyed but restrained myself. At George's very last appearance in Russia, the same writer came up to me again and apologized. He had followed George everywhere and established for a fact that he did not speak Russian.

After Moscow, we went to Riga, where George again sang Boris and gave a recital. Riga was the capital of Latvia, an independent country until World War II, when it was annexed by the Soviet Union. It is again an independent country today. In 1960 the population had been forced to speak only Russian and to submit to Soviet rule. Only fifteen years had passed and the people were far from being assimilated by the Russians. The concert hall was packed and when George sang the aria from *Prince Igor* in which the prince, taken prisoner, laments about his fate and sings "Give me freedom," the whole audience rose and applauded until he repeated the aria.

London was well aware that the applause was not only for him but for the incarnation of freedom that he represented. After the concert, when he left the hall, hundreds of people were waiting backstage to greet him, some just to touch him. "Come back, please come back," they begged. He talked with groups here and there for a long time in the cold night and when he finally left many people were crying.

The next stop was Leningrad, now again St. Petersburg, where we arrived toward evening. The taxi driver who drove us to our hotel pointed out some landmarks. At the Nevsky Prospekt, which was sparsely lit, he turned around, grinned and said "Broadvai" with great satisfaction.

George sang several performances at the Maryinsky Theater, which had been preserved exactly the way it was under the czars. It was one of the most beautiful halls in the world. The walls were gold and the seats and curtains were aquamarine. It was smaller than the Bolshoi and had wonderful acoustics.

London went to a great performance of Tchaikovsky's *Pique Dame* there, and the next night he was on stage singing Méphisto in *Faust*. There had been just a short rehearsal covering only the scenes in which he was involved. All went well and the opera was coming to its close with the last scene where Marguerite ascends to heaven. Suddenly, however Marguerite was led away in chains by an irate mob. Because

Marxist dogma did not recognize religion, Marguerite could not be redeemed and Gounod's heavenly music accompanied her death march. This was *Faust* Soviet-style. Since he was no longer on stage at this point, George did not know what happened, but when he found out he was furious about the desecration of this masterpiece.

George loved to go to museums and spent as much time as possible at the Hermitage. He was awed by the wealth and majesty of the czars' palace, not to mention the collection of paintings. Leningrad was beautiful and the people were more like Europeans and more considerate than in the rest of Russia. In 1960, the West had put the memories of the war to rest; yet in Russia it seemed still very close and was talked about very frequently. These people were frightened at the idea of another conflagration, and the government constantly refueled this feeling with their propaganda about American "imperialism."

Some of the artists we met were permitted to invite us to their homes. We became friends with Pavel and Mara Lisitsian. Pavel was the baritone who came to the United States in exchange for George's trip to Russia. They always managed to have fruits and salad, which were unavailable anywhere else, on their table. They toasted us with sweet wine and strong vodka, which was hard to swallow. George, as the guest of honor, had double rations and became more and more enthusiastic about the food and the company.

We liked the Lisitsian family. We met their married daughter and their twins, a boy and a girl, all with beautiful velvety dark eyes and warm smiles. For many years we exchanged notes at Christmas. When we returned to Moscow the last time, in 1966, Pavel was ill with serious back trouble and we went to see him in a hospital on the outskirts of the city. The hospital was clean and roomy, situated in a lovely park, and Pavel was immensely pleased with our visit. He told us he had been overworked; he was forced to travel and perform constantly in remote provinces. Pavel was an honored Soviet singer and entitled to first-class care. His services belonged to the state and as a useful subject of the state it was advantageous to restore him to good health. Pavel was guaranteed engagements, but he could not choose them. "It is true that artists often have a hard time getting work in our country, but we always have freedom of choice," George proclaimed, "and that is essential to artistic growth."

We sadly said good-bye to Pavel and his family, fearing that we were not likely to see each other again. There was little chance of our returning to Russia and the Lisitsians had no prospect of coming back to the United States. Pavel lived with his dear wife and family in Moscow until his death at 93 in July 2004. In a book dedicated to his remarkable career, he wrote of his friendship with George London. There is a photograph of Lisitsian with Leonard Bernstein and George London in front of Carnegie Hall and a picture of Lisitsian visiting George during the Boris performance.

Through Pavel, George met an Armenian sculptor who made a striking bust of George. Our friend, the conductor, Igor Markevitch, who was in Moscow at the same time, introduced us to a young painter called Zverev with the advice, "He is very talented, but he paints only if you give him a bottle of vodka." So we invited Zverev to our hotel room for a drink, he liked George and admired him and agreed to paint our portraits.

A few days later we went to his place, which consisted of one room, with a mattress in one corner and a chair in another. He proceeded to make a fascinating likeness of George, full of tormented insights, and also a charming but glib portrait of me. We carried these aquarelles with us to our house in Switzerland, and they hung there until one day in May 1977, when George's portrait fell from the wall and the glass broke into many pieces, a bad omen for the future.

Today the portraits are in the United States, treasured evidence of a long-ago voyage to Russia.

The last stop of the tour was Kiev, capital of the Ukraine,

where London was scheduled to give a recital. He had an interview with a young journalist who spoke perfect English, having been raised in Canada, where his father was the Soviet ambassador. As they were walking along the wide but bleak avenues of Kiev, the young man tried to convince George that his city was as beautiful as "Paris in the spring." George laughed later about the extent of self-deception people are capable of. Forever after when a place was gray and depressing he would say it was "like Paris in the spring."

By now it was the beginning of October, almost winter in Russia. It was unusually cold in Kiev and there was no hint of heating anywhere. For George's recital I decided to wear a blue satin dress from Paris with a matching coat lined with mink. I thought it was a bit too showy for the Soviet Union, but I had nothing else sufficiently warm with me. I was quite shocked when I entered the large concert hall to discover that I was seated way up front, in the middle of the center aisle in an armchair that had been placed there especially for me. The local organizers felt they were doing George a great honor this way.

When he arrived on the stage and bowed to the audience, he could almost touch me. He was surprised to see me there, but controlled himself and just winked imperceptibly at me. Then he proceeded to perform with his usual passion and dedication. I thought that there was extra warmth in the voice, an extra depth in his expression, and soon I was convinced that this one time he was singing just for me. It was the only time I ever felt this, and I will never forget the sensation. I thought how fortunate I was and forgot all about my awkward seat. Indeed, only after a while did I realize that it was so cold I could see George's breath while he was singing.

He was due to sing another recital in Moscow in a few days. He was worried about catching a cold and demanded hot tea during the intermission and at the end of the recital. The demand had not been foreseen and created a tremendous crisis, but in the end someone managed to bring some tea from a nearby restaurant.

On the following day we were supposed to fly back to Moscow. When we arrived at the airport, it was covered with fog; no plane could possibly arrive or leave. The airport was not heated, since there was an electrical breakdown, and for some unknown reason no food was available. Dejected, cold, and hungry, we waited all day, George getting angrier by the minute. We played cards all day in coats and scarves with gloves on, barely able to see in the gray daylight, and blessed Paola for having taught us our game. Finally an Aeroflot plane managed to land and carried us to Moscow. Olga apologized for the mishap and accused the Kiev officials to be responsible for this inefficiency.

London loved the Russian people but resented the oppression of the iron communist regime upon them, although most of them seemed used to it. At that time, his Armenian friend told us with contempt, "The Russians are like sheep, they follow the leader blindly."

The Soviet people were suspicious because of their lack of freedom and lack of information. They were constantly frustrated and exhausted from their efforts to procure daily necessities or obtain permits to travel, to change apartments or jobs. After a month in this stifling atmosphere, deprived of news (the only Western news came from an occasional paper from the U.S. Embassy), London could not wait to go home, in spite of all the honors and the success. He decided that he had to leave immediately after his last concert.

He asked me to call the Gosconcert people and tell them that he wished to go that Thursday, instead of Saturday as originally scheduled. They informed us that this was impossible because there was no Aeroflot plane leaving that particular day. I replied that I knew that an SAS plane was going to London on Thursday. The answer was: "Impossible." We could not leave, no reason given. I knew they wanted us to use Aeroflot because the fare would be collected by the Soviet government. Furious, I said, "If we cannot leave on Thursday, my husband will not sing on Wednesday."

I knew that the concert in the huge Tchaikovsky Hall was completely sold out and that it would be a great scandal if the recital did not take place. I was told, "Please wait a moment." There was much discussion at the other end of the line. In the meantime, I explained the conversation to George, who waited anxiously for the results. After a short pause, the answer came back, "You can leave Thursday with the Scandinavian Airline." I breathed a sigh of relief; my threat had worked. I don't know what George would have done had they refused, coming from a democracy he could not tolerate being told that he could not come and go as he pleased.

The last concert was very moving. The audience applauded on and on and shouted to George, "Come back, come back." George wondered if he would ever be able to return to sing in Russia. He loved the audience even if he detested the government. He would always remain ambivalent about Russia. He had tears in his eyes as he bowed and applauded them, as is the custom in Russia. We left the next day, on a gray morning with snow flurries, full of love and sadness. Yet as soon as we boarded the Scandinavian plane it seemed that a weight had been lifted, and upon arriving in London we appreciated to its fullest the meaning of democracy and freedom.

George London returned to Moscow in May 1963. This time Herb Fox had negotiated for George the recording of *Boris Godunov* with Mezhdunarodnaya Kniga, the Soviet state organization that is responsible for all Russian recordings as well as the publishing of books. George was to record all the scenes in which Boris appears, and these scenes would be incorporated into a recording of the whole opera. The complete recording with George as Boris was then sold in the United States by Columbia Records. Boris appears only in four scenes in the entire opera and has fewer than thirty minutes of singing. It took three sessions to record his role. Alexander Melik Pashaev was again the outstanding conductor.

We spent nearly two weeks in Russia and were happy to see all our friends again, including Kiril Kondrashin and his wife, Nina. He was a well-known conductor who eventually defected to the West. George indulged again in his passion for caviar, which he ordered every morning for breakfast while Mara Lisitsian managed to bring him some salad leaves from their *dacha*. She knew of George's addiction and he was touched by her solicitude. George wrote in the notes for the recording:

> May in Moscow was delightful and balmy. The trees in the parks were in full bloom. Young girls in gaudy sum- mer prints, walking arm in arm with their swains, were to be seen everywhere. The city looked brighter and more prosperous than the last time we had been there. At the large recording studio of the Mezhdunarodnaya Kniga (International Book), which produces all records in the Soviet Union, I renewed my acquaintance with Melik Pashaev, who this time eschewed German and insisted on conversing in French. I was warmly greeted by my colleagues, all of whom had sung with me at the Bolshoi. But my most profound impression of these recording ses- sions was of the Bolshoi chorus. The women's voices possess a quality of what may be described paradoxi- cally as cultivated vulgarity. It is a folk sound so well suited to the scenes of the populace in such operas as *Boris, Khovanshchina* and *Prince Igor*. And yet there is a perfect discipline of musicality and intonation. The tenor voices are high and lyrical, but cutting, and the basses are of unequalled sonority and profundity. Mussorgsky felt that the true protagonist of his opera was the chorus, the Russian people. Our sessions went smoothly and without incident. We listened to the final playback on May 10, 1963.

The weeks went by quickly and we did not have time to get homesick. When we left, the Kondrashins surprised us with the gift of a large lacquer box representing Boris Godunov against a colorful background of St. Basil's Cathedral and the Kremlin. George had admired this box while visiting the Gum department store with them and he was overwhelmed by their generous gift.

Back in the States, George suggested that a picture of the box be used for the cover of the *Boris Godunov* album, and Columbia Records adopted his idea. This complete opera recording was reissued recently on compact disc by Sony Classical with the same picture.

George expressed his feelings in the conclusion of the *Boris* album notes when he wrote: "I felt that were I never to sing another note, I would at least have this unique documentation of my most beloved role."

Chapter 12
The Fragile Voice

In 1959 George London had very little to complain about, he had more offers than he could possibly accept; his only regrets were that often he had to forgo a prestigious offer at La Scala, for instance, because he had already committed that time slot to Vienna. He never went back on his word and insisted on having enough time to recuperate between engagements. The intensity of his performances was costly to his nerves and he needed several days to unwind. His involvement in his roles was part of his success and he could not have behaved differently had he wanted to.

By the time his summer vacation came around he was in need of rest. A summer house, shared by the family, was the obvious solution. Long periods in Bayreuth together were difficult, because of the lack of distractions for the children and the difficult climate, either too hot or too rainy. In 1959 George performed *The Flying Dutchman* with Wieland Wagner but he did not sing in *Parsifal* that year and was free after August 5. He loved Switzerland and decided that there he could find the ideal place for his family. There was entertainment for the children, the air was wonderful, and, above all, Switzerland would provide the calm and beauty that he enjoyed.

That summer we rented the Villa Bella Vista in Bellevue overlooking Lake Geneva. It had a fabulous view, as its name suggested, but was in fact a white elephant. No one would buy it, in spite of its location near the water, because it was a huge mansion, with innumerable rooms and a second floor inhabited by bats. For this reason it could be rented at a reasonable price. By closing off the upper part of the house, including the bats, there were enough rooms left for all of us. Making the house habitable was well worth the effort for it came with a marvelous garden and private beach.

Coming from Bayreuth, London was delighted with the place. He loved to be with the children all day, enjoyed loafing on the beach with the older boys and Marina, and admired his infant son. He had grown to love Andy and Philip as if they were his own and was involved with their playtime as well as their school curriculum. The summer started perfectly. We hardly ever went out but many friends visited: the conductor Eugene Ormandy and his wife Gretl, Henry and Ginny Pleasants, and friends from Paris. George was relaxed and enjoying himself. He was at his most exuberant, joked a lot and was acutely aware of his good fortune, for he wrote to his parents, "One must always count one's blessings and be grateful for every good day in one's life."

During the end of August he returned to Rome for a few days to complete some minor scenes for a *Tosca* recording with Renata Tebaldi and Mario Del Monaco, which had been started in previous months. When he returned he felt tired. Even after a week of rest and sleeping twelve hours each night he did not feel better and could not digest his meals. He did not look right and his eyes seemed blurred. He agreed to see a physician. The diagnosis was clear: George had viral hepatitis and he was immediately hospitalized in Geneva. The staff in the hospital was extremely kind and efficient and the doctor assured him that after three weeks in the hospital and an equal amount of rest at home, he would recover completely. It was hard to believe that George was so ill. He always seemed strong and took such good care of himself.

He was horrified at having to cancel some engagements and worried about it. His peace of mind was very important to his recovery, so I reassured him as best I could. The doctor was positive that by autumn he would be well again.

He lay in his hospital bed, jaundiced and weak. He agreed to everything and promised not to worry. It was devastating to see him so subdued. His managers in New York and Europe were informed of his illness so that they could cancel London's engagements for the coming six weeks. It was agreed that he would hold on to a planned *Don Giovanni* in San Francisco for October 20, which would give ample time for a full recovery.

He was overwhelmed with get-well wishes from all over the world. While trying to respond, we wondered how he could have contracted this disease. For now he was too ill to think about this. But later, when George felt somewhat better, he recalled his experiences during the past three months and found that during the arduous tour in Israel he had been given vitamin B injections, which he believed gave him added energy. He had noticed that the needle was not new and did not seem too clean (disposable needles were not in common use at that time), but he was assured that they were sterile. No doubt the needles were the cause of his illness, for the time between the injections and the hepatitis was the exact incubation period for this disease.

The summer was coming to a close and as soon as George was strong enough to be moved, he decided that he would be more comfortable in our apartment in New York. School was about to start for the boys and the whole family moved back to the United States, including a Swiss nanny, but leaving behind our beloved maid Sasha, who returned to Paris.

George recuperated quickly. There was a lovely Indian summer in New York and that fall he spent lazy afternoons on the terrace admiring the changing colors of Central Park. The children were delighted to have Daddy home for such a long time. He played for hours with Marina and watched the development of baby Marc, now six months old. He wrote to his parents with great perspicacity: "Marina has a simply devastating personality, enormous charm and humor and great warmth too. Marc has a very special sweetness."

He spent more time with the older boys and helped with their homework, especially English. He had an unusually large vocabulary and perfect command of the English language; he prided himself on being able to finish the crossword puzzle in *The New York Times* every Sunday. He tried to inculcate his love for words in all of us, although he declared with a smile that I managed to confuse everybody's English with my idiosyncratic pronunciation. However, in the end I think he succeeded in teaching us a reverence for the wealth and power of the language of Shakespeare.

Soon he became impatient at being condemned to inactivity. He argued with me about his ability to exercise and to go out and I complained that he needed a gendarme, not a wife to take care of him. To keep him entertained, I invited his friends to visit and distract him with political dissertations or opera gossip.

When he felt stronger, George started to vocalize and found with relief that all was well with his voice. In fact, soon he was once again his former self except that he had to forgo the sweets and desserts that he loved. Although he sighed with frustration, he was quite good about it. He was never again able to eat two banana splits in a row but he did recover completely from the hepatitis.

He left our cozy domesticity to go to San Francisco for peformances of *Don Giovanni,* which went very well. In fact, the 1959/60 season turned out to be one of George's most successful ones. It was the season of the triumph of the first *Flying Dutchman* with Leonie Rysanek at the Met, a great colleague and close friend and the creation of the role of Golaud in Debussy's *Pelléas et Melisande* with Anna Moffo and Theodor Uppmann under the direction of Ernest Ansermet.

All through the autumn, George worked hard to prepare for the Golaud role. Spending so much time in the French part of Switzerland, George had become fluent in the language. This made the study of a new Gallic work easier, but, as usual for him, he had to delve deep into this new character. He was able to consult Carlton Gould, a singer who had performed this role in France and had known Mary Garden the original Melisande. Golaud is another one of those complex, tormented personalities with whom George could identify because he understood them and had the ability to project their inner conflicts on the stage. Golaud became one of his most moving roles and a great personal success for George, although the opera has never been very popular.

The Flying Dutchman premiere took place in January 1960. It was followed by one of London's longest seasons at the Met, during which he sang a variety of roles: Amonasro in *Aida*, Méphistophélès in *Faust, Don Giovanni*, and *Flying Dutchman*. His singing was so secure that he performed almost without apprehension.

In April he left on the Met tour, doing the Count in seven performances of *The Marriage of Figaro* all over the United States. He did not travel with the tour but flew home between performances. After the second *Figaro* he came back and I could tell right away that he was disturbed. He told me that the previous night his voice cracked on the F-sharp, the high note, toward the end of his third-act aria, "Vedrô mentr'io sospiro." This had never, never happened before and he was terribly upset. He had prepared for the high note as usual, supported the voice perfectly, and could not understand how the crack had happened. "Such an accident," he said, "should never happen to a singer of my standing. I am mortified."

He talked for hours, alluding to his tiredness from traveling, uncomfortable housing, heavy meals, all the possible reasons. Finally, he was persuaded that this could happen to anyone and that one single note could not erase the accomplishments of his entire career. I had seen in many singers' eyes the look of terror when they approached a high note they dreaded.

He had to go back and sing more *Figaros* in the next few

weeks. I told him that this F-sharp was unimportant, that the whole aria was the thing, that he was a magnificent Count, that the people came for his interpretation of the role, not to hear one note. He practiced the dreaded phrase over and over until he was partially reassured. He went off again and finished the tour without further mishaps, but for the first time fear had entered his singing. The performances, which came in close succession, were a trial for him and took a heavy toll on his nerves. When the last one, on May 25, was behind him he was greatly relieved.

Afterwards, we were going to Europe. Our first stop was Geneva. We stayed at our beloved Hotel de la Paix, with a view of the lake and Mont Blanc, to celebrate George's birthday. He wrote to his parents on May 29, 1960:

> Tomorrow I shall be forty years old. I'd just as soon not go into details about this or even to philosophize. I hereby leave my youth behind and take the first timid step into middle age. On the other hand, I feel a flowering of my vocal and intellectual powers which previously had eluded me.

Switzerland did not have its usual soothing effect on him. Although he seemed to be in good health, he was traumatized at the thought that he was leaving behind his thirties, during which he had been so fortunate. He still worried about the *Figaro* incident. Did he have a foreboding of what was to come? He was terribly gloomy and I consoled him as best I could, pulling out all the jaded arguments about the forties being the best years of a man's life. Eventually he emerged from his depression, but was concerned about his strained nerves and decided to cancel a concert in Vienna and six performances in Bayreuth. This way, he argued, he would be in perfect condition for the forthcoming recording of *The Flying Dutchman* in August and for the all-important Russian tour in September.

He talked again about needing complete relaxation and total rest for his nerves. It seemed that, in spite of appearances, he had not completely recovered from his bout with hepatitis. He became very quiet and gloomy, kept to himself, and read. Gone was the boisterous, gregarious man so full of life from before. We decided that a prolonged stay in Switzerland would provide the right atmosphere.

This time we rented a chalet in Villars up in the mountains about an hour from Lausanne. The mountain air was beneficent and invigorating. Our good friends, the conductor Igor Markevitch and his wife Topazia were helpful because George could take just so much nature and needed intellectual and artistic stimulation before long. He spent two weeks alone just resting while I went back to the States to fetch the family. Everyone including Socrates, our wise beagle, moved safely from New York to Villars.

The summer turned out to be a great success. George and the two younger children were soon beautifully tanned. Marc was walking, holding on to his dad who seemed gigantic next to him. Philip had his first flirtation, with the daughter of the family in the chalet next door, and Socrates begged around the kitchens of nearby hotels for additions to his meals. George dressed his wife and daughter in dirndls, which he had bought, deciding against type that they were perfect for us. He did not get bored thanks to the evenings with Igor and Topazia, during which they argued about the merits of various pieces of music (they did not like Rachmaninoff as he did) or about politics. They were more indulgent toward the Soviet regime than we were; they had been there and gave us advice about our forthcoming trip.

Soon London was rested, optimistic, and his usual noisy and joyous self. He forgot about the shame he always felt when he canceled a performance and began to look forward to the *Dutchman* recording. The glamour of the career did not always make up for all the sacrifices, the tension, and the frequent separations. The love and care that George lavished on the children was a joy to watch. This was what he had always dreamed about.

When we left our mountain refuge, London was eager to go; he was ready for work. His vocalizing was going well. Since we had no piano, he practiced with an accompanist at the Markevitches every day and was pleased and confident with the results: He would be in top form in London and in Russia.

The Flying Dutchman was to be recorded in London. There he met Leonie Rysanek, one of his favorite colleagues, who sang the role of Senta, and Antal Dorati, the conductor. In spite of uninterrupted rainy weather, the recording went extremely well. After the sessions, which were long and strenuous, there was much togetherness and joking among the artists. George was full of verve and swapped jokes with Toni Dorati and Giorgio Tozzi, who was also part of the cast. When the recording was finished, we went back to New York to prepare for the Russian trip. After that, George had a somewhat shorter season at the Metropolitan, which included *Boris Godunovs, Arabellas, Don Giovannis,* and *Toscas.* No *Figaros* were foreseen, and it seemed that last year's incident had been forgotten.

London left for a long and profitable concert tour that kept him away for weeks in a row. He hated to be gone so long and swore that next season he was going to insist that his concertizing be cut into two separate periods.

In May I went with him to Stuttgart where he did a television performance of *Tosca* with Renata Tebaldi, which was seen all over Europe. He wrote about it to his parents:

> To be known by the average person one needs either TV or films. It depends on what you want out of life. Believe me, I'm aware of these things and I'm proud and ambitious too. I am sure I will leave my mark in operatic history and that is what counts.

In spite of the Russian triumph a certain wistfulness crept into his outlook. He was no longer the young singer ready to climb mountains. He had been wounded, and it was not quite the same again.

During the summer of 1961, we went back to Villars, renting a more comfortable chalet for four months. There George spent happy periods before and after his performances in Bayreuth. Once, as we left to go to Germany, we drove off in our new four-door white Mercedes and we both kept waving to the children standing in front of the door. We waved so frantically that George forgot about the driveway and drove down the four steps of a footpath. There was a clatter and tremendous laughter as everybody ran over to assess the damage. Miraculously the Mercedes survived without a scratch and served us perfectly for ten years. The mishap postponed our departure for a few minutes and afforded an excuse for more kisses and good-byes.

It was one of George's busiest and most satisfying summers in Bayreuth. He sang Amfortas twice and the Dutchman three times and came back in a great mood. A few weeks later he went alone to Munich for some performances of *Don Giovanni* and brought back a surprise especially for me. In his arms he carried a small basket, which he put on my lap with a look of great joy and expectation. He could not wait to see my face when I discovered that the basket contained a two-month-old wirehaired dachshund, silver and black, brown eyes like shiny buttons, a tiny wet nose, and a pink tongue that licked my hands with immediate devotion. I was overjoyed. George knew how much I loved this breed, and had driven from Munich without stopping to be sure to get home with the little dog on the eve of our anniversary.

At the end of the summer, just before coming home to New York with the new family member, we started to look for a piece of land near Lake Geneva where we could eventually build our own house. The couple who had rented the chalet in Villars to us, lived near Lausanne and knew of land for sale not far from their own house. So one day we stood proudly on our own property, six acres over-looking a vineyard, some rolling fields, and below, Lake Geneva with the Alps on the far side. Far away you could see Mont Blanc when the weather was clear, and just to our left was a fourteenth-century castle that gave the name of Vufflens-le-Château to our village. We stood arm in arm on the property making plans for the house and our future life in it. Someday we hoped to spend most of the year in Switzerland, just keeping a small pied-a-terre in New York for the Metropolitan Opera season.

During the following winter London caught a cold and, as is usual for singers, he went immediately to see his throat specialist. Dr. Leo Reckford took care of most of the Metropolitan Opera's artists. In addition to being medically expert, he also knew how to handle his patients' delicate psyches. After George's visit Dr. Reckford called to warn me that one of George's vocal cords was not responding. He was not sure, because the throat was inflamed, but if it was the left cord that was injured, it could have serious implications. The nerve to that cord loops around the aorta, the main artery leaving the heart, and George might be seriously ill. Dr. Reckford had not said anything to George, expecting to see him again in a few days when the swelling went down, but he told me to keep George home and prevent him from getting agitated. I barely heard the physician's advice. What did this mean? What kind of heart problem? Could it be fatal? How could this strong giant be so ill? But already George was home giving a report about his sore throat, and I smiled and went about the household chores as usual.

A few days later George went back to Dr. Reckford and I went along. The swelling was gone; the cold was cured. Dr. Reckford asked me to look over his shoulder into George's throat while he was examining him with his instruments. George's throat was so wide and open that I could clearly see his vocal cords, two short rather thick membranes that met in a central position when he said the letter a. I could also see what the doctor now diagnosed: that the left cord was moving back and forth diligently while the right one seemed sluggish and vibrated only slightly when touching the left. The doctor explained to George that because the right cord was the affected one, it had nothing to do with the aorta. Still, it seemed that the nerve which activated the right cord was paralyzed. Possibly the nerve and cord were affected only temporarily, as a result of the throat infection, and would recover in time. In the meantime he advised as much vocal rest as possible.

I was somewhat relieved to be free of the terror of the past few days—at least it wasn't his heart—but we left the doctor's office in silence, each wondering what this meant for the future. I wondered if there was anything seriously wrong in the magnificent vocal apparatus I had just inspected.

Evidently George had the same thoughts. He did not know the exact prognosis of his ailment. Of course he was deeply disturbed by the doctor's discovery, but it was not in his nature to accept any misfortune without a fight. His voice was his capital and he was determined to take any measures needed to preserve it.

He remained as loving and considerate as ever with his family but his nerves paid a heavy price. He had to resort to sedatives more and more frequently. At night he often got up to read for hours. The constant search for a cure kept him busy at least and sustained him with hope of improvement.

At first the diagnosis had no influence on his singing. His cold was cured and he went back to his busy season at the Metropolitan, his recitals and the performances in Cologne. But from that time on, between operas and concerts, wherever he went, he would consult every throat specialist he heard about. In the beginning it often seemed that the right cord was moving, and the doctor could reassure George. Then he went back to the stage and performed as if nothing had happened. In 1964, Dr. Zimmermann, a German doctor, convinced him that an operation to straighten the septum in his nose would help. He went ahead and was disappointed once again. As the years went by, it became obvious that the right cord was definitely not moving; would never move again. Another operation opening the base of the neck to find out if some muscle was pressing on the nerve proved useless; the laryngeal nerve was not functioning. Recently, it has been discovered that hepatitis sometimes attacks a nerve; this was probably the only valid explanation.

Because the cord was not moving, it eventually became atrophied. The left cord compensated and moved over farther and farther to meet the affected one. As long as the cords met sound was produced and George could continue to sing. Because of his excellent technique and breath support, he was able to perform for a few years without too much trouble. On January 19, 1963, Winthrop Sargeant wrote in *The New Yorker:*

> George London, in his role as the Dutchman, ought to be commemorated by a statue in the lobby. I have never encountered a finer interpretation of the Dutchman, and I suspect it will be many seasons before any other artist anywhere undertakes this brooding, romantic role with comparable authority, either in voice or in physical presence.

This extravagant praise was particularly welcome at that time. Yet some high notes were becoming increasingly difficult, and then little by little he did not have the customary thrust in the voice. He was painfully aware of these faults.

At the end of 1963 we sold the apartment on Central Park West—the building had gone co-op the previous year—and moved to 1155 Park Avenue. The apartment was very roomy with four bedrooms, living room, dining room, and den. There was a rumor that Caruso had once lived there. We also started building our house in Switzerland, hoping to go there within two years. Andy started at Yale that year and nephew Patrick had gone to Cornell a year earlier. So we were left with only three children. Philip was picked up every morning by the Riverdale Country Day School bus and Marie Claire took Marina to the French Lycée two blocks away on her way to the park with Marc and Zorro, the dachshund.

In January 1964 George sang the title role in *The Last Savage*, a new opera by Gian-Carlo Menotti, which was given at the Metropolitan Opera. Roberta Peters and Nicolai Gedda were the soprano and tenor leads. George was carried onstage in a cage where he stood dressed in a leopard skin, showing his splendid physique. During the remainder of the story, he became exposed to the benefits of civilization. The libretto was rather silly but there was some charming music. After his entrance George had a lovely aria, set fairly high in his range, and he was nervous about it. However, at the general rehearsal all went well and we had a party full of good cheer in our new apartment with Gian-Carlo Menotti, Samuel Barber, and Thomas Schippers, the conductor. We had just moved and everyone sat on boxes and packing crates eating the food displayed on a huge buffet. At the premiere, three days later on January 23, the cage was brought in to great applause and set down center stage. When George started singing, the cage, which had evidently not been well fastened to the floor, began to sway alarmingly and it appeared to be falling over, righting itself at the last moment. There was an audible sigh from the audience. Combined with his fear of the aria, this incident was terribly disturbing for him. He managed to finish the aria reasonably well but afterward he came to dread his entrance at every performance.

By the end of 1964 every appearance was an ordeal for him. The carefree performer of the past was gone; his instrument was no longer dependable and all his know-how could not help. He took tranquilizers before each performance, and waged a heroic battle against his awful fate. Without complaining, he forced himself with superhuman dedication to try different tricks: take a deeper breath, or place the tone preceding a high tone somewhat higher, or cheat with the pronunciation of a vowel to make it sound like *A,* which is easier. He could have transposed some arias one tone down, but considered that dishonest.

The situation was all the more difficult because besides the doctor and Paola Novikova, his teacher, no one knew that there was anything wrong with him, since that in itself would have been damaging to his career. No one would engage a singer who had a problem with his vocal cords.

At home, he was quieter than usual and would stay for hours in his room with a book. He was always affectionate with the children, who did not suspect anything. He worked on many of Philip's English compositions; they were a challenge to both. Then he waited anxiously for Philip's marks to find out if they had done well. He was naturally competitive in everything he did and had strong opinions about literature and politics. He was furious if the teacher did not like his/Philip's work as if they were his own school marks.

In September 1964 London went on a four-week tour of recitals in Japan. He tailored his program to his current capacities, performing arias without too many high notes and relying on relatively easy song cycles. We went to Tokyo, Kyoto, and Osaka; the faithful Leo Taubman was his accompanist. The concerts were a great success. The Japanese, usually not demonstrative, gave him an effusive welcome. The audience was extraordinarily attentive. They had been told to refrain from applauding between songs of the same group, which they understood to mean no applause until the end of the first half. There was total silence until the intermission, which seemed ominous to the artists, but then came huge prolonged acclamation, which more than made up for everything. Sony issued a George London solo recording especially for the Japanese market. George was relaxed and loved Japan. This was to be his last extended tour abroad.

During the season 1964/65 at the Met, London had a

fairly heavy schedule, which included his first *Walküres* in New York, *Tosca, Last Savages* and a number of *Flying Dutchmans*. The *Walküre* performances were in February and the beginning of March. Miraculously they went well. Although the voice lacked luster and carrying power, he had some good nights, but each performance took a heavy toll on George's nerves and required twice as much energy as usual.

The atrophy of the affected cord progressed faster during these months, and by the spring of 1965, George's singing voice was a fraction of what it had been. I remember that his last *Flying Dutchman,* at the Met, was in mid-April. He was in agony and just prayed his voice would hold out until the end. He knew he had to sing three additional *Flying Dutchmans* on tour; however each appearance was a trial for him and each high note had become a torment.

London was acutely aware of his condition and realized that he would not be able to sing opera too much longer. When he was offered a role in a Broadway musical, he jumped at the opportunity. It was scheduled for November 1965. George was to play the male lead in the story about Anastasia, the daughter of Czar Nicholas who allegedly escaped the massacre of the imperial family during the revolution. The show sounded promising and was to be directed by George Abbott, who was famous for his musical theater productions. London thought that he would be able to do this kind of singing without problems. Also, he would be well paid and that would be a big help, for the cancellations had mounted steadily and consequently George was earning only a fraction of his former income.

In the summer of 1965 London was scheduled to sing the role of Wotan in Wieland Wagner's new staging of *The Ring of the Nibelungen*. This had been planned for years with great expectations both from Wieland and George. The trial performances in Cologne had gone well in the previous years. Now George wondered how he could get through those grueling parts. The weather did not help. It rained nonstop from the moment of his arrival. He immediately caught a cold that would not go away. Karl Böhm, the conductor replacing Wolfgang Sawallisch, the Cologne conductor who had been more accommodating, insisted on opening up all the cuts of Wotan's declamations in *Siegfried*, cuts that had been promised to George in his contract. This situation gave him the opportunity to withdraw gracefully from the whole engagement.

This was the first major disaster resulting from London's infirmity and he had to face it. But first he had the sad duty of saying goodbye to Wieland. Both men were heartbroken to see their dreams shattered. Wieland could find another Wotan but it would not be the same. George was dejected; this was one of the worst moments of the long, tormented path from stardom to the end of his career.

We left the gloomy, wet town for the Swiss mountain resort of Gstaad carrying with us the secret of George's real malady. By now many people in the music business had guessed that there was something wrong with George, but no one knew what it was. Over the years new excuses had been invented — sometimes a hernia, sometimes colds, or various indispositions— but the sacred words *vocal cords,* the death sentence for an opera singer had never been mentioned.

George hated the lying, the cover-up. It was particularly difficult for somebody who was such an extrovert and who liked to talk openly about all his concerns. He became gradually more uncommunicative and less sure of himself.

During the fall of 1965 London's voice became less and less dependable. From time to time even his speaking voice was a little hoarse. At last George realized that he could not even go through with the musical-comedy project. The doctors suggested an operation to free possible pressure on the paralyzed nerve. It was announced to the press as a hernia operation and George withdrew from the musical. He had pinned his hopes on the operation, but it turned out to be useless. Once again the doctors had found no cure. He was still hoping that there would be some improvement, but the cord did not move. It was risky to undergo surgery but he felt that if there was a millionth of a chance for the operation to succeed, he had to do it.

On his forty-sixth birthday he wrote to his parents:

> The current season has not been very agreeable. But I've had a lot of success and joy and fulfillment in my life and I should not complain too bitterly." And he added, "There is so much to be thankful for—it's true I've had my share of bad luck this past year, but I've developed a good broad back and have most certainly grown and become wiser and perhaps better for the experience.

After his supposed "recovery from the hernia operation" he sang one last Amfortas at the Met. The voice was no longer there but the performance was deeply moving. Inevitably George identified with the wounded knight. He did not know that this would be his last opera performance. His retirement from the stage would be a great loss to the opera world.

In the spring he was asked to be the American judge for the singers' contest of the Tchaikovsky competition in Moscow, to be held from June 10 to 26, 1966. The two weeks in Russia provided a wonderful change of scenery for him. He could forget about his own problems and just think about the voices of the competitors. He again had caviar every day for breakfast and spent most of his free time advising and helping the American contingent, which included the eventual two bronze medalists, Veronica Tyler and Simon Estes. George was received with great honor by the Russians, who listened respectfully to his opinions. Watching his interest in the young singers was the first hint of an activity that would satisfy him after his career was over.

Suddenly the voice problem became even more serious

than before. Now his speaking voice was getting weaker from day to day. A visit to a specialist in Moscow resulted in the usual diagnosis and sad shaking of the doctor's head. He, too, could offer no cure. Although he knew that Soviet medicine was generally backward, George wanted to try every possibility; at that point he would have consulted a witch doctor.

After Moscow, he planned to go to California to visit his parents. On the way, George had been scheduled to give a recital in San Francisco, which he had to cancel, using a sore throat as his excuse. Although he did not suspect the seriousness of the disease, Kurt Adler, the director of the San Francisco Opera, recommended that George see an outstanding throat doctor in Los Angeles. Dr. Henry Rubin not only realized immediately what the trouble was but could offer a remedy. He proposed to inject the paralyzed right cord, now much shrunken, with silicone. The implantation of plastic material into the atrophied cord would fill it out and push it back to the center; then the two cords would again meet as if both were healthy.

We took a long walk along the ocean in Santa Monica to discuss the proposed treatment. Healthy youths and tanned children were playing in the waves. We walked in the shallow water. George was talking to me, but I could not hear what he said. The great voice that had sung on stages all over the world was reduced to a whisper. It was the lowest point of his ordeal.

The next morning George had the injection, and two days later he could talk almost normally. It was miraculous. Dr. Rubin advised him to start vocalizing slowly to see how he would progress. George was not overly optimistic, but the immediate result of the injection was so spectacular that one could have high hopes. George was still a little hoarse, but both the speaking and the singing voice retained the same quality and exact tone as before the paralysis.

Encouraged, we returned to Switzerland and the village

of Vufflens-le-Château. We had moved into our new house the preceding spring with the two younger children. Both Andy and Philip were at Yale now. All our belongings were sent over from New York, where we kept just a two-room apartment on Madison Avenue. The house was everything he could have hoped for, and George adored it. He picked the colors of the walls, the wallpaper, the curtains, and the furniture, and the joy of having his own place made up a little for the hardship that he was enduring. He was in a good mood, as loving and playful as ever with the children.

George's vocal progress was astonishing and he could re-alistically think of singing again. He did not talk about opera but recitals seemed perfectly possible. His voice sounded good, as warm and rich as ever, yet he wondered if it had the strength and the sustaining power. He worried about his return to sing-ing.

In March 1967 he gave a recital, which was respectable and got good reviews, at the Metropolitan Museum of Art in New York. Paola Novikova had the great joy of hearing her Georgie sounding his old self again. She died a few months later. George was guardedly optimistic. He had been able to complete this recital without too much trouble. Could he sustain the effort and how long would the improvement last? There was a problem with silicone injections: they were some-times reabsorbed.

On May 17, 1967, he was scheduled to give a recital in Vienna and I decided that I would drive there from our home in Switzerland and take Marina, Marc, and Marie Claire. I wanted the children to see Vienna and above all I wanted them to see their father on stage and witness the cheering crowds, the applause, the flowers. I was hoping that at eight and eleven they would be old enough to remember the con-cert when they were grown up.

The concert hall was full. George ended his program with the "Farewell and Death of Boris," and although the voice did not have its former power, his artistry was such that the audience was as enthusiastic as always. Marina and Marc witnessed the applause with starry eyes and George described the concert in a letter to his parents:

> My concert here was a great success. I had a wonderful reception from the audience when I first appeared and the applause grew in intensity after each group so that at the end it was quite frenetic. Certainly the Viennese public has remained faithful to me. Marina and Marc came. It was the first time they had ever heard me in a recital. They sat so quietly, quite transfixed. It was such a pleasure to look out at those four intense, chocolate-brown eyes. Afterwards, Marc helped carry my flowers to the dressing room. He asked Nora how come nobody asked for his autograph. Nora explained that Daddy had sung and that he was the one who should sign autographs. Marc said to this, "But I'm daddy's son"—it's quite an argument. Marina looked so grown up—really a young lady. We took them with us to the restaurant where we had supper afterwards with close friends. When she kissed me goodnight, Marina whispered in my ear, "It was just great."

Some weeks later, back in Vufflens, I sat on the bed looking at the familiar landscape of fields, lake, and mountains in front of our window. George came in and sat down next to me. He put his arm around my shoulder and for a while we sat in silence. At last he said quietly but forcefully, "You understand, what I can do now is not good enough. I have come to a decision. I will not sing anymore." In a few words he put an end to six years of torture and concluded the career to which he had dedicated his life.

In a letter to me after two last concerts in Germany that had been booked earlier, he summed it up:

> Giving public appearances on this basis is simply not worth it in terms of morale and personal satisfaction. I

know I gave the people great pleasure. I was also relaxed and able to concentrate on my interpretations. However, for me the experience was not exultantly satisfying—as it should be—and can only be if I have vocal strength to spare. I may never again achieve that—and then again I may—but I will go ahead now—without pressures or deadlines. I'm sure you agree with this. And believe me I'm not depressed in any way, truly not. I just feel that when I sing in public it must be representative of my best standards. Otherwise I harm my inner self even if the public buys it.

This paragraph was George London's own epitaph to his singing career; it marked the end of his struggle. He said that without his voice he felt emasculated. He could not stop singing all at once. He had to give up first the opera, then the recitals, until at last he was able to face the world without his voice but with his soul intact.

A few years later, in November 1971 George gave an interview to Bob Sherman for his WQXR "Listening Room" program and talked openly for the first time about the end of his career. He said:

You reviewed a concert [at the Metropolitan Museum] in which I sang a varied, rather substantial program where I was working with a paralyzed vocal cord which had been artificially reconstituted with silicone. It's a miracle and therefore we ask ourselves, where does the quality of the human voice come from? What is the secret of that special sound? Because I have always flattered myself that people who are keyed to voices could recognize George London if they heard him on a record. They say, "That's the sound that *he* made."
From a hoarse, resonanceless state I went to a situation where a reviewer of *The New York Times* can say, "Well he has made a fine comeback and this is the voice we always knew." That is a miracle.
I continued to work in this way for the better part of

two years but by the very nature of the situation, which is not a normal thing—this is like working with a prosthesis of some kind, with a crutch—structurally the voice is not what it was, and therefore under stress and under certain conditions I could not be expected to maintain the top standard with which I believed I had been identified. And so rather than do less than what was expected of me, I decided to give it up and so I went into other areas that interested me. It is an unfortunate thing but I had about sixteen years at the very top, I made a lot of good recordings and I think I left my mark on certain parts in a rather special way and so I have a great deal to be grateful for. It's regrettable because singing was great fun and a great satisfaction.

His friend Simon Bourgin reports that he said to him "Sy, nothing, absolutely nothing will make up for losing my voice" but Sy also wrote in a speech that "George never gave up - putting the same energy, passion, experience and dedication into his future work at the Kennedy Center, The Washington Opera, the Opera Institute as he had into his singing career."

Chapter 13
A New Career

We loved our Swiss home which we called "Les Muses." It was the first house he owned and George was immensely proud of it. He had designed the floor plan with the architect. The master bedroom decorated, in blue and white, was on the main floor far away from the children's and guest rooms, which were on the second floor. Since he liked to sleep late, undisturbed by the youngsters, his sleeping habits were always a problem for the household and were best solved in Vufflens.

Marina and Marc went to school close by. Marie Claire drove Marina to her school in Lausanne, twenty minutes away, and Marc was dropped off at the village school in Vufflens. In the summer months Andy and Philip came to visit. George took part in all the children's games. Most of all he enjoyed touch football and ping pong, at which we were all very good. There were fierce battles; everyone was very competitive and no one would give up, including the adults.

London was content to remain at home. He could spend hours on the terrace reading and watching the vineyards below the property, or the white-capped mountains beyond the lake, or the little Disneyland train climbing across the fields from the lake to the village.

His pleasure in the ownership of the property helped him in this time of change. The solid brick house, the peaceful landscape, everything proved to be a tangible possession that no one could take away from him.

During the inexorable progress of the paralysis, London became more and more aware that he could no longer support his family by singing. Having been deprived as a youth, he always worried about financial security and had taken life insurance and even health insurance that covered his voice. So he did receive some compensation when he could not perform, but it could not compare with what he was earning when he was well.

In 1965 he began looking at positions for which he would be qualified. He was best prepared for the directorship of an opera company. He had a thorough knowledge of the whole repertoire; unlike some of his colleagues, he had not been content simply to perform his own roles. Frequently he listened to the other artists and gave them advice about their careers. As a result he was unusually well informed about the capabilities and availability of most singers.

Aside from this, London was also interested in all forms of music; his taste was eclectic and if he preferred classical music, he also loved jazz, the Beatles, and Broadway musicals. At that time, there were fewer opera companies in the United States than today, and the important ones, such as San Francisco, Chicago, and the Metropolitan Opera, were all led by capable directors. Another possibility was as director of a music school. There had been precedents of appointing singers into such positions. George enjoyed teaching, particularly coaching young singers. He found out how good he was at this during classes given in Cincinnati in February 1968.

In May of that year he was approached by Julius Rudel, director of the New York City Opera, who intended to recommend him for a position at the John F. Kennedy Center for the Performing Arts, which was constructed in Washington, D.C. Julius had been engaged as the artistic director of the Kennedy Center, but his obligations with the New York City Opera, a position that he intended to keep, would make it impossible for him to give full time to Washington. For that reason, another artistic expert was needed to reside in the capital.

The Kennedy Center, a complex with 3 auditoriums, was scheduled to open in 1971, but the staff had to be in place long before, as planning for any artistic event had to be done years in advance. George would be in charge of artistic matters, Rudel told him, and although the offer was not definite yet, it prompted him to write to his parents on May 30:

> Today is my birthday [his forty-eighth] and in spite of all the setbacks which life has presented me with these past couple of years, I still consider myself a most fortunate man. My children are happy, healthy and well adjusted, I have an excellent marriage and I am perhaps on the threshold of challenging new activities.

George met William McCormick Blair, Jr., former United States Ambassador to Denmark, now appointed director of the Kennedy Center, and the meeting went well. As a result Roger L. Stevens, chairman of the board of the Kennedy Center, its founder and animator, signed a contract appointing George London artistic administrator in June 1968. He was to start in September of the same year.

The title was a compromise as there was already an artistic director and a general director. George London was hired on the basis of his artistic expertise; he could not boast any previous administrative experience. However, his conversations with Bill Blair and Roger Stevens had evidently convinced them that he had the intelligence and common sense to implement the artistic plans for the future of the Kennedy Center.

This would be an interesting and stimulating position for London with a measure of prestige. At least it would make up somewhat for the tragic blow that had hit him, and it would guarantee a steady income. George had invested in real estate in California but this was not an auspicious time to sell. He could not bear to sell the house in Vufflens, where every stone, every tree meant so much to him. True, the family would have to move to Washington, but could return to the Swiss house every summer for a few months. Marina and Marc were growing; the older boys thought that the younger children's education should be continued in the States. Otherwise, they said, they would become European and they would never "belong." We welcomed the opportunity to take them back to the States.

On August 28, 1968, I wrote to George's parents:

> The difficult adjustment will be for George who is going into such a different kind of work under difficult and challenging circumstances. I am sure that in time with success he will find it exciting and satisfying but I know that he still feels much heartache at leaving his artistic career. He will see little by little that he is just as needed in this type of work where his knowledge and his enthusiasm will be so important.

Once more we were moving. We had rented a house on Chain Bridge Road, in a beautiful residential part of Washington. We decided to transport only a few pieces of furniture but George could not part from his favorite paintings: a large dramatic Appel, a colorful Chagall, a striking Jenkins, several sculptures and two views of Paris by a French impressionist.

London was somewhat apprehensive about his new obligations. He had been self-employed, at the top of his profession, recognized by all those he came in contact with. Now he would be an employee in a large organization and in a city where most people knew nothing about him. It was almost like starting from the beginning, and it would be difficult for him to be in a subordinate position, no matter how cheerfully he seemed to accept it.

We had found a fine school for Marina and Marc, the Maret School, which emphasized the teaching of French. We hoped that this way the transition would not be too traumatic for them. Our dear Marie Claire remained in Switzerland; the children were too old for a nanny now. The farewells were very difficult for everyone as she was like a member of the family. We could not bear to leave our dogs behind. That meant taking Zorro, the intrepid dachshund, which posed no problem; and Tessa, our huge Bernese mountain dog, almost the size of a Saint Bernard—which meant a big problem indeed. George was traveling together with the family. Marina was a grown-up twelve-year-old and Marc a serious nine. We felt very close and adventurous. The trip was uneventful; we arrived at Kennedy Airport just after Labor Day, and it seemed that the whole world had arrived on that same day.

We had ten pieces of luggage that required customs inspection, and had to retrieve the dogs from a special section. It looked as if it would take hours. When we opened Tessa's cage, the huge black dog jumped with joy on me and anyone nearby while Zorro barked incessantly. We created havoc. The customs officials couldn't get rid of us fast enough. They glanced at our passports, declined to look at our luggage, and showed us out in five minutes. We laughed about the scene for days. Washington, here we come!

The nine years in the capital turned out to be happy ones. London traveled less and spent more time with his family. His work was interesting and satisfying; he made great new friends and kept in touch with old ones.

He was relieved to know that his whole life no longer depended on his voice. The constant tension was over, but he was fighting new battles daily. His job was a test of unknown capabilities; and his voice, even for speaking, gave him problems from time to time. The day of our arrival Bill Blair and his wife, Deeda, paid a friendly call with flowers. We were touched by this gesture and thought it augured well.

The following Saturday Roger Stevens gave a cocktail party to introduce George to Washington society. Except for the Blairs, the host and his wife Christine, we did not know anyone of the hundred and fifty guests. We circulated bravely among the crowd, which included Senators Fullbright and Percy, Chief Justice Abe Fortas, several ambassadors, and other influential Washington personalities. There was much talk about the forthcoming presidential election. The host and most of the guests were Democrats, and everyone hoped that Senator Humphrey would be elected, although they all feared that it was unlikely.

London, as always, was completely at ease. He was interested in politics and he had testified before Congress in favor of the establishment of the National Endowment for the Arts. He was well informed and had an excellent memory so he could converse intelligently with this political crowd. I established an immediate rapport with our hostess, Christine Stevens, who was committed to saving endangered animal species. I volunteered to work for the Washington Humane Society. This meant lobbying in the Senate with her.

A few weeks after his arrival, George was invited to tea at the White House by Lady Bird Johnson. She was interested in the arts and wanted to know all about George's plans. He found her very charming and intelligent. Sometime later we were invited to a reception at the White House by President and Mrs. Johnson. For the first time we experienced the glamour of these official dinners. There were extensive security checks when you drove through the gates of the White House and once more as you entered the house itself, but afterward you could walk around quite freely. At the entrance level there were several rooms with exhibits of the china used by various presidents and a gallery of portraits. As you went up the marble stairs to the reception rooms, the marine band was playing. We stood in line and an aide introduced us to the president, who shook hands with George and then with me and said a few pleasant words.

Later we were invited to the White House quite often, particularly by President Carter, who liked opera. We also went to special performances there, such as the Alvin Ailey Dance Theater and concerts by Vladimir Horowitz or by young singers. No matter how often we went to the White House it was always with some excitement.

The social highlights were only a small part of Washington life. Marina and Marc had to get used to a new school, but soon they made new friends and were old enough to take care of themselves.

George, of course, was away from home all day like any businessman. He launched into multiple projects all dealing with music, to which he brought imagination, hard work, and tremendous know-how. Aside from his activities at the Kennedy Center, he directed a number of operas culminating in Seattle in 1975 with Wagner's complete *Ring of the Nibelungen,* in both English and German. He coached young singers, he created and supervised a grants program, he gave numerous master classes here and in Europe, and finally he became director of the Washington Opera Company. In retrospect, it seems that he crowded as many activities as possible into these years, as if he were racing against time.

His forceful and exuberant personality created problems for him. London was given to strong statements and outbursts, which might lead people to think of him as mercurial and difficult, whereas actually he was just the opposite, infinitely serious and totally dedicated. Eventually he proved to everyone that he was not a temperamental opera singer but a reliable and successful administrator.

Those who knew him realized that the rhetoric was just an outlet for his theatrical personality. Although he was getting older, he remained slim and elegant. He was vain about his figure and exercised religiously every day. To his dismay, his hairline was receding.

Through the influence of a friend, London became interested in vintage cars and first bought a white Bentley convertible dating from the 1950s and then a four-door Bentley sedan, both of which required constant repairs, but gave him enormous satisfaction. He spent hours polishing them with special wax and chamois on Sunday afternoons. It was great therapy for him.

Meanwhile the work at the Kennedy Center was interesting but often frustrating. George had to discuss most decisions with Julius Rudel, who did not spend much time in Washington. George was very grateful to Julius for recommending him for the job and said that, "Julius and I see eye-to-eye in all musical matters."

The Kennedy Center, as conceived by the architect Edward Durell Stone, is composed of three theaters enclosed in one building. There is a concert hall with twenty-seven hundred seats, an opera house of two thousand one hundred seats, and the Eisenhower Theater for dramatic performances. George was in charge of the first two halls. He had several ideas for the opening season but the actual opening spectacle had already been planned by Roger Stevens before George's arrival. This was to be a Mass commissioned specially from Leonard Bernstein to be performed in September 1971 at the opera house. A good number of events had already been booked in the concert hall by the Washington Performing Arts Society before his arrival as well. This organization had existed in Washington for many years; formerly their concerts had taken place in cavernous Constitution Hall or the theater of George Washington University, which were previously the only halls suitable for music in the nation's capital.

Three evenings weekly were taken by the National Symphony Orchestra, which also moved into the Kennedy Center's Concert Hall, eventually under the dynamic leadership of London's close friend Antal Dorati, whom he had recommended for this position. On free evenings, George was eager to arrange for some special events in the concert hall but the Kennedy Center's budget was small. Roger Stevens's efforts had managed to convince Congress to vote for the funds necessary to build a performing arts center in Washington, but there was not much money to run it.

In 1969 George was able to persuade friends and colleagues from the classical and popular music world to perform during the opening season of the Kennedy Center. The artists most generously donated their performances. In return they received a replica of the Kennedy Center in white marble and silver and the assurance that their names would be engraved in the building as "Founding Artists." This way George put together an extraordinary series of thirty-five concerts divided into a jazz series, a pop series, and a classical series. The concerts included many great names in music, from Dionne Warwick to Pearl Bailey to Dizzy Gillespie, from Isaac Stem and Van Cliburn to Joan Sutherland, and Placido Domingo. As time went on, there were disagreements between George and Julius Rudel, and Roger Stevens was put in the position of mediator between the two music administrators. Eventually London adapted to the wishes of the different directors of the center, although he resented being interfered with when he felt that the interests of the Kennedy Center were at stake.

He conceived a plan for bringing great European opera companies to the Kennedy Center Opera House. This, he felt, would generate great prestige for the new theater. Julius, who intended to bring the New York City Opera to the Center, feared the competition. George was convinced that the foreign companies would not interfere with the American opera company. He thought that if the Washington public became acquainted with international-caliber grand opera, it would only whet its appetite for more opera at home. He was right, as was proven in time.

The greatest difficulty in realizing such ambitious plans was financial. Even sold-out houses have never been able to support the lyric theater and there was an added problem because the Kennedy Center Opera House, which is a perfect size acoustically, is small in terms of financial return.

La Scala, the Vienna State Opera, or the Berlin Opera could come to Washington only if the Italian government, the Austrian government, or the West German government heavily subsidized their appearance. London talked to his friends at the Vienna and Berlin operas and started negotiations with the director of La Scala with the help of the Italian ambassador, Egidio Ortona. The negotiations progressed slowly; and George traveled to Milan to meet Antonio Ghiringhelli, then director of La Scala. He hoped that La Scala would open the second season of the Kennedy Center.

George's efforts came to fruition a few years later, when he was no longer head of the Kennedy Center. All the big European companies eventually came—the Berlin Opera arrived with *Lohengrin* under the baton of Lorin Maazel in November 1975. The Bolshoi Opera came in July of 1975 and Richard Kidwell, manager of the Opera House remembers a touching moment:

> I asked George if he planned to see any of the performances and he said he didn't think so; that it might be too hard for him emotionally. However, a day or so later, at one of the *Boris* performances I was standing in the rear of the theatre and turned around to see George standing next to me. Watching the same *Boris* production (sets, costumes etc) that he had performed in years before in Moscow! A very moving moment for me (and I'm sure, him!).

For the opening of the Berlin Opera, there was a gala performance in the presence of the German ambassador Berndt von Staden, a good friend of George's. We were seated in the center of the orchestra and as usual we were early, for George hated to be late to any performance; he felt it was an insult to the artists. While we were getting settled, George noticed that two young men seated immediately in front of us were wearing swastikas in their lapels. He was incensed and asked the men who they were. They answered rudely and said it was none of his business. George said it was very much his business. The men snickered malevolently. Now George was furious. He got up from his seat, towering over the short youths. He took both of them by their coat collars, lifted them out of their seats, and literally carried them to the door where the police took over. Later it was established that the two individuals were indeed part of a plot to disrupt the performance. Ambassador von Staden sent George a formal note of gratitude.

Most of the time, however, there were no incidents like this one. There were many official receptions at the Kennedy Center and the Washingtonians liked and admired London.

On Christmas 1968, the whole family celebrated together. Philip, Andy, and nephew Patrick had come and everyone helped decorate a huge tree in the living room. To spite us the furnace broke down on Christmas Eve on a bitter cold night, and we huddled together around the tree until a good-hearted repairman mercifully arrived that very evening.

We proudly looked at our three young men who were ready to start life on their own. But we knew they would always remain close to us and we felt full of love and contentment. We watched Marina and Marc, so much like their father. They needed us for some years yet but they, too, would grow into special people. It was important that they all be close to each other; it would be a great strength for them.

At the end of December, George wrote to his parents, "Our children are wonderful and make up so much of what I am feeling grateful for as this old year passes."

But with the new year, there were renewed concerns about his voice. It seemed that the silicone was slowly being absorbed into the tissue. Consultation with Dr. Rubin confirmed this, and he recommended another injection into the vocal cord. However, as this could not be done too frequently, he advised George to wait a few months.

George went to California in February to have another injection. The result was good but he had more difficulty recovering than the first time, becoming hoarse on and off. I wrote him suggesting that perhaps Dr. Rubin had over-injected the cord a little but that it would settle soon and added, "I got your long, sad letter last night. I am so dreadfully distressed that you continue forever to have troubles and tortures. You, who are the nicest, dearest, most humane person I know. I miss you acutely at all times and must watch myself not to talk about you all the time."

During the following years, the quality of London's speaking voice varied. Sometimes it was clear and strong, sometimes less weighty, sometimes slightly hoarse. He had two additional injections, the last one with Teflon, a newer substance that was not expected to be absorbed.

It was a constant concern for him. He had to use his voice all day, on the phone, teaching, coaching, staging, for an occasional speaking engagement, in interviews. During interviews on radio, or television he was conscious of every variance in his speaking voice and he could not believe that most people did not notice anything. However he faced his trials with unending courage and fortitude.

Fortunately, his voice was no longer crucial for his livelihood and in time he learned to live with this problem. But over the years it remained a recurrent torment that he was never allowed to forget.

Chapter 14
The Washington Years

The following seventies were characterized by unfulfilled hopes and opportunities and by the creation of an organization that carried his vision into the twenty first century. He found his work at the Kennedy Center challenging. It provided him with valuable new experience. However, he could not help feeling that he was spending too much time on administrative duties and not enough in dealing with artists. He missed direct contact with opera. He felt deprived without the singing and the music. Although glad at first to be removed from the source of his pain, he began to be aware of a great void in his life.

The long reign of Sir Rudolf Bing as general manager of the Metropolitan was coming to an end in 1972. There were several rumors about his successor and George's name was mentioned repeatedly, even though he had made no effort to approach anyone for the job. Obviously the prospect of the Met excited him, and eventually he started making inquiries and talking to people he knew on the Met board. George was bursting with new ideas, although he was aware of the Met's financial problems. But the people in power had no confidence in George's managerial capabilities. It became clear to him that he had little chance to be nominated and he did not expect anything to happen. It was 1970, and he had as yet no references as an administrator. Bing did not feel that he could recommend George, and it was questionable that his support would have helped. The board's attention turned to Goeran Gentele, the successful director of the Stockholm Opera, and in December 1970 Gentele was appointed general manager starting in the 1972-73 season.

Because opera seasons are planned many years in advance, the new general manager had to begin working in New York in the fall of 1971 to ensure a smooth transition. He needed to assemble a new staff and to set as soon as possible the repertory and the casts for the 1973/74 and 1974/75 seasons. (The previous season had already been booked by Rudolf Bing.) Therefore, Gentele started looking for assistants in the beginning of 1971 and George was recommended to him. He contacted George and they had a number of conversations. Gentele was a charming and cultured man; they were in agreement on all artistic subjects and London became hopeful that he would be hired.

On April 16, 1971, Gentele wrote him a letter with the following paragraph:

> As to the specification of your job at the Met, I want you as "assistant manager." One of your tasks will be to take over part of the planning job, which is now handled by Bob Herman. The chief stress should be laid upon the casting problems— to find the right persons with the right voices for the right parts which, up to now, has not always has been the case—besides the fact that you should take part in the planning and proposing operas for the repertory in consultation with the music director, an eventual other assistant manager and myself. In other words: you will be holding one of the key positions in the team of persons, who will handle the artistic side of the theatre.

The proposal was very attractive to George. He reasoned that he would be giving up a more glamorous title at the Kennedy Center to become only assistant manager at the Met, but he would be doing what he loved best, involved once more with opera and opera singers.

In the beginning of May, George was in Germany and decided to go to Sweden and see Gentele once more. When he returned, he was convinced that the matter was settled. But unknown to George, Gentele had approached Schuyler Chapin as early as February for the position of assistant general manager. Schuyler Chapin had been instrumental in the appointment of Gentele for the general manager job. On March 18, 1971, Chapin had accepted the position.

Therefore, when Gentele wrote the April letter to London, he had already appointed somebody else, but he never mentioned this to George.

On the other hand, Chapin did not mention London's name at all in his memoirs. Possibly he did not know of Gentele's offers to George. The announcement was made that Gentele had appointed Schuyler Chapin as assistant manager and the conductor Rafael Kubelik as music director. There was no mention of a position for George. When he asked, he was informed that he would work with Chapin and have some position to be decided upon in the future.

He was more angry than sad but discussed the situation calmly. He consulted a number of friends. Some told him he should sue for breach of promise. He dismissed this idea and considered the possibility of accepting a lesser position at the Met. Eventually he rejected this offer.

Schuyler, who had been an old friend and had been part of George's management at Columbia Artists, must have known about Gentele's conversations with George by then. He begged George to work with him, but London refused.

Looking back, it seems that Gentele never intended to give George a position of control. He was probably frightened by George's strong personality. Schuyler Chapin wrote in his book *Musical Chair:* "Gentele had one bothersome habit: he hated making final decisions." But if he had openly explained his intentions from the beginning, George might have considered a lower position. This might have been a happier solution for all concerned, considering future events.

In July 1972 Goeran Gentele was killed in an automobile accident and Schuyler became general manager of the Metropolitan. Kubelik was not able to spend enough time in New York and did not get along with the rest of the staff. He resigned from his post in February 1974.

Ten years later, when I first returned to the Metropolitan Opera House in New York, I was amazed to find that George London was still beloved by everyone, even after such a lapse of time. He might have been happy there, working with people who admired and appreciated him.

The board of the Metropolitan and particularly its president, George Moore, had accepted Schuyler Chapin as general manager by default and kept looking on and off for another candidate. By the spring of 1974 there was a new wave of rumors and soon an article in *The New York Times* predicted the demise of Chapin and named some front-runners for the position, one of whom being George London.

The phone started ringing. George answered truthfully that he had not been approached. However, he asked his friend Gabor Carelli, long-time tenor at the Metropolitan and active with the Met Auditions, to find out what was going on. Gabor met with several members of the board and discovered that indeed they were thinking of replacing Chapin and that London had been mentioned.

Eventually Gabor saw Mr. Moore and convinced him to meet with George London. George had several meetings with Moore and evidently made a very good impression, for the two men agreed on many points. It seems that Moore had decided to recommend George for the position of general manager when he went to the next meeting of the board of directors in the summer of 1974. By then, however, Moore was no longer president of the board. He had been replaced by William Rockefeller, who liked and respected George London. But there was a new mood in the board. One of their own, Anthony Bliss, became general manager and the young conductor James Levine became music director.

London remained sanguine during these months of suspense. The heartbreak had occurred in 1971 when he really believed that he was going to the opera house and was looking forward so eagerly to casting and choosing repertoire. Three years later he no longer believed it would happen, it always remained remote.

Being in charge of the Metropolitan might have been the only position that would have made up for the loss of his voice. He would have been an excellent administrator and a fine artistic influence on the house, as he proved he could be for smaller organizations. "It is not in the cards—I am not a member of the establishment," George said with some sorrow but with newly acquired serenity.

In 1971, London had resigned from the Kennedy Center, there was no job at the Met, and he would be out of work the following autumn.

During that summer he came only briefly to Switzerland, but he was there for our anniversary on August 30, 1971. I gave him a lithograph of Sarah Bernhardt by Mucha that he admired and wrote, "Only something very beautiful could celebrate the beautiful relationship between us—How could I ever find anything which could even begin to express my love, my devotion and my admiration which has grown continuously over the years." We could really celebrate, for George had arrived with good news: he had another job.

In 1969 Roger Stevens, with George's help, had incorporated a new organization, named the National Opera Institute, which was dedicated to the support and encouragement of all matters pertaining to opera. Now he appointed George as director of the institute, with an office in the Kennedy Center. George was pleased and greatly relieved. He was beginning to do more and more stage directions, and those together with the institute job would provide him with enough income. In addition, his duties at the institute would allow time for other work. He threw himself into his new occupation with his usual enthusiasm. The institute started giving grants for apprentices in all fields of opera, management, staging, composing of new works. But the program that was closest to George's heart was the one designed to help young singers.

George said, "No one ever helped me when I started my career," but he remembered his long and painful road to success and he wanted to help devise a way to make the road a little easier for future generations of singers.

George created a grants program whereby young American singers with some professional experience could receive financial assistance during the difficult and expensive early years of their careers. The program started modestly. In the first year, 1971, there was only one grant recipient, Richard Stillwell. Richard turned out to be a model for many of his followers. He was hardworking as well as talented, developed rapidly, and today has an important international career. The awards program grew rapidly and established the routine that would be followed thereafter.

Yearly auditions were held in several cities: Chicago, Washington, New York, and Los Angeles or San Francisco. Each singer had to be a professional with some opera experience to qualify for a grant. Every year there were ten grants of five thousand dollars each. George went to each city and heard all the candidates, an average of two hundred fifty singers each year. He was assisted by local judges who were asked to write their recommendations on each candidate's description sheet. Back in Washington, George would go through all the lists and pick the ten best artists. These artists could receive an equal grant for a second year if the results of their coaching or their engagements showed serious effort and progress.

After a few years George found that there were some artists who were not quite ready for a career and did not qualify for the prize, but were talented. He hated to deprive them completely and so he started one-thousand-dollar encouragement prizes. The recipients also could come back another year and compete again.

During the following six years London attended and supervised all the auditions in New York and Washington, Chicago and San Francisco. As with everything he did, he was intensely involved in the proceedings. He greeted each singer very pleasantly, but they were awed by his presence and obviously nervous. Each performer sang one aria of his or her choice and then would be asked to sing another chosen from a list that he or she had submitted to George and the other judges. Sometimes George did not agree with the choice of a particular singer and would suggest some other piece. When he liked an artist, he became more absorbed in the performance. He was delighted with the discovery of talent, and he always talked with the candidate, asked questions about his or her experience, teacher, and repertoire.

The grants program was the beginning of a new phase in George London's career, for now young singers entered his life. He was not content to give the grants and check on the use made of the money. He insisted on getting reports of the activities of each grantee, and often got in touch with them personally. This started a personal relationship with a number of young artists. They came to his house or to the office and he gave them advice on their teachers and their repertoire, and helped them with possible engagements. Occasionally he would get an accompanist and coach a singer in a special aria or show him some special technique that would improve his vocal production. After working with a young singer and future teacher, Erik Thorendahl, who was preparing the role of Siegmund in *Die Walküre,* he followed up with a letter on February 27, 1971:

> The pianissimo involves exactly the same production of tone as for forte; the position is identical. Try practicing crescendo and decrescendo. If the soft tone is right, the crescendo should work smoothly as well as the decrescendo. If not, it will be difficult to crescendo the tone smoothly. In decrescendoing one must think very high and increase the support.

His influence was powerful. He convinced Rockwell Blake, a young tenor with a wonderful top with exceptional flexibility, that he could do all the Rossini and Bellini repertoire in opera. Rocky developed a successful international career.

One night the phone rang. A young artist, on tour in Switzerland, had become ill and called for advice about a doctor. George found what she needed through friends and within a short time he called her back with the information. A few days later he called her again to find out how she was doing.

These young people became almost part of our family. George was very fond of many of them. To some degree he was reliving his own beginnings through them, and he was most eager for them to succeed. He wanted them to be aware of his support. Whenever they had an engagement, he tried to attend the performances and gave encouragement and sometimes constructive criticism.

An avalanche of calls began coming in from young hopefuls who begged to be heard. If George had the time he obliged. These auditions often filled his weekends, and he said, "they are so anxious to get my advice." He could be very abrupt and uncompromising at times. After listening to a young man who had come with his parents all the way to Washington from Cleveland, he told them nicely but unequivocally that the youth had neither the voice nor the talent to make a career. When told that he had been cruel to squash the youth's hope, he said, "Not at all, I prevented him from paying teachers and coaches for years, saving every penny to be able to live and giving up in the end anyway because he will never make it."

George was realistic and down to earth when necessary. He thought of music making as serious work that required total commitment. He detested dilettantes. He could never accept the concept of nice young girls playing the piano or singing for pleasure, although he acknowledged that people did this in past centuries. However, when someone was serious about a career and showed real talent, George had endless patience.

At the end of his speech to young singers during his master class in Cincinnati, London spelled out his credo:

> I would urge every young singer to immerse himself in all the arts—everything which stimulates the aesthetic nature. An understanding of life is important to the developing artist whatever his field. Human development and artistic development are concomitant. The cultivated and versatile human being can be sensed in the work of every distinguished artist. So I urge you to be content not merely with producing mellifluous sounds but with building a fully rounded human and artistic personality. It will be the attention to such details which will make the difference between the talented singer you are now and the compelling artist you can become.

When George became director of the newly named Washington Opera in 1975, there were some murmurs about conflict of interest, and in 1977, with a heavy heart, he felt forced to resign from the National Opera Institute. One hundred twenty grants to young singers were given between 1971 and 1977.

John Ludwig, who followed London as Director of the Institute, wrote in the program notes to George London's memorial gala:

> London founded the Singer Career Program in 1971 and until his retirement in 1977, he supervised it personally, giving its grantees the benefit of his artistry, managerial expertise and great warmth of spirit. His career had been built on talent, knowledge, and perseverance, and he made it his mission to pass on to the singers what he had learned and—more importantly perhaps—some of his

own spirit.

In 1978 the grants were named the George London Awards in his honor.

The internationally acclaimed soprano, Catherine Malfitano, one of George's protégés, said in a television interview in 1982: "Each one of us received from him this gift and we all think that we were special. And each one of us was special to him. But the amazing thing was that he was able to give this to so many people."

Ruth Welting, another soprano who went on to a successful career, added, "George gave me criticism but it was with love, it was with encouragement. He said 'You can work on this but you are like a raw diamond that needs to be polished.' He was one of the few people who gave me the incentive to keep going at all."

Although he would not be able to supervise his young artists in the future, the foundations of his program were laid so perfectly that it has been possible to continue the competitions and grants for over thirty years. The George London Foundation for Singers has given over 300 awards in his name to date. The example of his caring and his enthusiasm has been followed by this organization and through it, his spirit lives on into another century.

In spite of his involvement, the National Opera Institute was not a full-time job and George made other commitments during those years. On July 17, 1972 he gave a master class at the University of Southern California and, while there, investigated the possibility of founding an opera company in Los Angeles.

A number of friends and a consortium of business men, committed to the arts appointed George London General Director of the Music Center Opera Association to have its first season in 1973-74. George started at once to plan for this season. He began negotiating with managers to produce two operas: *La Fille du Régiment* with Beverly Sills and

Norman Treigle, and *Otello* with Jon Vickers and Sherrill Milnes. He had reached the point of discussing fees and schedules when, in spite of all the efforts of the board to raise enough money for this enterprise, the season was cancelled. The reason given was that the "cost exceeded available funds". It would take many more years until Los Angeles was ready for a major opera company.

London was disappointed. However he wrote to his parents:

> One must constantly count one's blessings, particularly when one has health and wonderful children. That is more important than the search for glory—especially when one has had it in good measure. I'm a lucky man.

The family was elated to be back in Switzerland in the summer of 1973. George expressed over and over his love for the house and the landscape. As soon as he arrived, he installed himself on the terrace with his binoculars and looked at the lake of Geneva and the chain of mountains behind it. Every now and then he called me over and thrust the binoculars in my hands, "Look at Mont Blanc, isn't it incredible? Can you see the little cabin near the top?" Then he ran for his camera and took pictures of the sunsets on the white slopes.

At the end of July, London went to Salzburg to give a master class and had the courage to go back to Bayreuth for the first time since Wieland's death. Although he was very fond of Wolfgang Wagner and was received with great respect, he found a lack of major voices at the festival. He left after a few days, disappointed and sad.

The month of August was beautiful that year. We had many friends in the region and there were dinner parties with much joking and good food. George's cousins, Ed and Lorna Mann, who came to live nearby, even convinced him to go on a picnic with all of us, to the delight of the children. His horror of ants and other insects was overcome only with the promise of a portable table and a sophisticated picnic basket, so that he sat on a lawn in the middle of nowhere just like at home, declaring, "I am definitely not a nature boy."

But he could sit for hours on the terrace and be content. The vineyards below the property were heavy with golden grapes and behind the house the wheat in the fields swayed in the wind. In the evenings we took long walks on the deserted country lanes to the nearest village and back.

George enjoyed this life and had visions of us, years later, being able to retire there to spend our old age together in this ideal setting.

When we returned to Washington in the autumn, it was time to move again. The house on Edmunds Street was too big and too expensive now that our circumstances were less affluent. We moved to Bethesda to a pleasant house on Glengalen Lane, which had the advantage of a huge playroom in the basement with enough room for a bar, a pool table, and living quarters for our Bernese Mountain dog Tessa and her son Samson, who grew to a size commensurate with his name. The disadvantage was that the house sat on top of a hill and on cold winter nights we had to crawl up to the door on all fours to avoid slipping.

During the previous two years we had been helped by a warm-hearted Haitian woman who followed us to Bethesda. Ricilia worshiped George, she was a great cook and constantly made special dishes for him. She could also whip up an elaborate buffet dinner for forty people, which got huge praise from the guests. She stayed with us throughout the Washington years.

At that time London was pleased to hear that some of his records were being reissued. He was prompted to write to his parents: "If I have achieved that, it is more important than whether I was able to sing some years longer than I did." He was in his fifty-fourth year and, although he would always regret that he could no longer sing, the acute pain had gone; he was at peace.

Chapter 15
The Stagings and the Washington Opera

During the Washington years, George London became involved in many activities. It was as if he wanted to prove that he could help the cause of opera in a number of ways, even if he could no longer sing. He was constantly busy, perhaps anxious to cram as many events as possible in the shortest time.

He became actively involved in staging. His first assignment was in 1971, when he directed *The Magic Flute* for the Juilliard School in New York. It was well received and opened opportunities for more engagements.

In 1973 he staged *The Marriage of Figaro* for the Dallas Opera Company with a distinguished cast headed by Evelyn Lear and Sir Geraint Evans. The premiere was a great success and was received with enthusiasm by a large audience. As is often the case with regional companies, one of its benefactors gave a party afterward for the cast and members of the board. The artists were taken by car on a twenty-minute ride to a palatial home in the outskirts of the city and arrived with mighty appetites. George had waited for the singers to remove their makeup before leaving the theater, so the party was in full swing when they arrived.

There were some dainty finger sandwiches and the single ham supposedly meant for the cast was almost gone. Barely greeting the hostess, the singers ran to the buffet, but in vain; within minutes not a crumb of food was left. The drinks too were distributed grudgingly and in small glasses. After a very short visit, the performers left the mansion to return to the hotel and managed to get a late meal. They ate and drank and joked into the morning hours. Much bitter humor was directed at wealthy patrons too stingy to feed starving artists. George proclaimed that there was a residue of eighteenth-century haughtiness that allowed the artists into the drawing room only when they were performing, at other times they were sent to the kitchen.

During the same year George London directed Wagner's *Die Walküre* in Washington, conducted by Antal Dorati, a performance that brought together the forces of the Washington Opera and the National Symphony with great success. In the beginning of 1974 he staged another *Walküre* with a different cast for the San Diego Opera and in December 1976 there was another *Walküre* in Philadelphia with Jon Vickers, Rita Hunter and Johanna Meier. It seemed a little like old times, although now he was directing the singers, not standing on the stage.

We went together to San Diego and enjoyed our stay. The weather was beautiful and we spent a lot of time walking around, just the two of us. I persuaded George to visit the famous San Diego Zoo with me and at night we went window-shopping. He was in a good mood. His successful stagings had prompted Glynn Ross, the director of the Seattle Opera, to engage him to direct a complete *Der Ring des Nibelungen.*

Glynn was a friend of George from early days in Los Angeles. In 1964 he had single-handedly created a successful opera company in Seattle, and by 1975 had a yearly winter season, as did most regional companies. Now, at a time when there were no complete Ring productions in the United States, not even at the Met, Glynn conceived a daring project: he was going to create an American Wagner Festival. Each summer the Seattle Opera would present *Der Ring des Nibelungen* on consecutive nights, like in Bayreuth. Since sur-titles did not yet exist, to make it more attractive to American audiences there would be a Ring in German one week alternating with a Ring in English the following week.

George agreed to stage both versions with two different casts, to open July 15, 1975. He was touched by Glynn's confidence in his talent. It was a tremendous challenge. He was excited at the prospect and sure of himself: he knew that he could draw from his years of work in Bayreuth. "But the time for abstract stagings is past," he said. "nothing can be added to Wieland's concepts and we must go back to realism."

This idea has been upheld by subsequent stagings of the *Ring*, including the recent stagings in Bayreuth, which returned to naturalistic interpretations. It is not inconceivable, had London lived longer, that he might have returned to the Festspielhaus as a stage director.

Probably he did not fully realize that he would be staging eight operas, all performed for the first time, within a period of two weeks—a feat that had never been done before or repeated since. He did know that he would need at least six to eight weeks of rehearsals to accomplish his task, especially because a good number of the artists had never performed their roles before. So he decided that he needed to spend June and July in Seattle.

As usual, he wanted his family with him and some kind of living quarters that would permit him to eat home-cooked meals instead of depending on restaurants. By then all our children were almost grown up and arrangements were no longer so complicated. Marc elected to stay in Washington. Marina wanted to come with us and took a summer counseling job in Seattle.

The Seattle Opera Company found a pleasant apartment for the three of us. I had plenty of leisure time to go to the rehearsals with George. He had an able assistant director, Lincoln Clark, but found that I could be helpful in many ways. George told me what he wanted and I took notes throughout the sessions. Since he had so much to do and was so absorbed in his work, the singers sometimes found it more convenient to come to me with their problems.

At first the rehearsals took place in rooms, in lofts, any-place where a piano could be installed. A few chairs and props marked the limits of the stage. Theaters and orchestras are expensive so most rehearsals for opera take place in small rooms with piano accompaniment. Onstage rehearsals with orchestra are reserved for the last two weeks or less of a pro-duction, depending on the wealth of the opera company.

George worked long hours with incredible energy. He coached every performer separately, then in groups like the Rhinemaidens, then put together successive scenes. With end-less patience, he demonstrated what he wanted and explained the importance of the text to the young singers.

He lavished special care on the role of Wotan, which had been his own and which was now sung by a young American bass, Noel Tyl. Noel had a beautiful voice and a tall, com-manding appearance. George taught him every phrasing, ev-ery gesture. He told him never to make an aborted move-ment with his arms. "Do nothing or make a wide, meaning-ful gesture."

It was not surprising that he knew all about *Rheingold*, *Walküre*, and *Siegfried*: after all, he had appeared in these operas often. But how could he handle *Götterdammerung*, the fourth opera of the *Ring* cycle? He said "I saw it many times, in Bayreuth. I studied the score and I remember all my discussions with Wieland."

He wanted to infuse his own knowledge and intensity into his cast. He did not mind repeating the same scene over and over. Eventually when the artists did not duplicate his instruc-tions, he became frustrated and angry and shouted, "No, no, that's not the way." He would jump up and run on the stage and demonstrate what he wanted.

When he complained that he would never achieve the right effects, I told him that the performance was already very good, that it would improve, and that he was too exacting. Paci-fied, he admitted, "I know. I'm a perfectionist and will never be satisfied."

He had demonstrated his fanatical sense of detail the previous year while working with Sherrill Milnes. The Met had asked him to coach Sherrill, who was to make his debut in the role of Don Giovanni that season. So Sherrill came to Washington and George taught the part he had sung so many times in his own career. He was thrilled to be able to bequeath his knowledge to the young baritone who had such a beautiful voice. He was terribly eager for Sherrill to have a great success and later went to the rehearsals at the Met. Sherrill tells the following: "After the first dress rehearsal, he stormed backstage and argued with the lighting director, complaining that the Don did not have enough light while singing his aria. "But, Mr. London," replied the attending engineer, "this is exactly the same lighting that *you* had in this scene." "That just shows you that I didn't have a bastard like me watching in the hall when I was rehearsing," George said, and he did not give up until there was more light on Sherrill.

In Seattle he pursued the same kind of thoroughness. He checked every detail of the costumes: the tunic was too long for the tenor; the sandals had to be a darker shade. Brünnhilde's hair was too light, she looked like a bleached blonde, not a natural Nordic. Used to the lavish facilities of the costume and wig ateliers in Bayreuth, he was frustrated with the production level provided by Seattle's modest budget and tried his utmost to make things look their best, coaxing Glynn to get a handsomer wig or another new costume, as if the whole show depended on it.

Finally it was time for the premieres. London could do nothing more except be nervous for everyone. It was worse for him to be a spectator than to be on stage. He sat in the third row and watched on successive nights the four operas of *Der Ring des Nibelungen* unfurl in front of him. In the darkened theater, George was mouthing all the words, particularly for Wotan.He whispered, "Do it, do it" during decisive moments, or grumble audibly if someone made a mistake. People sitting next to him were not too pleased, for George's whisper carried well around him.

In the end, he was satisfied. The singers came through with moving performances and during the last measures of *Götterdammerung* he had tears in his eyes. There was a huge ovation for the cast and for the director who had all worked so hard. The success of these performances, which fulfilled Glynn Ross's dream, started a tradition of Wagner Festivals in Seattle continuing to this day.

The summer days of the Ring production were among the happiest and most relaxed in many years. London could enjoy his success and look forward to other achievements; the future looked safe. He had left for Seattle with the knowledge that upon his return to Washington, he would be involved in new work which would give him great satisfaction.

In the spring of 1975 George had meetings with Christine Hunter, the daughter of his good friend, the philanthropist William Fisher. She had grown into a great lover and patron of opera in her own right. Chris and Bill Hunter had settled in Washington with their three little boys and she had been asked to become the president of the Board of Trustees of the Washington Opera Society. Chris told George that she would accept on the condition that he became director of the company. George later told the press that his decision to take the job was due to the fact that "I feel she is somebody I can work with in a most congenial way and someone who is supportive of my ideas." Indeed, during the next two years, the two were to work together in perfect harmony.

At the next board meeting on May 5, Chris simply announced that she accepted the presidency and that George London would be the new director. George was thrilled to head his own company at last, although he did not have any illusion about its size. He quickly announced that he would revise the unpopular plans of his predecessor, who favored contemporary works. He was planning for three operas in the 1975/76 season, the same in 1976/77, and would expand to four operas in the 1977/78 season.

He knew that plans had to be made well in advance because of booking problems, and the operas chosen with great care because of casting and financial problems. He could not, for example, stage an *Aida,* which required bank-breaking sets, a chorus, and crowds of supernumeraries. But the modest budget of the Washington Opera Society permitted outstanding performances of works that did not require elaborate sets and a huge chorus, such as *Madame Butterfly* or *L'Italiana in Algeri.* "We must have both great international artists and productions which will feature young American singers who will be the stars of the future," George announced in the May 7, 1975, *Washington Post.* Through the Opera Institute he was in touch with the best young singers in the country, and now he would be able to cast them in vehicles that would show off their talent.

One of his first decisions was to change the name of the company by removing the word *Society* and calling it simply the Washington Opera. He said the word *Society* reminded him of a meeting of old ladies sitting around a tea table. "It doesn't sound professional," he said.

At the Opera Institute he had had a most capable and efficient associate, Ruth Sickafus, but in the beginning, to save money, he did not even have a secretary at the Washington Opera. He did his own typing with two fingers, describing himself as a diligent and well-meaning but not very competent secretary.

Later George was able to get a few rooms in another part of the Kennedy Center specifically for the opera company. They were tiny rooms without windows, like most of the offices in the building; George referred to his office as "a broom closet."

George brought two key employees to Washington. First he engaged a serious and industrious young man, Gary Fifield, as business manager and managing director. Then he asked Jerry Shirk to join the company. Jerry had worked with

George on the *Walküre* staging in Washington and had proved to be a gifted and resourceful helper; he became stage manager and technical director. They worked together with great success during the next two years, and in a letter Jerry wrote about his fond recollections of this period:

> Our system was that George would make the arrangements, then Gary would issue the contract. I remember at least one occasion when George worked out an engagement for an important artist and the moment would arrive when George would call Gary and say, "I have just engaged Miss X to sing the role of Y in our production of Z. Her fee is $5,000, so please send off the contract." At this point, Gary would have a fit of apoplexy over the amount, and would say, "Do we have to pay that much? I'm sure we could have gotten her for less." George would merrily respond, winking at me as he said, "Of course, I could have gotten her for less, but that happens to be exactly what she's worth!
> Especially in the area of fees, he often expressed his conviction that managements and agents so often take advantage of artists, that he was determined to be on the artist's side. "Maybe it won't make any difference," he would say, "but maybe this artist will be a little happier to be here, and maybe she (or he) will be a bit more willing to cooperate with our difficult situation, and *maybe* she (or he) will sing just a little bit better, knowing that this is a good job, not some kind of favor for George London.
> He especially wanted to engage the young American artists whom he knew from auditions. Many of them did not have agents, and he always got a special charge out of sending contracts to them unannounced, not negotiated, just as a surprise in the mail. In the days when I typed the contracts, I recall one situation where he instructed me to send a contract to a singer for a fee of $600 per performance. Since I was quite sure he had not actually negotiated this fee with anyone, I asked if this

was a definite agreement. He assured me, "She will accept this, and we will hear from her the day she gets the contract and my letter."

Predictably enough, he was right, and she was thrilled. Also predictably, Gary wondered if it might not have been possible to get her for less, but by that time, of course, the contract was already out.

In everything he undertook, George always strived to accomplish it in the classiest and most honest way possible. Whether it was in the casting of the tiniest bit parts, or in the style with which international artists were met at the airport, he refused to cut corners. Once committed to a project, he would consider his commitment final and total. He said, "I would pawn the family silver if that would make a difference to this production."

In view of his past, it was normal for George to favor the artists. He needed some big names to sell the season, but he knew he could lower the budget of any production without harming the quality of the show by engaging many unknown artists commanding lesser fees. He was able to look at a score and calculate in minutes how much it would cost to produce the work.

During his first season the Washington Opera presented *Otello* with such established stars as Evelyn Lear and James McCracken and also introduced young singers such as Rockwell Blake, Noelle Rogers and a young conductor, James Conlon. The following year, George persuaded his friend Nicolai Gedda to do his first *Werther* in Washington with the promise that London himself would stage it. He engaged a young Japanese artist, Yasuko Hayashi, to do *Butterfly* and asked Frank Rizzo, a gifted young director, to stage it. Frank joined the company and stayed as artistic director for ten years.

George was making plans for the years ahead. Every night he brought home the score of another opera, which he studied with intense pleasure. He murmured, "Such a wonderful aria" or "What a great part for a mezzo." When asked, "Can you do this opera in Washington?" he answered, "Maybe, perhaps in a few years, if I can find the right artists." He only wanted to present a work if he felt that he had the perfect performers for its roles. George foresaw the renewed interest in French opera and scheduled two Massenet operas, *Thais* and *Werther.* Then he tried without success to put together a cast for *Carmen* with the thought of persuading Shirley Verrett, a beautiful singer, to play the title part. He loved Russian opera and was familiar with lesser-known repertoire. He started talks with Mstislav Rostropovitch, director of the National Symphony, concerning the possibility of doing Rimsky Korsakov's *The Czar's Bride* starring Rostropovitch's wife, Galina Vishnevskaya. This project would be realized many years later in 1986.

In spite of his enthusiasm, he could not get to his office before nine-thirty; his metabolism was geared to late hours forever. He would stay late, rarely coming home before seven. He said, "When I work, I work with total concentration and accomplish as much as anyone on a given day." In fact, he took his work home with him. He was involved with programs and casting until late at night.

He was enjoying his life. On December 31, 1975, he wrote to his mother, "This is the last day of what was in many ways a good year for us and for that I am very grateful."

As planned, the first three operas of George's season at the Washington Opera were *L'Italiana in Algeri, Otello,* and *Thais,* given during February, March, and April 1976. He wrote to his mother: "I have my first short season of opera behind me, and I believe I have made the public aware of a new style and new standard of opera in Washington. Plans proceed for the next two seasons and look very good indeed. I am optimistic."

The whole tone of his letters was different. He could visualize a future with a rewarding and secure place for himself. At fifty-five, had he been singing, George would be nearing the end of his career. He noticed that some of his contemporaries were slowly leaving the stage.

We came to the conclusion that we were in Washington for good and that it was foolish to keep renting houses. Bethesda was too far away if George wanted to come home to change for a performance at night. Marc was graduating from high school in June 1976 and had been accepted to a six-year medical program at Northwestern University. So we were free to move anywhere.

After some searching, we found an attractive brick house in an excellent neighborhood, near Fox Hall Road, just "eight minutes from the Kennedy Center," as George proclaimed. He liked this house at first sight and decided to buy it even though it was a bit more than we had planned to spend. It was not huge but had enough rooms to accommodate my mother, now living with us, Marina and Marc when they came home, and our housekeeper, Ricilia, who followed her restless employers everywhere. The living room was not large but there was a spacious dining room. The pool table had to go, as there was no basement, and the dogs had to be content with the couch in the den or the small garden; but these were a small sacrifices compared to all the conveniences.

We were due to move in the beginning of April 1976. George was busy with the opera, which was just as well, since Ricilia and I were more efficient without him. But during the previous weekend George and Marc proceeded to hang our paintings in all the rooms. Every wall was measured exactly and each painting hung precisely in the center at the same distance from the floor as all the others.

He enjoyed this task and decided where each work was to go. It did not matter too much, for a few months later, I would find him one night changing everything around, including the furniture, to give our house "a new look." "Much better, don't you think?" he would say.

As soon as we were settled, we gave a party that coincided with the opening performance of *Thais*. There was a big crowd but the buffet table was loaded with delicious dishes from Ricilia's kitchen, which satisfied the appetites of the hungry cast and all our friends.

These were good times. I went to the rehearsals with George and sat next to him with my yellow pad as in Seattle. Now that he was dealing with his own company, he was even more exacting about everything. Although he was not directing most of the time, he was still responsible for the final product. He made sure the wigs were becoming, the men's coats the right length; he checked every detail, down to the size of the buckles on the women's pumps. Always there were long rehearsals for lighting, which he considered so important. He made sure that the musical preparation was thorough before the show came on stage, because orchestra rehearsals in the opera house were costly and had to be kept to a minimum. He engaged conductors familiar with the style of the works he was presenting, such as a French conductor for the Massenet operas.

In May he went to Cincinnati to perform the speaking part of Moses in a concert version of Arnold Schonberg's *Moses and Aaron*. He gave a profound, moving performance to great acclaim. However, he was not satisfied with the quality and volume of his voice and decided to go back to Dr. Rubin in California for another injection into his paralyzed cord. George was told not to use his voice for a few weeks and was warned to be careful about not catching any food in his throat, because the passage was somewhat reduced now due to the rigidity of the injected cord.

In the summer of 1976, George met me in Switzerland where I had preceded him with the children. We spent an idyllic month of July. He reported to his mother, "The mountains were clear, the Mont Blanc was out in all its glory, it was just heavenly. I am so happy we have this place. It's just good for the soul."

The Geddas, who were our friends, had visited us some years earlier and had been so delighted with the landscape that they had bought a beautiful house with a swimming pool in a nearby village. We spent many joyous summer days with Nicolai and his wife Stacey. George, taking advantage of their proximity, had arranged rehearsals at his house for the forthcoming *Werther.*

For a couple of weeks Nicolai and Joann Grillo, who was to sing Charlotte with him in Washington, came every day, and George staged all the scenes in which they appeared together in the opera. The high ceilings of the living room resounded with the passionate oaths of Werther's love against a background of vineyards, lake, and white mountain peaks. It was a perfect setting for the opera and a joy to hear it this way.

George was irritated because his speaking voice sounded hoarse much of the time. He called Dr. Rubin for advice. He assured him that the harshness would pass, and indeed it went away at the end of the month. When London left for Graz to give two weeks of master classes there, he was well rested and in excellent disposition.

After the summer, we would be without children for the first time in our lives. Marina returned for her senior year at Yale and Marc was off to Northwestern as a freshman. George knew he would miss them, and went on last-minute shopping sprees with them. He bought all kinds of fancy stereo equipment for Marina, which they smuggled secretly into the house to avoid my objections. They giggled so much and I admired their obvious delight with each other. After Marc's departure, George wrote to his mother, "Marc was a bit sad to leave, just as we were. But when the family is that close, that is the price one pays when separating."

He did not have much time to think about the void left by the children. In November he went on his yearly circuit to Los Angeles, San Francisco, Houston, and New York for the National Opera Institute's auditions. In December, the 1976/77 season of the Washington Opera started auspiciously with successful performances of an early Verdi opera, *Attila,* with

Justino Diaz in the title role.

On January 2, 1977, George wrote to his mother, "With a bit of luck, a few smiles of Providence, the new year can move us closer to some of our goals. I persist in being optimistic and I believe there are good reasons for being so. The one important thing is good health."

In February 1977, *Butterfly,* directed by Frank Rizzo with Yasuko Hayashi, a young Japanese soprano, in the title role, was a triumph. This Italian-trained singer had a beautiful voice and moved with inimitable grace in her own splendid Japanese kimonos. President Carter heard about the success from his elder son, Chip, and decided to come to the performance with Mrs. Carter and their daughter Amy.

The news spread quickly. The whole company was tremendously excited and outdid itself. Afterward the president and his party came backstage, guided by George London, and congratulated all the performers. Mr. Carter had obviously enjoyed himself and demonstrated his knowledge of the story. He congratulated Ermanno Mauro, the tenor, who had played Pinkerton, adding jokingly, "You've disgraced the U.S. Navy, but you're an asset to opera."

The newspapers were full of accounts of the president's visit, and of course it was great press for London as well. Unfortunately, his enjoyment of this acclaim was marred by problems with the Kennedy Center. La Scala and the Paris Opera finally came to Washington in the fall of 1976 under the guidance of Martin Feinstein, George's successor as director of the Kennedy Center. Evidently these performances kindled a desire in Martin to have his own opera company, and he made plans for his company to be part of the Kennedy Center.

George was thunderstruck when he heard of this scheme. He realized that if the Kennedy Center sponsored an opera company it would mean the end of an autonomous Washington Opera, which depended on the Opera House of the Kennedy Center to stage performances. Even without this new competition, it was always difficult to get the house's schedule of availability far enough in advance to book the artists. (The intimate Terrace Theater, ideal for small-scale productions, did not yet exist at that time.)

George was nervous and agitated but he had proved again and again that he was tough and incredibly resilient; he was not going to abandon his promising opera company so easily. He told Chris Hunter about the rumors. She was disturbed. They decided to see Roger Stevens together and confront him with the story. Apparently Roger did not deny it but assured them that Martin would not be given the means to transform his plans into reality.

Chris and George left somewhat reassured, but they had not been able to finalize the dates for the 1977/78 season at the Opera House. Without the dates, George could not sign contracts for the artists he wanted to engage and everything remained up in the air.

More rumors kept spreading and Christine Hunter scheduled another meeting with Roger Stevens to ask for a definite commitment of dates for the next two seasons. I had gone to Switzerland for a week to prepare the house which had been rented out for a year, and George wrote to me at the end of April:

> I met with Chris for a talk before the meeting. . . Chris is prepared to tell Roger that if the Kennedy Center insists on proceeding with Feinstein's plans, we are prepared to pay off our contract obligations and cancel our next season. Chris persists in believing that Roger is, au fond, too sensible to preside over the destruction of this company in order to extend Feinstein's power base. It would be a major scandal, and she and I believe he doesn't want that.
>
> It's a risk we have to be prepared to take when we go into that meeting. And apart from the gamble, there is no doubt that if the Kennedy Center announces their own future operative plans, we will have a desperate

job to raise our money for next season. I agreed with Chris, and when our talk was over I felt as though a stone had dropped from my heart. I am confident that I will always find productive ways to use my talents. But I will not work under such dreadful conditions. As I write this I feel more relaxed than I have in many months, and it's a good feeling. I love you. Your George.

I answered from Vufflens-le-Château on May 1, 1977:

Your letter disturbed me. I wonder if the threat to cancel next season is the right approach. How can you give up all you would eventually accomplish for opera in this position, all that you love and do so well.
I do know that I love you as ever with unfailing admiration, respect and passion, such a wondrous feeling after these many years. How lucky I am to be with a man like you. I wish you with all my soul to be well and happy, I suffer with your pain and I am happy with your joys. I love you. Your Nora.

These were our last letters to one another.

In the midst of his anxiety, London staged *Werther,* which was a solid success and a personal triumph for his friend Nicolai Gedda. But George could not rejoice in his achievements while agonizing about the very existence of the company.

Then, possibly prompted by George's steady successes with the opera and by fear of a big deficit for the Kennedy Center, Roger Stevens gave George firm commitments for the dates at the opera house for the coming years. Chris and George felt like celebrating. Later we heard that the board of the Kennedy Center rejected Martin's plans; they were not willing to finance an opera company. Some years later Martin Feinstein resigned.

George bounced back with his usual resiliency, but it all took its toll and he looked tired. He was persuaded to have a checkup. He wrote to his mother:

> We are all well, no complaints. The doctor found the results of my recent physical 'superb.' Nothing wrong at all, with blood pressure at 120 over 70. So that, too, is something to be very grateful for.

Now he could concentrate on the planning of the future seasons and at the end of April he wrote, again to his mother:

> I am busy these days setting repertoire and casting for the season after next and hopefully soon we will know what periods we can have in the Kennedy Center in 1979/80. One has to plan that far ahead in order to be able to get the artists and conductors one wants. We have established strong ties to the Washington public, and with a little luck and cooperation I think the future looks very good. I will be gone for the first two weeks of May. I will be staging *Don Pasquale* in Grand Rapids, Michigan, again with a cast of outstanding young artists. You may recall I did *Cosi fan tutte* there two years ago which was a big success and gave me a lot of pleasure.

In a rare reflective mood, he remembered singing the role of Dr. Malatesta in *Don Pasquale* many years ago at City College. "Imagine, I was only twenty-one years old. It is a long time ago!"

George London went in good spirits to the Opera Ball in June. It was hosted by the Swedish Ambassador and Mrs. Wachtmeister in the enchanting gardens of the embassy. Everyone applauded when George arrived. He was delighted and made conversation left and right with patrons of the opera. But he made sure to dance with his wife several times during the evening.

London's plans for the season 1978/79 were the most ambitious so far. The Washington Opera would produce four operas, *The Magic Flute, Elisir d'amore, The Seagull,* and

Tosca. The production of *The Magic Flute* was being borrowed from Toronto, and George decided that he had to see it before leaving for Europe, where he was to give some master classes, to make sure that it was right for Washington.

He flew to Canada, saw the performance, was quite pleased with it, and returned to Washington Thursday morning, July 28. He had to leave for Munich the same evening, on his way to Graz, where the classes were to be held.

I picked him up at the airport and took him to his office where he had last-minute matters to attend to. The director he had hired for *The Magic Flute* canceled. London was very annoyed but decided that if he could not find anyone else, he would direct it himself

I thought he looked drawn and begged him to stay overnight. He argued that he had to be in Graz by Sunday and could not disappoint the people there. He promised that he would rest during the two days he would spend in Munich. I wanted to go with him, but he was leaving for only two weeks and it seemed unreasonable for me to go. Moreover my mother had suffered a slight heart attack recently and I did not feel that I could leave her. Sometimes decisions that seem inconsequential turn out to be terribly important. If I had traveled with George, we would have stayed together in a hotel in the center of town and his fate might have been different.

That day George took a short rest at home, and in the late afternoon Marina and I drove him to Dulles Airport. It was a warm July evening. George was dressed in a red plaid blazer, white shirt, navy tie, and light-gray pants. I thought he looked refreshed and as handsome as ever. He was happier then he had been in a long time, relieved that the fate of the Washington Opera was secure. We walked with him as far as was allowed before he boarded the shuttle bus which takes passengers to the planes.

We kissed good-bye as tenderly as twenty years earlier; then he embraced Marina and walked toward the bus. I called him back, capriciously, and begged for "one more kiss." He turned around, gave me a kiss, laughed his joyous thunderous laugh and said, "I'll be back in just two weeks." Then he was gone.

Chapter 16
Last Years

CONFUTATIS
"I pray, suppliant and kneeling
My heart contrite as ashes
Take unto thy care my ending."
—Bass part, Verdi, *Requiem*

George London arrived in Munich on Friday, July 29 1977. He stayed at the apartment of his friend, Max Lipin. On Saturday he listened to some young singers and, as usual, spent time coaching them. In the evening he went out to dinner to one of his favorite restaurants "Zum Franziskaner" with close friends, among them Max and Franz Spelman, who had been a witness at his wedding. Franz found George in great form. He told wonderful anecdotes and seemed more cheerful and relaxed than he had been in years. Franz, who knew him well and who was very perspicacious, concluded that George had overcome the grief of losing his voice.

They parted quite late and George and Max drove back to Max's apartment, which was some distance from the center of town. At six o'clock in the morning, Max was awakened by George, who said apologetically that he had been having terrible pains in his left side for the last few hours. Max immediately called a doctor, but shortly before the doctor arrived George said he was feeling better. Apparently he suffered a mild heart attack.

When the doctor came, George was sitting at the break-fast table. He took George's blood pressure, which was normal, and he was about to speak, when George fell forward stricken with cardiac arrest. The doctor immediately started mouth-to-mouth resuscitation while Max called an ambulance and paramedics. The doctor was a slight man and could not do much; by the time the ambulance came Max was hysterical. He told the paramedics that George was a famous opera singer and that they had to save him. They continued their efforts to revive him for a long time—varying accounts say from ten to twenty minutes—until finally George London's heart started beating again in the ambulance on the way to the hospital.

The exact amount of time London's heart had stopped, a crucial factor in estimating how long his brain had been deprived of oxygen and how severely brain damaged he would be was not known. If he had been at the hospital when the heart stopped, he could have probably been revived rapidly without damage to his brain. For days all the headlines in the German papers reported that "Great Opera Star in Coma following heart attack on July 31." Some weeks later the headlines about London's illness were replaced by still larger headlines about Elvis Presley's death.

The doctors could not say whether George would live and, if he did, how long he would be in a coma.

Alerted by a call from Max at three o'clock in the morning, I arrived in Munich on August 1, stunned by the magnitude of the catastrophe. Two days later Philip came to Germany so that I would not be alone, and when he could not stay away from his business any longer, Marc came and remained in Munich until college started. Without exchanging a word, the four children established an extraordinary support system, which never weakened during the years to come. Andy helped consistently with the paperwork; Marina immediately started taking care of the household and shopping. Philip handled all our housing dilemmas. All four had their own problems and suffered their own loss in various degrees, but they did not let their worries and grief interfere with their devotion to their parents.

George's heart had suffered a grave injury but the cardiograms showed no further problems. He was in a deep coma, but it was possible to wake up from such a condition and recover.

I had generally excellent experiences with the physicians I dealt with. As soon as I arrived in Munich, I communicated with my Washington friend, neurologist Dr. Margaret Abernathy, who supported me selflessly for the following years with positive and constructive advice.

Philip put me in touch with Dr. Elisabeth Kubler-Ross, the author of *On Death and Dying,* and I called her in Chicago. She knew who George was and after I explained his condition, she told me: "Play music for him, play his favorite pieces and records of his own singing and talk to him. People in a coma can hear. Tell him that if he wants to go, you will understand and you will be able to take care of yourself. Tell him that if he comes back, you will take care of him."

Six weeks after the cardiac arrest, London was taken back to the U.S. in an army transport plane, thanks to Simon Bourgin's connections at the State Department. On September 9 he arrived at Georgetown Hospital. His eyes were open, he could move his hands, but he had contracted pneumonia during the trip.

Again, his life was in danger and, again, his body would recover. He was built to live until his 90s like his parents. Possibly the intensity of his successes and his misfortunes destroyed this strong constitution.

After months in the hospital he regained some faculties and was sent home. Every possible therapy was tried with little results. He was able to sit and eat, listen to music, at best say yes or no. He would never stand or walk by himself again. He needed to be cared for day and night and required nurses around the clock.

While we were still in Germany, Andy had begun to examine all of George London's insurance papers. He had established that George had some disability insurance, about $1,000 a month altogether, and that through the Washington Opera he had an excellent health insurance policy that fortunately also provided for private nurses.

The fees for the nurses started at sixty dollars a shift and eventually went up to seventy-five and eighty dollars for registered nurses. Thus the insurance paid temporarily an average of two hundred seventy-five dollars a day in nurses' fees, and I felt temporarily relieved. Every expense was reported in writing monthly to the court, which was now controlling London's finances since he was considered totally disabled.

The Washington Opera generously paid George's salary for one year after his illness. The operas he had planned so carefully were performed with great success at the Kennedy Center by the artists he had chosen with knowledge and love. His place was taken over with devotion by his assistant, Gary Fifield, who always hoped to hear that George was getting better and would come back to his job.

The financial burden of the household plus supporting the two younger children, who were still in college and graduate school, was enormous. Consulting with Andy, we came to the conclusion that we could not keep the house in Switzerland, and so it was sold. We needed the money but above all it was George's house; it was the symbol of his achievements, it was *his* terrace in front of his living room; it was *his* view of the lake and the Alps and the castle. It was the house he built; without him it became a burden.

When three years had passed the insurance company warned us that George London's coverage was running out; within a few months the company would no longer pay the nurses' fees. How could we afford payments of eighty thousand dollars a year for nurses alone, not counting food, mortgage, and transportation?

The artistic community rallied around their stricken colleague with extraordinary generosity.

First, the American Guild of Musical Artists, whose president George had been for four years, had a pension fund program, and voted to support his care generously each year. But in spite of great efforts, they could not provide such staggering sums. Then all at once Matthew Epstein from Columbia Artists Management, Bill Blair, Chris Hunter, and great singer after great singer gave their time and energy to organize a benefit concert to help their ailing friend and colleague.

The benefit took place on November 4, 1981, at the concert hall of the Kennedy Center, which had been donated by Roger Stevens. The concert was televised nationwide. The funds it raised provided security for George's care and demonstrated how much he was beloved by his colleagues, those with whom he had performed and those he had helped start their careers.

Beverly Sills was the master of ceremonies for the telecast. She had met George in 1946 and recalled the circumstances of their meeting:

> There was a lady on the West Coast whose name was Mrs. Burnstein and there was another lady living on the East Coast whose name was Mrs. Silverman. Mrs. Burnstein had a son whose name was George. Mrs. Silverman had a daughter whose name was Beverly. Neither of the children was married, they were both singers and they were both Jewish and both mothers thought they were made for each other.
> So they arranged a blind date, and George invited me to lunch at a little restaurant on West 57th Street called "Vim and Vigor Vitamin Bar." I think he was a little nervous how it was all going to turn out because he brought along an old buddy with him and his buddy's name was Mario Lanza. The three of us really hit it off and we had fabulous times together. But I think George always knew there was going to be his wonderful Nora and I always knew there was going to be my wonderful Pete, so noth-

ing really came of it and we all went our separate ways.

The program was composed of performances by the great-est operatic stars of the time, accompanied by the foremost conductors and pianists. Behind each magnificent perfor-mance was a personal story of generosity and friendship, which was being returned to George a thousand fold on that night. Marilyn Horne said, "It is a measure of your husband's character that not a single singer canceled tonight."

With financial security assured, I multiplied my efforts to give George as much distraction as possible. I showed him the videotape of the gala in small portions to suit his short attention span.

After the gala I went to Los Angeles to visit George's mother who was in a nursing home. She was past ninety but fairly well physically. However, her mind was wandering. She recognized me, then confused me with Marina. She refused to watch the telecast of the gala. She could not accept the reality of George's illness. For her, the beloved son would re-main eternally young, healthy, and successful. It was best this way. She died in 1986.

All four children were married the same year. In June 1983, George witnessed his daughter's wedding day in our garden although he could not lead her to the altar.

George would have been delighted to see his daughter so happy. He would have loved his new son and his new daugh-ters. How proud he would have been at his son's graduation from medical school.

The long illness had taken a heavy toll on the children. Their efforts to spend some time with us every week forced them to disrupt their lives. I tried to tell them that I could manage alone, but they sensed that I did in fact need their company. Marina felt the heaviest sense of obligation; her husband was very sympathetic, always ready to come with her.

The children's visits were difficult. They were expected to

spend some time with their father, and this was heart-breaking for them. They did not have a close daily relationship with George and they only saw a shadow of the man they loved and admired. They did not believe that he understood what they said to him, but if their presence provided George with just an instant of pleasure, their sacrifice was justified.

At the beginning of 1984 I began to worry again about expenses. The nursing fees were constantly rising; simultaneously it became more and more difficult to find personnel. Our friends in Austria heard about our problems and about the tribute in Washington. So in June 1984, a concert dedicated to George London took place in Vienna. Again his friends and colleagues gave generously of their time and Gottfried Kraus, who had been a fan of George's since 1949 - at age thirteen - organized the event.

I traveled to Vienna to be present at the concert. For their fellow artist, the chorus of the Vienna Opera sang Beethoven's prisoners' chorus from *Fidelio,* which George loved so much. Then Leonie Rysanek, Catherine Malfitano, Tatiana Troyanos, James King and Nicolai Gedda, among others, sang for him. The magnificent baroque concert hall was packed with George's Viennese fans who came back after so many years, as if he had just performed for them yesterday. The love affair between Vienna and George continued. As Gottfried said: "Vienna would never forget George London." When the singers pulled me in front of the audience to bow in place of George, we all had tears in our eyes. I knew the ovation was for him, for all the joy he had once given to this public and I wished George could have been there to experience this homage.

In 1983 London suffered another slight stroke. He recovered once again but his left side was slightly affected and now he was able to stand only with great difficulty. He never spoke again. For years I had deluded myself into believing that he would improve and be able to resume a somewhat normal life. I realized at last that there was no hope and that he no longer understood much of what was happening around him.

Every week brought slight changes for the worse. He did not enjoy his meals anymore. Even the famous Sacher torte, which friends sent from Austria at regular intervals, hardly tempted him. He had more and more problems drinking and had long coughing spells.

I could hear his voice in the prayer of the Verdi *Requiem*: "Take unto thy care my ending."

On Sunday evening March 24, 1985, I was alone in the house. The night nurse was expected at midnight. As usual, I went into George's room to make sure that he was comfortable. His hands were cold and limp, and I realized suddenly that he was not breathing. George London had died peacefully in his sleep after almost eight years of agony.

Postscript

That night I sat next to him and held his hand for the last time. There were so many things I wanted to tell him once more: feelings and promises and foolish nothings that suddenly seemed important. I thought I heard again his voice as Amfortas imploring: "Death! To die! Unique mercy!"

Now he was liberated and whole again.

I refuse to think of him as he lay that night, pale and emaciated. I think of George, radiant after a concert, or arms outstretched in front of the curtain at the Metropolitan Opera, or triumphant after the *Boris* in Moscow.

I remember him smiling proudly in the crowd at Marina's graduation and laughing tenderly at our last good-bye in Washington.

I know that in spite of the vocal torments and the years of torture, his life was a success. He achieved what he wanted; "he made his mark" and reached most of his goals. He gave joy, support, and inspiration to those around him. His CDs, videos and DVDs are a legacy to coming generations.

To me George gave the greatest gift of all: he gave me a sense of self, in addition to his love and respect. Through his artistry, his humanity, his vitality, I discovered new dimensions to life. Through his courage and fortitude I found unexpected strength and compassion. A great love makes you a better person. I try to become the woman he expected me to be and continue his work by helping young singers in the way he envisioned.

George's voice and artistry remain an inspiration for future generations.

AWARDS & TITLES

1954	Awarded title of Kammersänger from Austrian government
1967-1971	President of the American Guild of Musical Artists
1971	Received Mozart Medal from the city of Vienna
1972	Advisor, National Endowment for the Arts
1976	Austrian Government Decoration Litteris and Artibus
1978	Award for service to American opera from The National Opera Institute

Chronology

1949

September 3	*Aida* Milinkovic, Jlitsch, Svanholm, Riegler, London (Amonasro) Conductor: Ferencsik
September 8	*Carmen* Milinkovic, Roswaenge, Hellwig, London (Escamillo) Conductor: Ferencsik
September 24	*Fürst Igor* Schöffler, Zadek, Hermann, Loose, London (Vladimir) Conductor: Prohaska
October 2	*Fürst Igor* Schöffler, Zadek, Hermann, Loose, London (Vladimir) Conductor: Prohaska
October 21	*Aida* Milinkovic, Zadek, Friedrich, Riegler, London (Amonasro) Conductor: Solti
October 26	*Carmen* Giannini, Friedrich, Güden, London (Escamillo) Conductor: Ackermann
October 28	*Carmen* Giannini, Lichtegg, Hellwig, London (Escamillo) Conductor: Loibner
November 14	*Carmen* Milinkovic, Roswaenge, Güden, London (Escamillo) Conductor: Moralt
December 4	*Carmen* Höngen, Friedrich, Güden, London (Escamillo) Conductor: Ferencsik
December 9	*Boris Godunov* Koreh, Höngen, Gallos, Taubmann, London (Boris Godunov) Conductor: Ferencsik
December 30	*Boris Godunov* Gallos, Alsen, Höngen, Patzak, London (Boris Godunov) Conductor: Ferencsik

1950

June 5	*Boris Godunov* Gallos, Koréh, Patzak, Höngen, London (Boris Godunov) Conductor: Ferencsik
June 15	*Aida* Höngen, Zadek, Masaroff, Ernster, Riegler, London (Amonasro) Conductor: Ferencsik
June 20	*Carmen* Höngen, Roswaenge, Güden, London (Escamillo) Conductor: Ferencsik
September 19	*Aida* Milinkovic, Zadek, Masaroff, Weber, Siedl, London (Amonasro) Conductor: Moralt

227

Chronology

September 21	*Die Zauberflöte* Henner, Güden, Patzak, Kunz, Loose, London (Sprecher) Conductor: Moralt
September 29	*Carmen* Milinkovic, Masaroff, Hellwig, London (Escamillo) Conductor: Moralt
October 5	*Aida* Milinkovic, Zadek, Masaroff, Weber, Riegler, London (Amonasro) Conductor: Moralt
October 6	*Die Zauberflöte* Lipp, Seefried, Patzak, Kunz, Hensser, London (Sprecher) Conductor: Moralt
October 19	*Aida* Höngen, Zadek, Ralf, Koréh, Riegler, London (Amonasro) Conductor: Loibner
October 21	*Eugene Onegin* Welitsch, Rohs, Dermota, London (Onegin) Conductor: Zallinger
October 23	*Eugene Onegin* Welitsch, Rohs, Dermota, London (Onegin) Conductor: Zallinger
October 25	*Eugene Onegin* Welitsch, Rohs, Dermota, London (Onegin) Conductor: Zallinger
October 31	*Eugene Onegin* Welitsch, Rohs, Dermota, London (Onegin) Conductor: Zallinger
November 5	*Eugene Onegin* Welitsch, Rohs, Dermota, London (Onegin) Conductor: Zallinger
November 10	*Eugene Onegin* Rohs, Ludwig, London (Onegin) Conductor: Zallinger
November 14	*Eugene Onegin* Rohs, Ludwig, London (Onegin) Conductor: Zallinger
November 25	*Aida* Höngen, Goltz, Friedrich, Ernster, Ringler, London (Amonasro) Conductor: Moralt
December 1	*Die Zauberflöte* Lipp, Güden, Deruiota, Poell, Loose, London (Sprecher) Conductor: Moralt
December 5	*Carmen* Milinkovic, Roswaenge, Ringler, London (Escamillo) Conductor: Zallinger
December 16	*Carmen* Anday, Roswaenge, Ringler, London (Escamillo) Conductor: Kempe
December 21	*Boris Godunov* Gallos, Alsen, Friedrich, Jurinac, London (Boris Godunov) Conductor: Zallinger

Chronology

1951

May 31	*Aida* Milinkovic, Martinis, Roswaenge, Weber, Reigler, London (Amonasro) Conductor: Sebastian
June 1	*Eugene Onegin* Reining, Rohs, Dermota, London (Onegin) Conductor: Zallinger
June 8	*Die Zauberflöte* Lipp, Seefried, Dermota, Kunz, Loose, London (Sprecher) Conductor: Böhm
June 16	*Boris Godunov* Szemere, Koréh, Friederich, Kalin, London (Boris Godunov) Conductor: Kempe
June 18	*Eugene Onegin* Welitsch, Rohs, Dermota, London (Onegin) Conductor: Zallinger
June 22	*Boris Godunov* Szemere, Alsen, Patzak, Höngen, London (Boris Godunov) Conductor: Hollreiser
September 9	*Carmen* Milinkovic, Gostic, Güden, London (Escamillo) Conductor: Sebastian
September 15	*Eugene Onegin* Reining, Rohs, Dermota, London (Onegin) Conductor: Annovazzi
September 19	*Aida* Milinkovic, Martinis, Gostic, Weber, Seidl, London (Amonasro) Conductor: Annovazzi
September 27	*Aida* Milinkovic, Martinis, Friedrich, Weber, Seidl, London (Amonasro) Conductor: Annovazzi
September 28	*Eugene Onegin* Reining, Hermann, Dermota, London (Onegin) Conductor: Annovazzi
September 30	*Boris Godunov* Gallos, Frick, Friederich, Höngen, London (Boris Godunov) Conductor: Hollreiser
October 9	*Eugene Onegin* Welitsch, Hermann, Patzak, London (Onegin) Conductor: Annovazzi
October 14	*Don Giovanni* Hellwig, Patzak, Jurinac, Kunz, Loose, London (Don Giovanni) Conductor: Krauss
October 16	*Don Giovanni* Hellwig, Patzak, Jurinac, Vogel, Loose, London (Don Giovanni) Conductor: Krauss
October 19	*Carmen* Milinkovic, Hopf, Jurinac, London (Escamillo) Conductor: Moralt
October 20	*Don Giovanni* Hellwig, Konetzni, Vogel, Loose, London (Don Giovanni) Conductor: Krauss

Chronology

October 22	*Don Giovanni* Zadek, Welfing, Konetzni, Vogel, Loose, London (Don Giovanni) Conductor: Krauss
December 19	*Eugene Onegin* Welitsch, Rohs, Patzak, London (Onegin) Conductor: Zallinger
December 20	*Don Giovanni* Dermota, Jurinac, Kunz, Loose, London (Don Giovanni) Conductor: Ackermann
December 23	*Die Zauberflöte* Lipp, Seefried, Dermota, Kunz, Loose, London (Sprecher) Conductor: Böhm
December 25	*Don Giovanni* Weber, Welitsch, Patzak, Zadek, Kunz, Seefried, London (Don Giovanni) Conductor: Böhm

1952

May 5	*Don Giovanni* Goltz, Schock, Jurinac, Kunz, Seefried, London (Don Giovanni) Conductor: Böhm
May 15	*Don Giovanni* Goltz, Dermota, Jurinac, Kunz, Loose, London (Don Giovanni) Conductor: Böhm
May 19	*Eugene Onegin* Welitsch, Hermann, Dermota, London (Onegin) Conductor: Zallinger
May 23	*Fürst Igor* Schöffler, Zadek, Kalin, Loose, London (Vladimir) Conductor: Ackermanna
May 29	*Don Giovanni* Goltz, Dermota, Réthy, Kunz, Loose, London (Don Giovanni) Conductor: Ackermann
June 19	*Die Zauberflöte* Hellweg, Rethy, Anders, Berry, Loose, London (Sprecher) Conductor: Kempe
June 21	*Don Giovanni* Goltz, Dermota, Konetzni, Faulhaber, Loose, London (Don Giovanni) Conductor: Kempe
September 15	*Eugene Onegin* Welitsch, Hermann, Schock, London (Onegin) Conductor: Zallinger
September 23	*Don Giovanni* Welitsch, Patzak, Jurinac, Kunz, Seefried, London (Don Giovanni) Conductor: Moralt
September 30	*Boris Godunov* Gallos, Frick, Höngen, Madin, London (Boris Godunov) Conductor: Hollreiser

1953

June 3	*Don Giovanni* Welitsch, Dermota, Konetzni, Kunz, Seefried, London (Don Giovanni) Conductor: Moralt

230

Chronology

June 13	*Eugene Onegin* Welitsch, Kalin, Dermota, London (Onegin) Conductor: Zallinger
June 19	*Tosca* Welitsch, Roswaenge, London (Scarpia) Conductor: Loibner
June 21	*Die Zauberflöte* Weber, Hollweg, Guden, Dermiota, Kunz, Loose, London (Sprecher) Conductor: Moralt
June 22	*Carmen* Höngen, Roswaenge, Yeend, London (Escamillo) Conductor: Loibner
June 27	*Don Giovanni* Zadek, Dermota, Konetzni, Czerwenka, Hollweg, London (Don Giovanni) Conductor: Moralt
September 1	*Don Giovanni* Welitsch Schock, Konetzni, Kunz, Loose, London (Don Giovanni) Conductor: Kempe
September 5	*Boris Godunov* Gallos, Frick, Patzak, Kalin, London (Boris Godunov) Conductor: Kempe
September 8	*Die Zauberflöte* Frick, Lipp, Güden, Patzak, Kunz, Boesch, London (Sprecher) Conductor: Moralt
September 9	*Eugene Onegin* Welitsch, Kalin, Schock, London (Onegin) Conductor: Kempe
September 17	*Don Giovanni* Grümmer, Patzak, Konetzni, Kunz, Güden, London (Don Giovanni) Conductor: Moralt
September 22	*Carmen* Höngen, Gostic, Güden, London (Escamillo) Conductor: Loibner
September 25	*Don Giovanni* Grümmer, Terkal, Konetzni, Kunz, Seefried, London (Don Giovanni) Conductor: Hollreiser
October 4	*Don Giovanni* Zadek, Schock, Jurinac, Kunz, Loose, London (Don Giovanni) Conductor: Hollreiser
October 6	*Boris Godunov* Szemere, Koréh, Friedrich, Höngen, London (Boris Godunov) Conductor: Hollreiser
October 14	*Tosca* Martinis, Gostic, London (Scarpia) Conductor: Loibner

1954

May 18	*Carmen* Höngen, Roswaenge, Güden, London (Escamillo) Conductor: Klobuèar
May 20	*Eugene Onegin* Welitsch, Hermann, Dermota, London (Onegin) Conductor: Klobuèar

231

Chronology

May 29	*Don Giovanni* Zadek, Dermota, Dellla Casa, Czerwenka, Güden, London (Don Giovanni) Conductor: Moralt
June 9	*Don Giovanni* Goltz, Terkal, Konetzni, Czerwenka, Güden, London (Don Giovanni) Conductor: Koslik
June 17	*Boris Godunov* Szemere, Alsen, Patzak, Mödl, London (Boris Godunov) Conductor: Klobuèar
June 20	*Fidelio* Roswaenge, Mödl, Hofmann, Güden, London (Don Pizarro) Conductor: Hollreiser
June 21	*Carmen* Mödl, Hopf, Güden, London (Escamillo) Conductor: Klobuèar
June 22	*Don Giovanni* Goltz, Terkal, Rieglar, Kunz, Güden, London (Don Giovanni) Conductor: Moralt
June 30	*Don Giovanni* Martinis, Terkal, Rieglar, Kunz, Loose, London (Don Giovanni) Conductor: Hollreiser
September 3	*Boris Godunov* Szemere, Koréh, Patzak, Kenney, London (Boris Godunov) Conductor: Klobuèar
September 9	*Tosca* Martinis, Roswaenge, London (Scarpia) Conductor: Klobuèar
September 14	*Don Giovanni* Grümmer, Simoneau, Jurinac, Kunz, Streich, London (Don Giovanni) Conductor: Böhm
September 18	*Don Giovanni* Grümmer, Simoneau, Jurinac, Kunz, Loose, London (Don Giovanni) Conductor: Böhm
September 23	*Don Giovanni* Grümmer, Simoneau, Jurinac, Kunz, Loose, London (Don Giovanni) Conductor: Böhm
September 25	*Don Giovanni* Grümmer, Lichtegg, Jurinac, Kunz, Streich, London (Don Giovanni) Conductor: Böhm

1955

May 28	*Die Zauberflöte* Weber, Koth, Della Casa, Dermota, Poell, Loose, London (Sprecher) Conductor: Moralt
June 3	*Carmen* Mödl, Hopf, Güden, London (Escamillo) Conductor: Loibner
June 5	*Boris Godunov* Gallos, Frick, Hopf, Kenney, London (Boris Godunov) Conductor: Hollreiser
June 15	*Die Zauberflöte* Bohini, Köth, Guden, Dermota, Kunz, Loose, London (Sprecher) Conductor: Böhm

Chronology

June 17	*Eugene Onegin* Rysanek, Kalin, Dermota, London (Onegin) Conductor: Klobuèar
June 30	*Tosca* Golz, Friedrich, London (Scarpia) Conductor: Loibner
September 7	*Die Zauberflöte* Korel, Köth, Seefried, Patzak, Poell, Loose, London (Sprecher) Conductor: Böhm
September 18	*Carmen* Madeira, Schock, Rysanek, London (Escamillo) Conductor: Klobuèar
September 24	*Carmen* Madeira, Friedrich, Stich-Randall, London (Escamillo) Conductor: Klobuèar
September 26	*Carmen* Höngen, Hopf, Loose, London (Escamillo) Conductor: Loibner
September 30	*Die Zauberflöte* Korel, Köth, Seefried, Patzak, Poell, Loose, London (Sprecher) Conductor: Böhm
October 2	*Die Zauberflöte* Weber, Köth, Seefried, Hopf, Kunz, Loose, London (Sprecher) Conductor: Hollreiser
November 6	*Don Giovanni* Della Casa, Dermota, Jurinac, Kunz, Seefried, London (Don Giovanni) Conductor: Böhm
November 11	*Aida* Madeira, Rysanek, Hopf, Frick, Felbermayer, London (Amonasro) Conductor: Kubelik
November 13	*Aida* Madeira, Rysanek, Hopf, Frick, Felbermayer, London (Amonasro) Conductor: Kubelik
November 17	*Don Giovanni* Della Casa, Dermota, Jurinac, Kunz, Seefried, London (Don Giovanni) Conductor: Böhm
November 19	*Aida* Madeira, Rysanek, Hopf, Frick, Felbermayer, London (Amonasro) Conductor: Kubelik
November 21	*Carmen* Kalin, Hendriksen, Siebert, London (Escamillo) Conductor: Klobuèar
November 22	*Don Giovanni* Della Casa, Dermota, Jurinac, Kunz, Seefried, London (Don Giovanni) Conductor: Böhm
November 26	*Aida* Madeira, Rysanek, Hopf, Frick, Felbermayer, London (Amonasro) Conductor: Kubelik
November 27	*Carmen* Kalin, Hendriksen, Siebert, London (Escamillo) Conductor: Klobuèar
December 7	*Don Giovanni* Della Casa, Dermota, Jurinac, Kunz, Loose, London (Don Giovanni) Conductor: Böhm

233

December 8	*Aida*
	Madeira, Kunitz, Hopf, Frick, Felbermayer, London (Amonasro)
	Conductor: Kubelik
December 9	*Carmen*
	Kalin, Hendriksen, Siebert, London (Escamillo)
	Conductor: Klobuèar
December 11	*Carmen*
	Madeira, Hendriksen, Siebert, London (Escamillo)
	Conductor: Klobuèar
December 12	*Carmen*
	Miladinoviæ, Roswaenge, Siebert, London (Escamillo)
	Conductor: Klobuèar
December 16	*Aida*
	Madeira, Rysanek, Roswaenge, Weber, Felbermayer, London (Amonasro)
	Conductor: Kubelik
December 28	*Aida*
	Madeira, Rysanek, Roswaenge, Weber, Felbermayer, London (Amonasro)
	Conductor: Kubelik

1956

June 19	*Don Giovanni*
	Rysanek, Konetzni, Berry, Güden, London (Don Giovanni)
	Conductor: Moralt

1957

June 19	*Carmen*
	Madeira, di Stefano, Güden, London (Escamillo)
	Conductor: Karajan
June 24	*Carmen*
	Madeira, di Stefano, Güden, London (Escamillo)
	Conductor: Hollreiser
June 26	*Carmen*
	Madeira, di Stefano, Güden, London (Escamillo)
	Conductor: Hollreiser
June 29	*Don Giovanni*
	Zadek, Simoneau, Jurinac, Edelmann, Loose, London (Don Giovanni)
	Conductor: Kempe
September 24	*Don Giovanni*
	Zadek, Dermota, Hellwig, Berry, Seefried, London (Don Giovanni)
	Conductor: Moralt
September 26	*Tosca*
	Borkh, Fernandi, London (Scarpia)
	Conductor: Klobuèar

1958

May 29	*Tosca*
	Frazzoni, di Stefano, London (Scarpia)
	Conductor: Curiel
June 2	*Carmen*
	Madeira, di Stefano, Güden, London (Escamillo)
	Conductor: Karajan

234

Chronology

une 4	*Carmen* Madeira, di Stefano, Güden, London (Escamillo) Conductor: Karajan
une 21	*Tosca* Rysanek, Fernandi, London (Scarpia) Conductor: Von Karajan
ᶴeptember 2	*Don Giovanni* Zadek, Kmentt, Scheyrer, Kunz, Sciutti, London (Don Giovanni) Conductor: Moralt
ᶴeptember 9	*Aida* Simionato, Nilsson, di Stefano, Zaccaria, Felbermayer, London (Amonasro) Conductor: Karajan
ᶴeptember 11	*Carmen* Madeira, di Stefano, Güden, London (Escamillo) Conductor: Karajan
ᶴeptember 13	*Tosca* Nilsson, di Stefano, London (Scarpia) Conductor: Mitropoulos
ᶴeptember 21	*Tosca* Zadek, di Stefano, London (Scarpia) Conductor: Mitropoulos
ᶴeptember 24	*Don Giovanni* Nilsson, Zadek, Scheyrer, Edelmann, Loose, London (Don Giovanni) Conductor: Hollreiser
ᶴeptember 28	*Die Zauberflöte* Greindl, Köth, Guden, Kmerett, Kunz, Maikl, London (Sprecher) Conductor: Gielen
ᴐctober 5	*Die Hochzeit des Figaro* Grümmer, Streich, Kunz, Ludwig, London (Count Almaviva) Conductor: Monteux
ᴐctober 10	*Carmen* Madeira, Filacuridi, Jurinac, London (Escamillo) Conductor: Monteux
ᴐctober 12	*Carmen* Madeira, Filacuridi, Jurinac, London (Escamillo) Conductor: Monteux

1959

une 4	*Die Hochzeit des Figaro* Schwarzkopf, Seefried, Kunz, Ludwig, London (Count Almaviva) Conductor: Böhm
une 7	*Die Hochzeit des Figaro* Schwarzkopf, Güden, Kunz, Ludwig, London (Count Almaviva) Conductor: Karajan
ᴹay 30	*Don Giovanni* Zadek, Dermota, Schwarzkopf, Kunz, Güden, London (Don Giovanni) Conductor: Hollreiser
une 12	*Tosca* Tebaldi, Fernandi, London (Scarpia) Conductor: Von Karajan

235

Chronology

1963

June 17	*Der Fliegende Holländer* Kreppel, Rysanek, Windgassen, Höngen, Dermota, London (Der Holländer) Conductor: Mataèiæ
June 24	*Aida* Simionato, Rysanek, McCracken, Kreppel, Maikl, London (Amonasro) Conductor: Molinari-Pradelli

1964

June 26	*Don Giovanni* Scheyrer, Wunderlich, Güden, Kunz, Grist, London (Don Giovanni) Conductor: Krips
June 30	*Don Giovanni* Scheyrer, Wunderlich, Güden, Kunz, Grist, London (Don Giovanni) Conductor: Krips

METROPOLITAN OPERA CHRONOLOGY

1951

November 13, 17, 20, 22, 26 December 8, 12,	New York	*Aida* Milanov, Del Monaco, Nikolaidi, Hines, London (Amonasro) Conductor: Cleva

1953

January 9	New York	*Aida* Milanov, Del Monaco, Barbieri, Hines, Amara, London (Amonasro) Conductor: Cleva
January 15	New York	*Don Giovanni* Harshaw, Peerce, Lewis, Warner, London (Don Giovanni) Conductor: Rudolf
January 20	New York	*Carmen* Barbieri, Tucker, De Los Angeles, London (Escamillo) Conductor: Adler
January 24	New York	*Aida* Thebom, Del Monaco, Barbieri, Hines, Amara, London (Amonasro) Conductor: Cleva
January 30	New York	*Don Giovanni* Harshaw, Peerce, Peters, Warner, London (Don Giovanni) Conductor: Rudolf

Chronology

February 9	New York	*Aida* Rigal, Del Monaco, Nikolaidi, Roggero, Hines, London (Amonasro) Conductor: Cleva
February 28	New York	*Aida* Rigal, Siepi, Nikolaidi, Hayward, London (Amonasro) Conductor: Cleva
March 6	New York	*Boris Godunov* Hines, Thebom, Björling, Sullivan, London (Boris Godunov) Conductor: Stiedry
March 14	New York	*Don Giovanni* Harshaw, Peerce, Peters, Warner, London (Don Giovanni) Conductor: Rudolf
March 17	Philadelphia	*Boris Godunov* Hines, Rankin, Björling, Sullivan, London (Boris Godunov) Conductor: Kozma
March 21	New York	*Boris Godunov* Hines, Rankin, Björling, Sullivan, London (Boris Godunov) Conductor: Kozma
March 26	New York	*Tosca* Rigal, Baum, London (Scarpia) Conductor: Cleva
March 28	New York	*Boris Godunov* Hines, Thebom, Björling, Sullivan, London (Boris Godunov) Conductor: Stiedry
April 11	New York	*Carmen* Barbieri, Tucker, De Los Angeles, London (Escamillo) Conductor: Adler
April 3	New York	*Parsifal* Svanholm, Varnay, Madeira, Hines, London (Amfortas) Conductor: Stiedry
April 6	New York	Metropolitan Jamboree Conductor: Cleva
April 11	New York	*Carmen* Stevens, Vinay, Conner, London (Escamillo) Conductor: Reiner
April 16	New York	*Boris Godunov* Hines, Thebom, Björling, Sullivan, London (Boris Godunov) Conductor: Stiedry
April 22	New York	*Tosca* Kirsten, Conley, London (Scarpia) Conductor: Cleva
May 2	New York	*Tosca* Rigal, Del Monaco, London (Scarpia) Conductor: Cleva

237

May 4	New York	*Carmen* Stevens, Tucker, Güden, London (Escamillo) Conductor: Adler
May 12	New York	*Tosca* Kirsten, Peerce, London (Scarpia) Conductor: Cleva
May 17 London	New York	*Don Giovanni* Harshaw, Conley, Resnik, Baccaloni, Peters, (Don Giovanni) Conductor: Rudolf
May 21, 24	New York	*Tosca* Kirsten, Del Monaco, London (Scarpia) Conductor: Cleva
May 27	New York	*Tosca* Kirsten, Peerce, London (Scarpia) Conductor: Cleva
December 26	New York	*Tannhäuser* Vinay, Harshaw, Varnay, Hines, Peters, London (Wolfram) Conductor: Szell

1954

January 9	New York	*Tannhäuser* Vinay, Harshaw, Varnay, Hines, Peters, London (Wolfram) Conductor: Szell
January 10, 18,	New York	*Carmen* Stevens, Baum, Amara, London (Escamillo) Conductor: Kozma
January 23	New York	*Boris Godunov* Gari, Rankin, Miller, London (Boris Godunov) Conductor:
January 28	New York	*Le Nozze di Figaro* Siepi, Peters, Seefried, Steber, London (Count Almaviva) Conductor: Stiedry
March 2	New York	*Don Giovanni* Harshaw, Conley, Güden, Steber, London (Don Giovanni) Conductor: Rudolf
March 6	New York	*Boris Godunov* Gari, Rankin, Miller, London (Boris Godunov) Conductor: Stiedry
March 13	New York	*Don Giovanni* Harshaw, Conley, Corena, Conner, Steber, London (Don Giovanni) Conductor:
March 15	New York	*Boris Godunov* Gari, Rankin, Miller, London (Boris Godunov) Conductor: Stiedry

March 20	New York	*Faust* Hayward, Conner, Guarrera, London (Méphistophélès) Conductor: Adler
March 26	New York	*Parsifal* Kullman, Varnay, Madeira, Frantz, London (Amfortas) Conductor: Stiedry
April 1	New York	*Aida* Nelli, Penno, Rankin, Scott, London (Amonasro) Conductor: Adler
April 14	New York	*Le Nozze di Figaro* Siepi, Peters, Steber, London (Count Almaviva) Conductor: Stiedry
April 22	New York	*Aida* Milnov, Baum, Thebom, London (Amonasro) Conductor: Cleva
April 26	Boston	*Don Giovanni* Harshaw, Conner, Steber, London (Don Giovanni) Conductor: Rudolf
April 28	New York	*Carmen* Thebom, Tucker, Amara, London (Escamillo) Conductor: Kozma
May 3	New York	*Don Giovanni* Harshaw, Valletti, Steber, Kunz, Peters, London (Don Giovanni) Conductor: Rudolf
December 9	New York	*Le Nozze di Figaro* Siepi, Conner, Della Casa, Miller, London (Count Almaviva) Conductor: Stiedry
December 25	New York	*Tosca* Albanese, Conley, London (Scarpia) Conductor: Cleva

1955

January 1	New York	*Aida* Milanov, Baum, Thebom, London (Amonasro) Conductor: Cleva
January 5	New York	*Le Nozze di Figaro* Siepi, Conner, Steber, Miller, London (Count Almaviva) Conductor: Stiedry
January 12	New York	*Don Giovanni* Harshaw, Valletti, Amara, D. Wilson, London (Don Giovanni) Conductor: Rudolf
January 15	New York	*Aida* Milanov, Baum, Thebom, London (Amonasro) Conductor: Cleva

Chronology

January 26	New York	*Tannhäuser* Vinay, Harshaw, Varnay, Hines, London (Wolfram) Conductor: Kempe
January 29	New York	*Tannhäuser* Vinay, Rigal, Varnay, London (Wolfram) Conductor: Adler
February 5	New York	*Tosca* Rigal, Campora, London (Scarpia) Conductor: Cleva
February 10	New York	*Arabella* Steber, Güden, Thebom, Peters, London (Mandryka) Conductor: Kempe
February 15	Philadelphia	*Arabella* Steber, Güden, Thebom, Peters, London (Mandryka) Conductor: Kempe
February 16	New York	*Tosca* Milanov, Campora, London (Scarpia) Conductor: Cleva
February 19, 26 March 2	New York	*Arabella* Steber, Güden, Thebom, Peters, London (Mandryka) Conductor: Kempe
March 22	New York	*Faust* Campora, Conner, Guarrera, London (Méphistophélès) Conductor: Adler
March 24	New York	*Arabella* Steber, Güden, Thebom, Peters, London (Mandryka) Conductor: Kempe
April 2	New York	Gala Die Fledermaus guest artist Conductor: Kozma
April 8	New York	*Parsifal* Harshaw, Hines, Aldenhoff, Ernster, Madeira, London (Amfortas) Conductor: Stiedry

1956

January 27 February 4	New York	*Le Nozze di Figaro* Singher, Conner, De los Angeles, Miller, London (Count Almaviva) Conductor: Rudolf
February 11	New York	*Tosca* Albanese, Campora, London (Scarpia) Conductor: Mitropoulos
February 15	New York	*Boris Godunov* Resnik, Hines, Scott, Miller, London (Boris Godunov Conductor: Mitropoulos

240

February 20	New York	*Tosca*
		Rigal, Barioni, London (Scarpia)
		Conductor: Mitropoulos
March 1	New York	*Le Nozze di Figaro*
		Siepi, Peters, Steber, Ruggero, London (Count
		Almaviva)
		Conductor: Rudolf

March 8	New York	*Tosca*
		Albanese, Campora, London (Scarpia)
		Conductor: Mitropoulos
March 10	New York	*Boris Godunov*
		Thebom, Tozzi, Gari, Miller, London (Boris
		Godunov)
		Conductor: Mitropoulos
November 13	New York	*Aida*
		Stella, Bergonzi, Barbieri, Moscona, London
		(Amonasro)
		Conductor: Cleva
November 15, 19	New York	*Tosca*
		Callas, Campora, London (Scarpia)
		Conductor: Mitropoulos
November 29	New York	*Les Contes d'Hoffman*
		Tucker, Hurley, Amparán, Amara, London
		(4 Villains)
		Conductor: Schippers
December 5	New York	*Aida*
		Milanov, Baum, Siepi, London (Amonasro)
		Conductor: Cleva
December 7, 15	New York	*Les Contes d'Hoffman*
		Tucker, Hurley, Amparán, Amara, London
		(4 Villains)
		Conductor: Schippers
December 17	New York	*Le Nozze di Figaro*
		Siepi, Güden, Della Casa, Miller, London (Count
		Almaviva)
		Conductor: Rudolf
December 22	New York	*Les Contes d'Hoffman*
		Tucker, Hurley, Amparán, Amara, London
		(4 Villains)
		Conductor: Schippers
December 27	New York	*Carmen*
		Stevens, Tucker, Amara, London (Escamillo)
		Conductor: Mitropoulos
December 29	New York	*Les Contes d'Hoffman*
		Tucker, Hurley, Elias, Amara, London (4 Villains)
		Conductor: Schippers

1957

January 5	New York	*Tosca*
		Rigal, Tucker, London (Scarpia)
		Conductor: Mitropoulos

Chronology

January 7	New York	*Arabella* Della Casa, Güden, London (Mandryka) Conductor: Leinsdorf
January 12	New York	*Le Nozze di Figaro* Güden, Della Casa, Tozzi, Elias, London (Count Almaviva) Conductor: Rudolf
January 17 February 9	New York	*Arabella* Della Casa, Güden, London (Mandryka) Conductor: Leinsdorf
February 23	New York	*Aida* Stella, Baum, Thebom, Tozzi, London (Amonasro) Conductor: Cleva
April 9	New York	*Tosca* Curtis-Verna, Campora, London (Scarpia) Conductor: Cleva
April 20	New York	*Tosca* Tebaldi, Barioni, London (Scarpia) Conductor: Adler
April 27, May 2	New York	*Le Nozze di Figaro* Siepi, Hurley, Amara, Miller, London (Count Almaviva) Conductor: Rudolf
May 14	New York	*Tosca* Tebaldi, Campora, London (Scarpia) Conductor: Mitropoulos
May 16	New York	*Tosca* Albanese, Barioni, London (Scarpia) Conductor: Mitropoulos
May 26	New York	*Carmen* Baum, Stevens, Amara, London (Escamillo) Conductor: Mitropoulos
May 27	Toronto	*Le Nozze di Figaro* Tozzi, Hurley, Amara, Elias, London (Count Almaviva) Conductor: Rudolf
May 31	New York	*Tosca* Tebaldi, Barioni, London (Scarpia) Conductor: Mitropoulos
October 28	New York	*Eugene Onegin* Amara, Tucker, Elias, Tozzi, London (Onegin) Conductor: Mitropoulos
November 5	Philadelphia	*Eugene Onegin* Amara, Tucker, Elias, Tozzi, London (Onegin) Conductor: Mitropoulos
November 8	New York	*Eugene Onegin* Amara, Gari, Elias, Tozzi, London (Onegin) Conductor: Mitropoulos
November 13	New York	*Don Giovanni* Steber, Valletti, Della Casa, London (Don Giovanni) Conductor: Böhm
November 19, 25 December 7	New York	*Eugene Onegin* Amara, Gari, Elias, Tozzi, London (Onegin)

Chronology

		Conductor: Mitropoulos
December 12	New York	*Carmen*
		Madeira, Güden, Tucker, London (Escamillo)
		Conductor: Schippers
December 19	New York	*Le Nozze di Figaro*
		Siepi, Hurley, Della Casa, Miller, London (Count Almaviva)
		Conductor: Leinsdorf
December 30	New York	*Tosca*
		Curtis-Verna, Labò, London (Scarpia)
		Conductor: Mitropoulos

1958

January 11	New York	*Le Nozze di Figaro*
		Tozzi, Güden, Della Casa, Miller, London (Count Almaviva)
		Conductor: Leinsdorf
February 3	New York	*Le Nozze di Figaro*
		Tozzi, Hurley, Della Casa, Elias, London (Count Almaviva)
		Conductor: Leinsdorf
March 5	New York	*Tosca*
		Callas, Tucker, London (Scarpia)
		Conductor: Mitropoulos
March 22	New York	*Eugene Onegin*
		Amara, Gari, Elias, Tozzi, London (Onegin)
		Conductor: Mitropoulos
March 24	Baltimore	*Eugene Onegin*
		Amara, Gari, Elias, Tozzi, London (Onegin)
		Conductor: Mitropoulos
March 26	New York	*Le Nozze di Figaro*
		Tozzi, Wilson, Amara, Elias, London (Count Almaviva)
		Conductor: Leinsdorf
April 2	New York	*Eugene Onegin*
		Amara, Gari, Elias, Hines, London (Onegin)
		Conductor: Mitropoulos
April 4	New York	*Parsifal*
		Harshaw, Vinay, Edelmann, London (Amfortas)
		Conductor: Stiedry
April 5	New York	*Don Giovanni*
		Amara, Steber, Hurley, Corena, London (Don Giovanni)
		Conductor: Böhm
April 8	New York	*Don Giovanni*
		Amara, Steber, Peters, Corena, London (Don Giovanni)
		Conductor: Stiedry
April 11	New York	*Carmen*
		Madeira, Baum, Amara, London (Escamillo)
		Conductor: Adler
April 14	Boston	*Eugene Onegin*
		Amara, Gari, Elias, Tozzi, London (Onegin)

		Conductor: Mitropoulos
April 17	New York	*Don Giovanni*
		Amara, Steber, Wilson, Corena, London (Don Giovanni)
		Conductor: Leinsdorf
April 21	Cleveland	*Eugene Onegin*
		Amara, Gari, Elias, Tozzi, London (Onegin)
		Conductor: Mitropoulos
April 26	New York	*Don Giovanni*
		Amara, Steber, Wilson, Corena, London (Don Giovanni)
		Conductor: Leinsdorf
April 30	Atlanta	*Eugene Onegin*
		Amara, Gari, Elias, Tozzi, London (Onegin)
		Conductor: Mitropoulos
May 10	New York	*Eugene Onegin*
		Amara, Gari, Elias, Tozzi, London (Onegin)
		Conductor: Mitropoulos
May 16	Minneapolis	*Eugene Onegin*
		Amara, Gari, Elias, Tozzi, London (Onegin)
		Conductor: Mitropoulos
May 19	Bloomington	*Eugene Onegin*
		Amara, Gari, Elias, Tozzi, London (Onegin)
		Conductor: Mitropoulos
May 22	Chicago	*Eugene Onegin*
		Amara, Gari, Elias, Tozzi, London (Onegin)
		Conductor: Mitropoulos
May 26	Toronto	*Eugene Onegin*
		Amara, Gari, Elias, Tozzi, London (Onegin)
		Conductor: Mitropoulos
October 27	New York	*Tosca*
		Tebaldi, Del Monaco, London (Scarpia)
		Conductor: Mitropoulos
October 31	New York	*Les Contes d'Hoffman*
		Gedda, Dobbs, Elias, Amara, London (4 Villains)
		Conductor: Morel
November 4	New York	*Tosca*
		Tebaldi, Campora, London (Scarpia)
		Conductor: Mitropoulos
November 12	New York	*Tosca*
		Curtis-Verna, Fernandi, London (Scarpia)
		Conductor: Mitropoulos
November 26	New York	*Les Contes d'Hoffman*
		Gedda, Hurley, Elias, Amara, London (4 Villains)
		Conductor: Morel
December 5	New York	*Boris Godunov*
		Scott, Elias, Gari, Miller, London (Boris Godunov)
		Conductor: Mitropoulos
December 8	New York	*Les Contes d'Hoffman*
		Gedda, Hurley, Elias, Amara, London (4 Villains)
		Conductor: Morel
\		
December 13	New York	*Eugene Onegin*
		Amara, Gedda, Elias, Tozzi, London (Onegin)

		Conductor: Mitropoulos
December 18	New York	*Eugene Onegin*
		Amara, Tucker, Elias, Wildermann, London
		(Onegin)
		Conductor: Mitropoulos
December 25	New York	*Tosca*
		Tebaldi, Fernandi, London (Scarpia)
		Conductor: Mitropoulos
December 30	New York	*Eugene Onegin*
		Amara, Tucker, Elias, Tozzi, London (Onegin)
		Conductor: Mitropoulos

1959

January 26	New York	*Eugene Onegin*
		Amara, Tucker, Elias, Tozzi, London (Onegin)
		Conductor: Strasfogel
February 3	New York	*Carmen*
		Maderia, Amara, Tucker, London (Escamillo)
		Conductor: Morel
February 7	New York	*Les Contes d'Hoffman*
		Gedda, Hurley, Elias, Amara, London (4 Villains)
		Conductor: Morel
February 14	New York	*Don Giovanni*
		Flagello, Hurley, Steber, Valletti, Della Casa,
		London (Don Giovanni)
		Conductor: Böhm
March 12	New York	*Tosca*
		Steber, Morell, London (Scarpia)
		Conductor: Adler
March 24	New York	*Don Giovanni*
		Curtis-Vera, Gedda, Amara, Hurley, London
		(Don Giovanni)
		Conductor: Böhm
March 30	New York	*Boris Godunov*
		Scott, Elias, Vanni, London (Boris Godunov)
		Conductor: Mitropoulos
April 2	New York	Gala – Act II, *Tosca*
		Albanese, Fernandi, London (Scarpia)
		Conductor: Adler
April 3	New York	*Eugene Onegin*
		Amara, Tucker, Elias, Wildermann, London
		(Onegin)
		Conductor: Strasfogel
April 11	New York	*Tosca*
		Steber, Bergonzi, London (Scarpia)
		Conductor: Adler
December 2, 14	New York	*Pelléas et Mélisande*
		Uppman, De Los Angeles, Tozzi, London (Golaud)
		Conductor: Morel
December 24	New York	*Faust*
		Gedda, Elias, Söderström, London

Chronology

(Méphistophélès)
Conductor: Morel

1960

January 2	New York	*Pelléas et Mélisande* Uppman, De Los Angeles, Hines, London (Golaud) Conductor: Morel
January 13	New York	*Der Fliegende Holländer* Rysanek, Liebl, Tozzi, Amparán, London (Holländer) Conductor: Schippers
January 16, 22	New York	*Pelléas et Mélisande* Uppman, De Los Angeles, Hines, London (Golaud) Conductor: Morel
January 23	New York	*Aida* Baum, Dalis, Amara, London (Amonasro) Conductor: Cleva
January 29	New York	*Don Giovanni* Gedda, Steber, Della Casa, Peters, Corera, London (Don Giovanni) Conductor: Böhm
February 6	New York	*Der Fliegende Holländer* Rysanek, Liebl, Tozzi, London (Holländer) Conductor: Schippers
February 8	New York	*Faust* Fernandi, Serini, Vanni, Söderström, London (Méphistophélès) Conductor: Morel
February 12	New York	*Der Fliegende Holländer* Harshaw, Liebl, Tozzi, London (Holländer) Conductor: Schippers
February 15	New York	*Der Fliegende Holländer* Harshaw, Da Costa, Tozzi, Dunn, London (Holländer) Conductor: Schippers
February 23	New York	*Der Fliegende Holländer* Rysanek, Da Costa, Tozzi, Dunn, London (Holländer) Conductor: Schippers
February 25	New York	*Don Giovanni* Amara, Flagello, Dobbs, Steber, London (Don Giovanni) Conductor: Böhm
March 5	New York	*Der Fliegende Holländer* Rysanek, Liebl, Tozzi, Amparán, London (Holländer) Conductor: Schippers
March 10	New York	*Der Fliegende Holländer* Rysanek, Da Costa, Tozzi. Dunn, London (Holländer) Conductor: Schippers
March 19	New York	*Der Fliegende Holländer* Rysanek, Liebl, Tozzi, Amparán, London

Chronology

		(Holländer) Conductor: Schippers
April 21	New York	*Le Nozze di Figaro* Amara, Söderström, Siepi, Miller, London (Count Almaviva) Conductor: Leinsdorf
April 29	New York	*Le Nozze di Figaro* Della Casa, Söderström, Siepi, Miller, London (Count Almaviva) Conductor: Leinsdorf
May 7	New York	*Le Nozze di Figaro* Della Casa, Söderström, Siepi, Miller, London (Count Almaviva) Conductor: Leinsdorf
May 16	Oklahoma City	*Le Nozze di Figaro* Della Casa, Söderström, Tozzi, Miller, London (Count Almaviva) Conductor: Leinsdorf
May 18	Bloomington	*Le Nozze di Figaro* Amara, Söderström, Siepi, Miller, London (Count Almaviva) Conductor: Leinsdorf
May 21	New York	*Le Nozze di Figaro* Amara, Söderström, Siepi, Miller, London (Count Almaviva) Conductor: Leinsdorf
May 25	New York	*Le Nozze di Figaro* Della Casa, Söderström, Siepi, Miller, London (Count Almaviva) Conductor: Leinsdorf
October 27	New York	*Boris Godunov* Tozzi, Thebom, Sullivan, Roggero, Dunn, London (Boris Godunov) Conductor: Leinsdorf
November 2, 8	New York	*Boris Godunov* Tozzi, Thebom, Sullivan, Roggero, Dunn, London (Boris Godunov) Conductor: Leinsdorf
November 18, 28	New York	*Arabella* Della Casa, Morell, Hurley, London (Mandryka) Conductor: Leinsdorf
December 13, 28	New York	*Arabella* Della Casa, Morell, Hurley, London (Mandryka) Conductor: Leinsdorf

1961

January 7	New York	*Boris Godunov* Dunn, Stratas, Vanni, London (Boris Godunov) Conductor: Leinsdorf
January 21	New York	*Arabella* Della Casa, Dunn, London (Mandryka) Conductor: Leinsdorf
March 15	New York	*Don Giovanni* Peerce, Amara, Flagello, Steber, London (Don

		Giovanni) Conductor: Böhm
March 25	New York	*Don Giovanni* Price, Anthony, Curtis-Vera, Flagello, London (Don Giovanni) Conductor: Böhm
October 27	New York	*Tosca* Kirsten, Tucker, London (Scarpia) Conductor: Adler
November 2	New York	*Tosca* Curtis-Vera, Barioni, London (Scarpia) Conductor: Adler
November 11	New York	*Les Contes d'Hoffman* Gedda, Moffo, London (4 Villains) Conductor: Morel
November 15	New York	*Tosca* Morell, Kirsten, London (Scarpia) Conductor: Adler
November 18	New York	*Les Contes d'Hoffman* Gedda, Hurley, Elias, Amara, King, London (4 Villains) Conductor: Morel
November 20	New York	*Tosca* Milanov, Zampieri, London (Scarpia) Conductor: Adler
November 27	New York	*Les Contes d'Hoffman* Hurley, Elias, Amara, King, Gedda, London (4 Villains) Conductor: Morel
December 7	New York	*Les Contes d'Hoffman* Hurley, Elias, Amara, King, Gedda, London (4 Villains) Conductor: Morel
December 22	New York	*Les Contes d'Hoffman* Hurley, Dunn, Amara, King, Alexander, London (4 Villains) Conductor: Morel

1962

January 9	New York	*Les Contes d'Hoffman* Hurley, Elias, Amara, King, Gedda, London (4 Villains) Conductor: Morel
September 29	New York	*Atlántida* (Lincoln Center opening gala performance) Farrell, Madeira, London (Narrator) Conductor: Ansermet
November 17	New York	*Don Giovanni* Price, Gedda, Tucci, Flagello, Peters, London (Don Giovanni) Conductor: Graf
November 23	New York	*Don Giovanni* Steber, Gedda, Tucci, Flagello, Hurley, London

		(Don Giovanni) Conductor: Graf
November 30	New York	*Pelléas et Mélisande* Uppman, Moffo, Hines, Thebom, London (Golaud) Conductor: Ansermet
December 6	New York	*Pelléas et Mélisande* Uppman, Moffo, Hines, Thebom, London (Golaud) Conductor: Ansermet
December 10	New York	*Pelléas et Mélisande* Uppman, Moffo, Gedda, Thebom, London (Golaud) Conductor: Ansermet
December 22	New York	*Pelléas et Mélisande* Tozzi, Moffo, Gedda, Thebom, London (Golaud) Conductor: Ansermet
December 25	New York	*Don Giovanni* Peerce, Della Casa, Steber, Coreno, Peters, London (Don Giovanni) Conductor: Maazel
December 29	New York	*Pelléas et Mélisande* Uppman, Moffo, Gedda, Thebom, London (Golaud) Conductor: Ansermet

1963

January 11	New York	*Der Fliegende Holländer* Rysanek, Kónya, Tozzi, London (Holländer) Conductor: Böhm
January 19	New York	*Der Fliegende Holländer* Crespin, Kónya, Tozzi, London (Holländer) Conductor: Böhm
January 23	New York	*Der Fliegende Holländer* Rysanek, Kónya, Liebl, London (Holländer) Conductor: Böhm
February 6	New York	*Der Fliegende Holländer* Kuchta, Kónya, Tozzi, London (Holländer) Conductor: Böhm
February 9	New York	*Don Giovanni* Stich-Randall, Della Casa, Hurley, London (Don Giovanni) Conductor: Rich
February 12, 16, 18	New York	*Der Fliegende Holländer* Kuchta, Kónya, Tozzi, London (Holländer) Conductor: Böhm
March 16, 20	New York	*Boris Godunov* Flagello, Gedda, Elias, Chookasian, London (Boris Godunov) Conductor; Solti
December 30	New York	*Aida* Price, Labó, Gorr, London (Amonasro) Conductor: Adler

1964

249

Chronology

January 23	New York	*L'Ultimo Selvaggio* Peters, Stratas, Gedda, Flagello, Chookasian, London (*Selvaggio*) Conductor: Schippers
January 31	New York	*Faust* Gedda, Kirsten, Ruzdak, London (Méphistophélès) Conductor: Cleva
February 8	New York	*L'Ultimo Selvaggio* Peters, Stratas, Gedda, Flagello, Chookasian, London (*Selvaggio*) Conductor: Schippers
February 22	New York	*L'Ultimo Selvaggio* Hurley, Stratas, Gedda, Flagello, Chookasian, London (*Selvaggio*) Conductor: Schippers
February 26	New York	*L'Ultimo Selvaggio* Hurley, Stratas, Gedda, Flagello, Chookasian, London (*Selvaggio*) Conductor: Schippers
March 2	New York	*L'Ultimo Selvaggio* Hurley, Stratas, Gedda, Flagello, Chookasian, London (*Selvaggio*) Conductor: Schippers
April 18	New York	*Tosca* Nilsson, Corelli, London (Scarpia) Conductor: Cleva
April 25	New York	*Faust* Alexander, Amara, Martin, London (Méphistophélès) Conductor: Cleva
December 31	New York	*L'Ultimo Selvaggio* Peters, Stratas, Chookasian, Alexander, London (*Selvaggio*) Conductor: LaMarchina

1965

January 19, 25	New York	*Der Fliegende Holländer* Rysanek, Kónya, Tozzi, Kriese, London (Holländer) Conductor: Böhm
February 22	New York	*Die Walküre* Nilsson, Vickers, Rysanek, Dalis, London (Wotan) Conductor: Steinberg
March 12	New York	*Der Fliegende Holländer* Kuchta, Liebl, Tozzi, London (Holländer) Conductor: Böhm
April 3	New York	*Tosca* Crespin, Corelli, London (Scarpia) Conductor: Cleva
April 24	New York	*L'Uultimo Selvaggio* Peters, Stratas, Chookasian, Alexander, London (*Selvaggio*) Conductor: LaMarchina
May 1	New York	*Der Fliegende Holländer* Rysanek, Sergi, Tozzi, London (Holländer)

		Conductor: Rosenstock
May 3, 14	New York	*L'Ultimo Selvaggio*
		Peters, Stratas, Chookasian, Sergi, London
		(Selvaggio)
		Conductor: LaMarchina
May 22	New York	*Der Fliegende Holländer*
		Rysanek, Vickers, Tozzi, Kriese, London
		(Holländer)
		Conductor: Rosenstock
May 29	New York	*Der Fliegende Holländer*
		Rysanek, Sergi, Tozzi, London (Holländer)
		Conductor: Rosenstock

1966

March 10	New York	*Parsifal*
		Kónya, Crespin, Hines, London (Amfortas)
		Conductor: Prêtre

George London performances in Bayreuth (43)

1951	*Parsifal*	Amfortas July 30, August 7, 10, 18 22, 25, cond.
		Knappertsbusch, w/Van Mill, Weber, Windgassen, Modl, Uhde,
		staging Wieland Wagner, same for all Parsifal performances
1952	*Parsifal*	Amfortas August 1, 5, 10 19, 23, cond.
		Knappertsbusch, w/Modl, Windgassen, Weber, Uhde, Bohme, Sievert
1953	*Parsifal*	Amfortas July 24, August 2, 15, 19, cond.
		Clemens Krauss, w/Modl, Vinay, Weber, Uhde, Greindl, von Ilosvay
1956	*The Flying Dutchman*,	Title Role, July 25, August 1, 4, 9, 12 Cond.
		Keilberth , w/Arnold Van Mill, Astrid Varnay, Traxel, staging
		Wolfgang Wagner
	Parsifal	Amfortas August 8, cond. Knappertsbusch, w/Greindl, Vinay, Modl
1957	*Parsifal*	Amfortas July 25, August 5, 13, 23, cond. Cluytens, w/Van Mill,
		Greindl, Vinay, Varnay, Blanckenheim
1959	*The Flying Dutchman*,	Title Role, July 23, 29, August 2, 5 cond. Sawallisch w/ Rysanek,
		Greindl, Uhl, Paskuda, staging Wieland Wagner
1961	*Parsifal*	Amfortas July 25, August 5, Cond.
		Knappertsbusch, w/Dalis, Thomas, Weber, Hotter, Neidlinger
	The Flying Dutchman,	Title Role, July 24, 31, August 9, cond. Sawallisch, Greindl, Uhl, Anja
		Silja, staging Wieland Wagner
1962	*Parsifal*	Amfortas July 27, August 5, 10, cond.
		Knappertsbusch, w/Dalis, Talvela, Hotter, Thomas, Neidlinger
1963	*Parsifal*	Amfortas July 24, August 1, 8, cond.
		Knappertsbusch w/ Dalis, Nienstedt, Hotter, Windgassen, Neidlinger
		Beethoven's 9th Symphony July 23, cond. Bohm, w/Janowitz, Bumbry,
		Thomas
1964	*Parsifal*	Amfortas July 21, 29, cond.
		Knappertsbusch, w/Dalis, Hotter, Vickers, Neidlinger

OPERATIC AND CONCERT HIGHLIGHTS

1938	*Marriage of Figaro*, Antonio, Los Angeles City College Production,
1940	Los Angeles, Meet the People, Edwin Lester company
1943	October, San Francisco, War Memorial Opera House, *Rigoletto*, cond. Pietro Cimara, w/ Ivan Petroff (10/25), John Charles Thomas (10/28), Lily Pons, Jan Peerce, Christine Johnson, London (Count Monterone)
1943	November, San Francisco, War Memorial Opera House, *Rigoletto*, cond. Pietro Cimara, w/ Ivan Petroff (10/25), John Charles Thomas (10/28), Lily Pons, Jan Peerce, Christine Johnson, London (Count Monterone)
1946	*Desert Song*, London (Ali Ben Ali), touring company of Edwin Lester
1946	*Verdi Requiem*, Dallas, Antal Dorati, conductor
1946-48	Bel Canto Trio, Frances Yeend, Mario Lanza, George London 86 Concerts throughout the United States, Canada, Mexico, Hollywood Bowl, Josef Blatt, pianist.
1948,	December, Toronto Massey Hall, Toronto Symphony Orchestra, cond. Paul Scherman, guest artist, G.L., La Columnia, Boris Monologue,
1948	Edinburgh, *Marriage of Figaro*, role of Figaro
1949	November Vienna Brahms-Saal, Recital, Erik Werba pianist
1949	November Vienna, Verdi-Requiem cond. Von Karajan
1950	December Vienna Brahms-Saal, 2 Recitals, Erik Werba, pianist
1950	New York Philharmonic, Carnegie Hall, Mahler, *Symphony No.8* Cond. Stokowski,
1952	Salzburg, Benefit Concert Salzburg Mozarteum withSchwarzkopf, Guden
1952	La Scala, *Fidelio*, cond. Von Karajan, London (Don Pizarro), w/Moedl, Della Casa,Windgassen, Edelmann
1952	New York Philharmonic, Carnegie Hall, Boris Godunov Scenes, Cond. Mitropoulos
1952	May, Vienna Brahms-Saal, Recital Erik Werba Pianist
1952	June, Vienna, Grosser Musikvereinssaal, Recital
1952	Salzburg, July 26, August 2,8, 29 *Marriage of Figaro*, cond. Moralt, London, (Count Almaviva), w/Schwartzkopf, Seefried, Guden, Kunz
1953	May, Vienna, Brahms Saal, Recital, Erik Werba Pianist
1953	National Symphony, *Boris Godunov* Excerpts
1954	New York Philharmonic, Carnegie Hall, Brahms, *Ein Deutsches Requiem;* Irmgard Seefried, George London, cond. Bruno Walter
1954	May Salzburg Mozarteum, Recital, Erik Werba, pianist
1955	May Vienna, Brahms Saal Recital, Erik Werba, pianist
1955	June Vienna, Grosser Musikvereinssaal, Recital, Erik Werba, pianist
1955	December, Vienna, Brahms Saal Recital, Erik Werba, pianist
1956	June Vienna, Brahms Saal, Recital, Erik Werba, pianist
1956	July, Bayreuth, Benefit Wagner Foundation, recital, Maximilian Kojetinsky, pianist
1957	February, New York, Hunter College, Recital, John Newmark, pianist
1957	Carnegie Hall, Benefit, Symphony of the Air, cond. Rudolf Kempe w/Vinay, Harshaw, Resnik, Schoffler, London, All Wagner excerpts
1958	June 16, Brussels, Recital US Pavilion World Fair, Leo Taubman, pianist
1958	July, Vancouver, *Don Giovanni*, title role, w/Sutherland, Simoneau, Alarie
1959	Brooklyn College Concert Series, Recital, John Newmark, pianist
1959	April, May, Israel Philharmonic Orchestra, Concert Tour, cond. Josef Krips, *Boris Godunov* Excerpts (8 concerts)
1959	June, Stuttgart Opera, *Boris Godunov;* cond. Wilhelm Seegelken; title role w/ Eugene Tobin, Grace Hoffman, Otto v.Rohr
1959	June, Stuttgart Opera, *Don Giovanni;* cond. Ferdinand Leitner, title role w/Josef Traxel, Gustav Neidlinger, Lore Wissmann

Chronology

1959	October, San Francisco, War Memorial Opera House, *Don Giovanni*, cond. Leopold Ludwig, title role w/Sena Jurinac, Richard Lewis, Lorenzo Alvary, Leontyne Price
1959	November, San Francisco, War Memorial Opera House, *Don Giovanni*, cond. Leopold Ludwig, title role w/ Gabriella Tucci, Richard Lewis, Lorenzo Alvary, Leontyne Price
1959	November, San Francisco, War Memorial Opera House, *Aida*, cond. Francesco Molinari-Pradelli, w/Leontyne Price, Jon Vickers, Irene Dalis, Mino Yahia, Mark Elyn, London (Amonasro)
1959	United Nations, concert, New York
1960	April, Montreal Symphonic Orchestra, Salle Le Plateau, cond. Igor Markevitch, Wagner scenes from *Parsifal* & *Meistersinger von Nurnberg*
1960	September, Vienna Grosser Musikverein Saal Recital, Erik Werba Pianist
1960	September 17, Moscow, Bolshoi Opera, *Boris Godunov*, September, Russian tour, Leningrad, *Boris Godunov* & *Faust*, Mephistopheles; Riga, Boris Godunov; Riga, Kiev, Leningrad & Moscow, Recitals, Leo Taubman, pianist
1961	May, Venice, Gran Teatro La Fenice, *Der Fliegende Holländer*, cond. Cluytens, staging Wieland Wagner, title role w/Gre Browenstien
1961	June, Stuttgart Opera, *Tosca*, cond. Patane w/Tebaldi, Tobin, London (Scarpia)
1961	June, Stuttgart Opera, *Der Fliegende Holländer*, cond. Janos Kulka, title role w/ Anja Silja, Eugene Tobin
1961	June, Vienna, Boris Scenes, Konzerthaus, cond. Matacic
1961	August 15 - 17, Munich Opera Festspiele, *Parsifal*, London (Amfortas) *Don Giovanni*, London (Don Giovanni)
1962	April, New York, Festival of the Performing Arts, Televised Concert, Orchestra conducted by Jean Morel, Leporello's Aria, Ford Monilogue, Rheingold "Abendlich Strahlt Die Sonne", Lord Randall, An Die Musik, Death of Boris
1962	May, Cologne, *Das Rheingold*, Wieland Wagner staging, cond. Sawallisch, London (Wotan) w/Elisabeth Schartel, Helen Erwin, Gerhard Nienstedt
1962	June 8, 18, 29; Paris, *Don Giovanni*, cond. Maurice Roux; title role June 23, 25, *Faust*, cond Louis Fourestier, Palais Garnier, London (Mephistopheles)
1962	August 14, 21 *Don Giovanni*, title role; Aug. 16 *Parsifal*, Amfortas, Munich Opera Festspiele
1962	September, Berlin, *Don Giovanni*, Deutsche Oper; cond. Fricsay; title role, w/ Köth, Lear, Greindl, Grobe
1963	May, Cologne, *Die Walküre*, Wieland Wagner staging, cond. Sawallisch, London (Wotan), w/ Silja, Schartel, Erwin, Nienstedt, Martell
1963	Oct., Cologne, *Siegfried*, Wieland Wagner, staging, cond. Sawallisch, London (Wotan) w/ Silja, Windgassen, Schartel, Nienstedt
1963	Fall, Cologne, *Der Ring des Nibelungen*, staging Wieland Wagner cond. Sawallisch, London (Wotan)
1963	December 7, 13, 18 *Aida*, London (Amonasro), December 11,15, 20 *Don Giovanni*; title role, Munich Reopening of the reconstructed National Theater
1964	February , Montreal, *Tosca*, cond. Mehta, London (Scarpia) w/ Ella Lee, Richard Verreau, Bernard Turgeon
1964	May, Venice, Gran Teatro La Fenice, *Don Giovanni*, cond. Peter Maag, title role w/Stich Randall, Casellato, Tadeo, Malliponte
1964	June, Vienna, Theater an der Wien, Recital, Erik Werba, pianist
1964	September, Japan, 4 weeks tour, Tokyo, Kyoto, Osaka, recitals, Leo Taubman, pianist
1964	November, Chicago Orchestra Hall, recital, John Newmark, pianist
1965	April, Yale University recital, Leo Taubman pianist
1965	May, Boston, *Boris Godunov*, Sarah Caldwell, cond. & staging, Moussorgsky version, title role

253

Chronology

1965	Munich, Television, *Portrait of a Singer*
1966	June 10-26, Moscow, Member Tchaikovsky Competition Jury, winners Atlantov, Veronika Tyler, Simon Estes
1967	February, Salzburg, Recital, Leonard Hokanson, pianist
1967	May, Vienna Volksoper, *Die Tote Stadt,* cond. Lee Shanen, w/Alexander, Zschau, Codes
1967	May 17, Vienna, Brahms Saal, recital, Leonard Hokanson, pianist
1967	Lübeck, Benefit Concert w/ Silja, Mathis, Konya
1974	May, San Francisco, *Gurrelieder,* San Francisco Symphony; cond. Seiji Ozawa, Napier, Chookasian, McCracken, London (speaking role)
1974	August, Tanglewood, *Gurrelieder,* Boston Symphony cond. Seiji Ozawa, Napier, Chookasian, McCracken, London (speaking role)
1976	May, Cincinnati, Hebrew Union College Centenary) *Moses and Aaron,* Schöenberg, Moses (speaking role)

Discography

GEORGE LONDON DISCOGRAPHY AND VIDEOGRAPHY
By Robert Baxter

OPERA

Debussy: *Pelléas et Mélisande*. Theodore Uppman, Victoria de los Angeles, Giorgio Tozzi, Regina Resnik, Metropolitan Opera Orchestra and Chorus, conducted by Ernest Ansermet (live recording 16 January 1960). Bensar OL 11660 (CD)

Debussy: *Pelléas et Mélisande*. Nicolai Gedda, Anna Moffo, Jerome Hines, Blanche Thebom, Teresa Stratas, Metropolitan Opera Orchestra and Chorus, conducted by Ernest Ansermet (live recording 29 December 1962). Piscitelli 9788 (CD)

Debussy: *Pelléas et Mélisande*. Camille Maurane, Erna Spoorenberg, Guus Hoekman, Josephine Veasey, John Shirley-Quirk, Choeur du Grand Théâtre de Genève and L'Orchestre de la Suisse Romande, conducted by Ernest Ansermet (August 1964). Decca 473-351-2 (CD)

Menotti: *The Last Savage*. Roberta Peters, Teresa Stratas, Nicolai Gedda, Ezio Flagello, Lili Chookasian, Morley Meredith, Metropolitan Opera Chorus and Orchestra, conducted by Thomas Schippers (live recording 8 February 1964). Piscitelli 1643 (CD)

Mozart: *Don Giovanni*. Elisabeth Grümmer, Sena Jurinac, Léopold Simoneau, Erich Kunz, Emmy Loose, Ludwig Weber, Walter Berry, Orchestra and Chorus of the Vienna State Opera, conducted by Karl Böhm (live recording Royal Festival Hall, London, 15 September 1954). Archipel ARPCD 0234 (CD)

Mozart: *Don Giovanni*. Ludwig Weber, Hilde Zadek, Léopold Simoneau, Sena Jurinac, Walter Berry, Eberhard Waechter, Graziella Sciutti, Vienna Chamber Chorus and the Vienna Symphony, conducted by Rudolf Moralt (May 1955). Philips 438 674-2 (CD)

Mozart: *Don Giovanni*. Hilde Zadek, Ludwig Weber, Léopold Simoneau, Maud Cunitz, Benno Kusche, Rita Streich, Horst Günter, Chorus and Orchestra of the Cologne Radio, conducted by Otto Klemperer (17 May 1955). Testament SBT 2149 (CD)

Mozart: *Don Giovanni*. Ludwig Weber, Lisa della Casa, Anton Dermota, Sena Jurinac, Erich Kunz, Irmgard Seefried, Walter Berry, Chorus and Orchestra of the Vienna State Opera, conducted by Karl Böhm (live recording 6 November 1955). RCA Red Seal 74321 57737 2 (CD)

Mozart: *Don Giovanni*. Eleanor Steber, Ezio Flagello, Lisa Della Casa, Laurel Hurley, Theodore Uppman, Cesare Valletti, William Wildermann, Metropolitan Opera Orchestra and Chorus, conducted by Karl Böhm (live recording 14 February 1959). Metropolitan Opera Historic Broadcast MET 25 (CD)

Mozart: *Don Giovanni*. Gottlob Frick, Hildegard Hillebrecht, Nicolai Gedda, Sena Jurinac, Benno Kusche, Anneliese Rothenberger, Albrecht Peter, Munich Philharmonic and Chorus of the Bavarian State Opera, conducted by Joseph Keilberth (live recording 21 August 1962). Golden Melodram GM 5.0041 (CD)

Mozart: *Le Nozze di Figaro*. Erich Kunz, Irmgard Seefried, Elisabeth Schwarzkopf, Sena Jurinac, Elisabeth Höngen, Erich Majkut, Chorus of the Vienna State Opera and the Vienna Philharmonic, conducted by Herbert von Karajan (September 1950). EMI Classics CMS 7 69639 2 (CD)

Discography

Mozart: *Le Nozze di Figaro*. Lisa della Casa, Roberta Peters, Giorgio Tozzi, Rosalind Elias, Sandra Warfield, Fernando Corena, Gabor Carelli, Annie Felbermayer, Ljubomir Pantscheff, Chorus of the Vienna State Opera and the Vienna Philharmonic, conducted by Erich Leinsdorf (June 1960). Decca 444 602-2 (CD)

Mozart: *Die Zauberflöte*. Anton Dermota, Irmgard Seefried, Erich Kunz, Wilma Lipp, Ludwig Weber, Sena Jurinac, Singverein der Gesellschaft der Musikfreunde in Wien and the Vienna Philharmonic Orchestra, conducted by Herbert Von Karajan (November 1950). EMI Classics CHS 7 69631 2 (CD)

Mozart: *Die Zauberflöte*. Jerome Hines, Roberta Peters, Lucine Amara, Brian Sullivan, Theodor Uppman, Laurel Hurley, Paul Franke, Chorus and Orchestra of the Metropolitan Opera, conducted by Bruno Walter (live recording 3 March 1956). Historical Performances AS425-26 (CD)

Mussorgsky: *Boris Godunov*. Vladimir Ivanovsky, Irina Arkhipova, Veronika Borisenko, Alexei Ivanov, Evgeny Kibkalo, Maria Mitukova, Mark Reshetin, Georgi Shulpin, Yelizaveta Shumskaya, Chorus and Orchestra of the Bolshoi Theater, conducted by Alexander Melik-Pashaev (1963). Sony Classical SM3K 52571 (CD)

Offenbach: *Les Contes d'Hoffmann*. Léopold Simoneau, Pierette Alarie, Suzanne Danco, Lucretia West, Renato Capecchi, Renato Cesari, Chorus and Orchestra of Rai Milan, conducted by Lee Schaenen (6 January 1954). Voce della Luna VL2009-2 (CD)

Offenbach: *Les Contes d'Hoffmann*. Léopold Simoneau, Pierette Alarie, Suzanne Danco, Lucretia West, Robert Destain, Chorus and Orchestra of RAI Milan, conducted by Lee Schaenen (live recording 9 September 1956). Melodram 033 (LP)

Offenbach: *Les Contes d'Hoffmann*. Nicolai Gedda, Gianna d'Angelo, Elisabeth Schwarzkopf, Victoria de los Angeles, Jean-Christophe Benoit, Nicola Ghiuselev, Ernest Blanc, Michel Sénéchal, Robert Geay, Chœurs René Duclos and Orchestre de la Société des Concerts du Conservatoire, conducted by André Cluytens (recorded 1964 and 1965). EMI Classics 5 67983 2 (CD)

Puccini: *Tosca*. Eleanor Steber, Carlo Bergonzi, Lorenzo Alvary, Gerhard Pechner, Alessio D Paolis, Chorus and Orchestra of the Metropolitan Opera, conducted by Kurt Adler (live recording 11 April 1959). MYTO MCD 951.120 (CD)

Puccini: *Tosca*. Renata Tebaldi, Mario del Monaco, Silvio Maionica, Fernando Corena, Piero de Palma, Giovanni Morese, Ernesto Palmerini, Chorus and Orchestra of the Accademia di Santa Cecilia, conducted by Francesco Molinari-Pradelli (July 1959). Decca 411 871-2 (CD)

Puccini: *Tosca*. Birgit Nilsson, Franco Corelli, Fernando Corena, Chorus and Orchestra of the Metropolitan Opera, conducted by Fausto Cleva (18 April 1964). Bensar OL 41864 (CD)

Strauss: *Die Fledermaus*. Eberhard Waechter, Anneliese Rothenberger, Risë Stevens, Sándor Kónya, Erich Kunz, Erich Majkut, Adele Leigh, Chorus and Orchestra of the Vienna State Opera, conducted by Oskar Danon. RCA Victor Red Seal LSC-7029 (LP)

Strauss: *Great Moments from Die Fledermaus*. Sergio Franchi, Anna Moffo, Risë Stevens, John Hauxfell, Richard Lewis, Jeanette Scovotti, Chorus and Orchestra of the Vienna State Opera, conducted by Oskar Danon. RCA Red Seal 63468.2 (CD)

Strauss: *Arabella*. Eleanor Steber, Hilde Gueden, Brian Sullivan, Blanche Thebom, Ralph Herbert, Roberta Peters, Thelma Votipka, Chorus and Orchestra of the Metropolitan Opera, conducted by Rudolf Kempe (live recording 26 February 1955). Voce della Luna VL2014-3 (CD)

Discography

Strauss: *Arabella.* Otto Edelmann, Ira Malaniuk, Lisa della Casa, Hilde Gueden, Anton Dermota, Waldemar Kmentt, Eberhard Waechter, Harald Pröglhoff , Mimi Coertse, Judith Hellwig, Vienna Philharmonic, conducted by Georg Solti (May/June 1957). Decca 430 387-2

Tchaikovsky: *Eugene Onegin.* Valérie Bak, Anton Dermota, Hertha Töpper, Lilian Benningsen, Ruth Siewert, Gottlob Frick, Max Proebstl, Franz Klarwein, Heinz Maria Linz, Chorus and Orchestra of the Bavarian Radio, conducted by Richard Kraus (1954). MYTO MCD 971.153 (CD)

Tchaikovsky: *Eugene Onegin.* Polly Bastic, Leonie Rysanek, Mira Kalin, Hilde Rössl-Majdan, Anton Dermota, Gottlob Frick, Ljubomir Pantscheff, Peter Klein, Chorus and Orchestra of the Vienna State Opera, conducted by Berislav Klobucar (live recording 1955). MYTO MCD 005-233 (CD)

Tchaikovsky: *Eugene Onegin.* Lucine Amara, Richard Tucker, Rosalind Elias, Giorgio Tozzi, Belen Amparan, Martha Lipton, Louis Sgarro, Alessio De Paolis, George Cehanovsky, Chorus and Orchestra of the Metropolitan Opera, conducted by Dimitri Mitropoulos (live recording 7 December 1957). G.O.P. 707 (CD)

Verdi: *Aida.* Zinka Milanov, Mario del Monaco, Blanche Thebom, Jerome Hines, Luben Vichegonov, Lucine Amara, Thomas Hayward, Chorus and Orchestra of the Metropolitan Opera, conducted by Fausto Cleva (live recording 24 January 1953). Bongiovanni GB 1173/74-2 (CD)

Verdi: *Aida.* Leonie Rysanek, Hans Hopf, Jean Madeira, Gottlob Frick, Oskar Czerwenka, Erich Majkut, Anny Felbermayer, Chorus and Orchestra of the Vienna State Opera, conducted by Rafael Kubelik (live recording 10 May 1955). MYTO MCD 023.267 (CD)

Wagner: *Der Fliegende Holländer.* Astrid Varnay, Josef Traxel, Arnold van Mill, Elisabeth Schärtel, Jean Cox, Chorus and Orchestra of the Bayreuth Festival, conducted by Joseph Keilberth (live recording 25 July 1956). Golden Melodram GM 1.0057 (CD)

Wagner: *Der Fliegende Holländer.* Leonie Rysanek, Josef Greindl, Fritz Uhl, Res Fischer, Georg Paskuda, Chorus and Orchestra of the Bayreuth Festival (live recording 1959) Conducted by Wolfgang Sawallisch. Melodram MEL 26101. (CD)

Wagner: *Der Fliegende Holländer.* Leonie Rysanek, Giorgio Tozzi, Karl Liebl, Rosalind Elias, Richard Lewis, Chorus and Orchestra of the Royal Opera House, Covent Garden, conducted by Antal Dorati (1960). Decca 417 319-2 (CD)

Wagner: *Parsifal.* Martha Mödl, Arnold van Mill, Ludwig Weber, Wolfgang Windgassen, Hermann Uhde, Ruth Siewert, Chorus and Orchestra of the Bayreuth Festival, conducted by Hans Knappertsbusch (live recording 1951). Teldec 9031-76047-2 (CD)

Wagner: *Parsifal.* Martha Mödl, Wolfgang Windgassen, Ludwig Weber, Hermann Uhde, Kurt Böhme, Ruth Siewert, Chorus and Orchestra of the Bayreuth Festival (live recording 1952). Archipel ARPCD 0112-4 (CD)

Wagner: *Parsifal.* Martha Mödl, Ramón Vinay, Ludwig Weber, Hermann Uhde, Josef Greindl, Maria von Ilosvay, Chorus and Orchestra of the Bayreuth Festival, conducted by Clemens Krauss (live recording 1953). Archipel ARPCD 0171-4 (CD)

Wagner: *Parsifal.* Astrid Varnay, Set Svanholm, Hans Hotter, Lawrence Davidson, Luben Vichey, Jean Madeira, Chorus and Orchestra of the Metropolitan Opera, conducted by Fritz Stiedry (live recording 17 April 1954). Adonis 54001 (CD)

Discography

Wagner: *Parsifal*. Irene Dalis, Jess Thomas, Ludwig Weber, Hans Hotter and Gustav Neidlinger, Chorus and Orchestra of the Bayreuth Festival, conducted by Hans Knappertsbusch (live recording 1961). Golden Melodram GM1.0049 (CD)

Wagner: *Parsifal*. Irene Dalis, Martti Talvela, Hans Hotter, Jess Thomas, Gustav Neidlinger, Ursula Boese, Chorus and Orchestra of the Bayreuth Festival, conducted by Hans Knappertsbusch (live recording 1962). Philips 416 390-2 (CD)

Wagner: *Parsifal*. Irene Dalis, Gerd Nienstedt, Hans Hotter, Wolfgang Windgassen, Gustav Neidlinger, Chorus and Orchestra of the Bayreuth Festival, conducted by Hans Knappertsbusch (live recording 1963). Golden Melodram GM-10034 (CD)

Wagner: *Das Rheingold*. Kirsten Flagstad, Set Svanholm, Gustav Neidlinger, Kurt Böhme, Claire Watson, Jean Madeira, Vienna Philharmonic, conducted by Georg Solti. Decca 414 101-2 (CD)

Wagner: *Das Rheingold*. Irene Dalis, Ralph Herbert, Karl Liebl, Ernst Wiemann, Jerome Hines, Heidi Krall and Chorus and Orchestra of the Metropolitan Opera, conducted by Erich Leinsdorf (live recording 16 December 1961). Bensar OL 121661

Wagner: *Das Rheingold*. Elisabeth Schärtel, Ingeborg Kjellgren, Karl Sablotzke, Hermann Winkler, Herbert Schachtschneider, Zoltan Kelemen, Erwin Wohlfahrt, Gerd Nienstedt, Gürzenich Orchestra, conducted by Wolfgang Sawallisch (live recording 22 May 1962). Living Stage LS 1004 (CD)

Wagner: *Siegfried*. Hans Hopf, Birgit Nilsson, Jean Madeira, Martina Arroyo, Paul Kuen, Ralph Herbert, Gottlob Frick, Chorus and Orchestra of the Metropolitan Opera, conducted by Erich Leinsdorf (live recording 13 January 1962). Bensar Records OL 11362.

Wagner: *Tannhäuser*. Jerome Hines, Ramón Vinay, Astrid Varnay, Blanche Thebom, Heidi Krall, Chorus and Orchestra of the Metropolitan Opera, conducted by Rudolf Kempe (live recording 29 January 1955). Adonis 55002 (CD)

Wagner: *Die Walküre*. Jon Vickers, Gré Brouwenstijn, David Ward, Birgit Nilsson, Rita Gorr, London Symphony Orchestra, conducted by Erich Leinsdorf (1962). Decca 430 391-2 (CD)

SOLO RECITAL

"Mr. Lincoln and his Gloves" by Gerald Marks and "Absalom, My Son" by George Kleinsiger. Joseph Blatt, pianist (1948). RCA Victor 12-0238 (78).

The Record of Singing Volume Four. Mussorgsky: *Boris Godunov* "I have attained the highest power." Virginia Pleasants, piano (22 October 1950). EMI Classics CHS 7 69741 2 (CD)

George London in Dramatic Scenes from Russian and French Operas. Arias from *Prince Igor*, *The Demon*, *Don Quichotte* and *Patrie*, Orchestra of the Metropolitan Opera Association, conducted by Kurt Adler and Jean Morel (10 December 1951). Columbia ML 4489 (LP)

Of Gods and Demons. Arias and scenes from *Das Rheingold*, *Die Walküre*, *Le Damnation de Faust*, *Faust*, *Mefistofele*, *The Demon* and Mussorgsky's *Song of the Flea*. Vienna Symphony Orchestra, conducted by Rudolf Moralt, and the Orchestra of the Metropolitan Opera, conducted by Kurt Adler (10 and 11 December 1951 and June 1952). Columbia ML 4658 (LP)

Verdi: *Aida* "Ciel! Mio Padre" with Zinka Milanov, Metropolitan Opera Orchestra, conducted by Fausto Cleva (live recording 24 January 1953). Metropolitan Opera Historic Broadcast Centennial Collection 1935-1959 MET-100 (LP)

Discography

Mozart Opera and Concert Arias. Arias from *Le Nozze di Figaro* and "Mentre ti lascio," "Per questa bella mano" and "Rivolgete a lui lo sguardo." The Columbia Symphony Orchestra, conducted by Bruno Walter (7 and 8 May 1953). Columbia ML 4699 (LP)

Famous Operatic Monologues. Arias and scenes from *Die Meistersinger von Nürnberg, Boris Godunov, Falstaff, Rigoletto, Othello, Thaïs* and *Emperor Jones.* Columbia Symphony Orchestra, conducted by Jean Morel (29 and 31 March and 6 April 1955). Columbia 4999 (LP)

Mussorgsky: *Songs and Dances of Death* and Duparc: "L'invitation au voyage." "Phidylé," Chanson Triste," "Extase" and "Le Manoir de Rosamonde." Paul Ulanowsky, piano (8 April 1955). Columbia ML 4906 (LP)

George London on Broadway. Songs from *Oklahoma!, South Pacific, Paint Your Wagon, Brigadoon, My Fair Lady, Carousel, Show Boat, Very Warm for May.* Roland Shaw Orchestra, conducted by Roland Shaw. London Records 5390 (LP)

Wagner: Great Scenes for Bass-baritone. Scenes from *Der Fliegende Holländer, Die Meistersinger von Nürnberg* and *Die Walküre.* Vienna Philharmonic Orchestra, conducted by Hans Knappertsbusch. London OS 25044 (LP)

George London as Boris Godunov. Prologue and Coronation Scene, Boris' Monologue from Act II, Dialogue and Hallucination Scene, Boris' Farewell to his Son and Death of Boris. Howard Fried, Mildred Allen and Stanley Kolk, the Columbia Symphony Orchestra and Chorus, conducted by Thomas Schippers (23 to 27 March 1961). Columbia MS 6273 (LP)

Mussorgsky: *Songs and Dances of Death* and Brahms: *Vier ernste Gesänge.* Leo Taubman, piano (1962-1964). Columbia MS 6734 (LP)

George London im Theater an der Wien. Schubert: *Schwanengesang,* Ibert: *Chansons de Don Quichotte* and Mussorgsky: *Songs and Dances of Death* (live recording 10 June 1963). Erik Werba, piano. Arias and duets from *Le Nozze di Figaro, Don Giovanni, Les Contes d'Hoffmann, Faust* and *Aida.* Irmgard Seefried and Astrid Varnay, Orchestra of the Vienna Radio, conducted by Max Schönherr, and Bavarian Radio Symphony Orchestra, conducted by Hermann Weigert. Amadeo 413 821-1 (LP)

George London. Arias and duets from *Le nozze di Figaro, Don Giovanni, Les Contes d'Hoffmann, Faust, Aida, Boris Godunov, Prince Igor* and *Eugene Onegin.* Irmgard Seefried, Erich Kunz, Astrid Varnay and Valerie Bak. Orchestra of the Vienna Radio, conducted by Max Schönherr, Orchestra of the Vienna State Opera, conducted by Karl Böhm, and Orchestra of the Bavarian Radio, conducted by Hermann Weigert and Richard Kraus. Deutsche Grammophon 415 449-1 (LP)

George London. Arias from *Le nozze di Figaro, La Damnation de Faust, Faust, Mefistofele, Boris Godunov, The Demon, Patrie, Falstaff, Otello* and Mozart: "Rivolgete a lui lo sguardo" and Mussorgsky: *Song of the Flea.* Columbia Symphony, conducted by Bruno Walter and Jean Morel and Vienna Symphony, conducted by Rudolf Moralt. Orchestra of the Metropolitan Opera Association, conducted by Kurt Adler and Jean Morel. Preiser PR 135 027 (LP)

Gustav Mahler: *Kindertotenlieder.* Symphony Orchestra of the WDR Köln, conducted by Otto Klemperer (live recording 17 October 1955). Cetra LO 510 (LP)

Bass-baritone George London. Arias and duets from *Don Giovanni, Les Contes d'Hoffmann, Tosca, Boris Godunov, Aida* and *Die Walküre* and "Shenandoah." Maria Callas, Laurel Hurley and Birgit Nilsson, orchestras conducted by Karl Böhm, Lee Schaenen, Dimitri Mitropoulos, Donald Voorhees, Leopold Stokowski and Paul Paray (live performances from 1954 to 1960). Parnassus PAR 1002 (LP)

259

Discography

George London. Arias and duets from *Elijah*, *Le Nozze di Figaro*, *Don Giovanni*, *Les Contes d'Hoffmann*, *Faust*, *Der Fliegende Holländer*, *Die Walküre*, *Aida*, *Tosca*, *Prince Igor* and *Eugene Onegin* (live performances from 1953 to 1962). Erika Köth, Anny Schlemm, Antonietta Stella, Maria Callas, Gottlob Frick and Valerie Bak. Orchestras conducted by Cristoph von Dohnányi, Leopold Stokowski, Otto Klemperer, Rudolf Moralt, Joseph Keilberth, Hermann Weigert, Fausto Cleva and Richard Kraus. Melodram 097 (LP)

First Performance Lincoln Center. Vaughan Williams: *Serenade to Music* and Mahler: Symphony No. 8 in E-flat Major, Part One. Adele Addison, Lucine Amara, Eileen Farrell, Lili Chookasian, Jennie Tourel, Shirley Verrett, Charles Bressler, Richard Tucker, Jon Vickers, Ezio Flagello, Donald Bell. Schola Cantorum, Juilliard Chorus, Columbus Boychoir and New York Philharmonic, conducted by Leonard Bernstein (live performance 23 September 1962). Columbia L2L 1007 (LP)

George London Bass-Baritone Of Gods and Demons. Arias and scenes from *Faust*, *La Damnation de Faust*, *Mefistofele*, *The Demon*, *Patrie*, *Thaïs*, *Don Quichotte*, *Prince Igor*, *Boris Godunov*, *Das Rheingold*, *Die Walküre*, *The Emperor Jones* and Mussorgsky's *Song of the Flea*. Orchestras led by Rudolf Moralt, Jean Morel and Kurt Adler (recorded 1951 to 1955). Sony Classical MHK 62758 (CD)

The Singers. George London. Scenes from *Der Fliegende Holländer*, *Die Meistersinger von Nürnberg* and *Die Walküre* and songs from *Oklahoma!*, *South Pacific*, *Carousel*, *Brigadoon*, *My Fair Lady*, *Knickerbocker Holiday*, *Very Warm For May* and *Showboat*. Orchestras conducted by Hans Knappertsbusch and Roland Shaw. Decca 467 904-2 (CD)

George London 1953. Mozart: arias from *Le nozze di Figaro* and concert arias "Mentre ti lascio, o figlia," "Per queste bella mano" and "Rivolgete a lui lo sguardo" and selections from *Aida*, *Prince Igor* and *Die Walküre*. Orchestras conducted by Bruno Walter and Hermann Weigert. Preiser 90580 (CD)

George London Recital, 1952-1955. Arias from *La Damnation de Faust*, *Faust*, *Mefistofele*, *Das Rheingold*, *Die Walküre*, *Prince Igor*, *The Demon*, *Don Quichotte*, *Patrie*, *Thaïs*, *Rigoletto*, *Otello*, *Falstaff* and Mussorgsky's *Song of the Flea*. Orchestras conducted by Rudolf Moralt, Kurt Adler and Jean Morel. MYTO MCD 942 101 (CD)

Grosse Sänger Unseres Jahrhunderts George London. Arias and scenes from *Les Contes d'Hoffmann*, *Eugene Onegin*, *Prince Igor*, *Aida* and *Die Walküre*. Teresa Stich-Randall, Maria von Ilosvay, Valérie Bak and Astrid Varnay. Live recordings with the Bavarian Radio Symphony Orchestra led by Rudolf Moralt, Richard Kraus and Hermann Weigert. Orfeo C 502 001 B (CD)

Giuseppe di Stefano presenta 'Recitals Indimenticabili' George London. Arias and scenes from *Aida* (Metropolitan Opera 23 February 1957), *Boris Godunov* (Metropolitan Opera 7 January 1961), *Don Giovanni* (Vienna Staatsoper September 1955), *Die Walküre* (Metropolitan Opera 6 March 1965) and *Le Nozze di Figaro*, *Prince Igor* and *Faust* (Philadelphia Orchestra 25 July 1962). Antonietta Stella, Kurt Baum, Blanche Thebom, Giorgio Tozzi, Louis Sgarro, Teresa Stratas, Helen Vanni, Normann Kelley, Sena Jurinac, Irmgard Seefried, Erich Kunz, Walter Berry, Ludwig Weber and Birgit Nilsson. Orchestras conducted by Fausto Cleva, Erich Leinsdorf, Karl Böhm, William Steinberg and Leopold Stokowski. GDS 2204 (CD)

George London in Concert. Arias and songs by Piccinni, Falconieri, Schubert, Mussorgsky, Irish and Scottish folk melodies and songs. John Newmark, piano (live recording 15 February 1957). VAI Audio VAIA 1030 (CD)

George London und Seine Freunde Gala. Francisco Araiza, Simon Estes, Nicolai Gedda, Sona Ghazarian, Edita Gruberova, James King, Catherine Malfitano, Lucia Popp, Leonie Rysanek, Tatiana Troyanos with ORF Orchestra, conducted by Heinrich Hollreiser (1984). Amadeo 449 574-2 (CD)

Discography

ORATORIO and CONCERT

Beethoven: Symphony No. 9. Gundula Janowitz, Grace Bumbry, Jess Thomas, Chorus and Orchestra of the Bayreuth Festival, conducted by Karl Böhm (live recording 23 July 1963). Melodram CD 18005 (CD)

Brahms: *Ein Deutsches Requiem*. Irmgard Seefried, Westminster Choir and New York Philharmonic, conducted by Bruno Walter (December 1954). Sony Classical SMK 64 469 (CD)

Brahms: *Vier ernste Gesänge*. Leo Taubman, piano (1962-1964). Sony Classical SBK 48 176 (CD)

Haydn: Mass No. 9 in D minor ("Nelson"). Lisa della Casa, Elisabeth Höngen, Horst Taubman, Vienna Academy Chorus and Symphony, conducted by Jonathan Sternberg (1949). Haydn Society HSLP.2004 (LP)

Hindemith: *When Lilacs Last in the Dooryard Bloom'd*. Louise Parker, New York Philharmonic, conducted by Paul Hindemith. CBS Masterworks MPK 45881 (CD)

Mahler: Symphony No 8. Carlos Alexander, Eugene Conley, Uta Graf, Martha Lipton, Camilla Williams, Frances Yeend, Philharmonic Symphony Orchestra, conducted by Leopold Stokowski (live recording April 9, 1950). Archipel ARPCD 0108 (CD)

Mahler: *Kindertotenlieder*. Orchestra of the West German Radio, conducted by Otto Klemperer (live recording 17 October 1955). MYTO MCD 971.153 (CD)

Mahler: Symphony No. 8: Part 1. Adele Addison, Lucine Amara, Lili Chookasian, Ezio Flagello, Jennie Tourel, Richard Tucker, Lee Venora. New York Philharmonic Orchestra, conducted by Leonard Bernstein (live recording 23 September 1962). Sony Classical SMK 47639 (CD)

Mendelssohn: *Elijah*. Ingrid Bjoner, Waldemar Kmentt, Ira Malaniuk, Chorus and Orchestra of the Cologne Radio Symphony Orchestra, conducted by Christoph von Dohnányi (live recording 1962). Melodram GM 40058 (CD)

Menotti: *The Death of the Bishop of Brindisi*. Lili Chookasian, New England Conservatory Chorus, Boston Symphony Orchestra, conducted by Erich Leinsdorf (19 October 1964). RCA Victor 09026-63747-2 (CD)

Verdi: *Messa da Requiem*. Lucine Amara, Maureen Forrester, Richard Tucker, Westminster Choir and Philadelphia Orchestra, conducted by Eugene Ormandy (14 and 15 May 1964). Sony Classical SB2K 53 252 (CD)

Vaughan Williams: *Serenade to Music*. Adele Addison, Lucine Amara, Eileen Farrell, Lili Chookasion, Jennie Tourel, Shirley Verrett, Charles Bressler, Richard Tucker, Jon Vickers, Ezio Flagello, Donald Bell, New York Philharmonic, conducted by Leonard Bernstein (live recording 23 September 1962). Sony Classical SMK 61874

VIDEO

George London in Opera and Song. Arias and duets from *Boris Godunov, Maytime, Le Nozze di Figaro, Don Giovanni, The Desert Song, Naughty Marietta*, songs by Rodgers and Hammerstein and others. Nadine Conner, Dorothy Warenskjold and orchestras, conducted by Howard Barlow and Wilfrid Pelletier (live recordings from *The Voice of Firestone* 28 December 1953, 3 January 1955 and 27 February 1953). Kultur KLT 2418 (VHS)

Discography

Puccini: *Tosca* scene from Act 2. Maria Callas, orchestra conducted by Dimitri Mitropoulos (live recording from the Ed Sullivan Show 25 November 1956). House of Opera (DVD)

Great Stars of Opera From the Bell Telephone Hour. Telecasts from *The Bell Telephone Hour* 1959-1966. "Farewell My Son" from *Boris Godunov.* Bell Telephone Hour Orchestra, conducted by Donald Voorhees (live recording 19 May 1964). VAI DVD 4201 (DVD)

Cole Porter – An All Star Tribute. "Night and Day," "Were Thine That Special Face" and duet from *Wunderbar.* Jeanne Finn. VAI 2005 (DVD)
CD Recording VAIA 1239

A Salute to George London. Arias from *Das Rheingold, Boris Godunov, Tosca, Don Giovanni, Faust* and Schubert: "An die Musik" with Joan Sutherland, Shirley Verrett, Leonie Rysanek, Tatiana Troyanos, Ruth Welting, James McCracken, Marilyn Horne, Nicolai Gedda, Evelyn Lear, Thomas Stewart, James King, Richard Stilwell, Carol Neblett, Justino Diaz, Rockwell Blake and Beverly Sills, accompanied by Jeffrey Goldberg, Eugene Kohn, Mstislav Rostropovich, Julius Rudel and Warren Wilson (live recording from the Kennedy Center 1981). Premiere Opera 5121 (DVD).

George London – A Celebration. Arias from *Don Giovanni* and *Boris Godunov* with Francisco Araiza, Simon Estes, Nicolai Gedda, Sonia Ghazarian, Edita Gruberova, Margareta Hintermeier, James King, Catherine Malfitano, Thomas Moser, Lucia Popp, Leonie Rysanek, Tatiana Troyanos, Vienna State Opera Chorus and Vienna Radio Symphony Orchestra, conducted by Lothar Zagrosek, Heinrich Hollreiser, Hans Graf and Erich Binder. VAI 69224 (VHS)

Great Voices from the CBC. Gounod: *Faust.* Marian Anderson, Lisa della Casa, Maureen Forrester, Marilyn Horne, Sir Peter Pears, Irmgard Seefried, Richard Tucker, pianists John Newmark and Franz Rupp, CBC Symphony Orchestra and CBC Festival Orchestra conducted by Lucia Agostini and Ernesto Barbini. VAI 69412 (VHS)

Puccini: *Tosca.* Renata Tebaldi, Eugene Tobin, Wilhelm Baur, Hubert Buchta, Heinz Cramer, Siegfried Fischer-Sandt, Gustav Grefe, Claudia Hellman, Chorus and Orchestra of the State Opera Stuttgart, conducted by Franco Patane. (Live Performance June 3, 1961) VAI 4217 (DVD)

Puccini: *Tosca.* Renata Tebaldi, Eugene Tobin, Wilhelm Baur, Hubert Buchta, Chorus and Orchestra of the Wurttemberg State Opera, conducted by Franco patane. VAI 4217 (DVD)

ABOUT THE CD

The compact disk enclosed in this book documents the most important stages of George London's career in mostly unavailable recordings from 1948 to 1963.The program begins with two unknown recordings on 78rp from 1948 which already show the talent and unmistakable timbre, warmth and maturity of the 28 year old singer. The next three recordings come from George London's first period at the Vienna Staatsoper and give an idea of the singer's versatility and intense interpretations which immediately earned him a star position in the company. In the same way he put his own unmatched stamp on the role of Amfortas in the Wieland Wagner staging of *Parsifal* in the Bayreuth Festival. Then comes London as Amonasro in *Aida* documented by a technically imperfect excerpt. However it gives an idea of the impact the young singer made. George London's numerous performances as Count Almaviva in Vienna, at the Met, in Salzburg are documented in an excerpt from a Mozart recording with Bruno Walter which radiates a mixture of virility and aristocratic nobility. In 1954, the Bavarian radio recorded Tschaikovsky's *Eugene Onegin* to document London's success in the title role in Vienna and at the Metropolitan. He also performed Don Giovanni first in Vienna and then in all the great opera houses as well as in many recordings. The first excerpt is a live recording from a guest performance of the Vienna Staatsoper in London 1954 previously unpublished, the second from a performance during the Munich summer festival 1962. London sang Scarpia in Puccini's *Tosca* for the first time at the Metropolitan and subsequently with all the great prima donnas of his time. This excerpt highlights the aristocratic accents which redouble the effect of his frightening cruelty.The monologue from the *Flying Dutchman* is a live recording of London's first performance of the title role in Bayreuth with a staging by Wolfgang Wagner. The excerpt from *Rheingold* comes from a recording done by the Deutsche Oper in Cologne, a segment from the role of Wotan in the *Ring der Nibelungen* staged by Wieland Wagner. The end of the program documents most impressively George London's performance as Boris Godunov at the Bolshoi Theater in Moscow. It was the climax of his career.

Gottfried Kraus

Gottfried Kraus was born in Vienna. He studied Cello, Voice and Musicology. He has worked as music critic for leading Austrian newspapers and published several books, among them a comprehensive chronicle entitled Music in Austria. He was head of the music department of the Austrian Broadcasting Corporation for fifteen years. Since 1986 he has been producing recordings and films, among them documents of the Salzburg Festival, Vienna Staatsoper performances and numerous other historic performances.

George London

1. Gerald Marks: "Mr. Lincoln and his Gloves"   4:51
   Josef Blatt, Piano   (rec. 1948)

2. George Kleinsinger: "Absalon, my son"   4:11
   Josef Blatt, Piano   (rec. 1948)

3. Offenbach: *Les Contes d'Hoffmann* – Aria of Dapertutto   3:51
   Orchestra of Austrian Radio, Max Schonherr cond., rec. Vienna 1951

4. Gounod: *Faust* – Mephistopheles' Serenade   2:55
   Orchestra of Austrian Radio, Max Schonherr cond., rec. Vienna 1951

5. Moussorgsky: *Boris Godunov*, Act 2 – Monolog of Boris   5:48
   Orchestra of Austrian Radio, Max Schonherr cond., rec. Vienna 1951

6. Wagner: *Parsifal*, Act 1 – Wehvolles Erbe Scene of Amfortas 8:10
   Live recording Festival Bayreuth 1951, Hans Knappertsbusch cond.

7. Verdi: *Aida*, Act 2 – Suo padre – Amonasro's entrance   3:01
   Ensemble, Chorus and Orchestra, 1954

8. Mozart: *Le Nozzee di Figaro*, Act 3 – Hia gia vinta la causa 4:41
   Columbia Symphony Orchestra, Bruno Walter cond. , rec. May 1953

9. Tschaikovsky: *Eugene Onegin*, Act 3 Scene Gremin,Tatiana,Onegin   3:04
   Valerie Bak, Gottlob Frick, Bavarian Radio Orchestra, Richard Kraus cond., rec. Munich July 1954

10. Mozart: *Don Giovanni*, Act 1 – Alfin siam liberati – Rec. and Duo with Zerlina   4:55
    Emmy Loose, Vienna State Opera, Karl Bohm cond., Live rec. Covent Garden London Sept. 15, 1954

11. Puccini: *Tosca*, Act 2 – La povera mia cena –   4:28
    Scene Scarpia, Tosca, Excerpts

12. Wagner: *The Flying Dutchman*, Act 1 – Die Frist ist um – Monolog of Hollander 11:38
    Live recording Festival Bayreuth 1956, Joseph Keilberth cond.

13. Wagner: *Das Rheingold* – Abendlich strahlt der Sonne Auge – Wontan, Fricka   4:39
    Elisabeth Schartel, Wolfgang Sawallisch cond., Live rec. Deutsche Oper Koln May 22, 1962

14. Mozart: *Don Giovanni*, Act 1 – Finche dal vino – Aria of Don Giovanni   1:46
    Joseph Keilberth cond., Live rec., Bavarian State Opera, Munich August 14, 1962

15. Moussorgsky: *Boris Godunov*, - Boris Farewell   10:17
    Chorus and Orchestra Bolshoi Theater Moscow, Alexander Melik-Pachaev cond., rec 1963

A

Abbott, George 166
Adler, Kurt 169
Adler, Peter 15
Aida 10, 26-27, 34, 38, 41, 52, 60,
  70, 77, 85, 96, 109, 156, 204
Albanese, Licia 96
Ali Ben Ali 14
Allen, Steve 99
Alvin Ailey Dance Theater 180
Amara, Lucine 95
American Guild of Musical Artists
  22
American Wagner Festival 199
Amfortas 33, 36-38, 40, 105, 116,
  131, 160, 168, 225
Amonasro 26-27, 33-34, 39, 52,
  70, 81, 96, 109, 131, 156
Anday, Rosette 76
Ansermet, Ernest 155
Arabella 49, 86-87, 125, 159
Attila 210

B

Bailey, Pearl 182
Barber, Samuel 164
Barrymore, John 139
Batistini 40
Bayreuth Festival 35-39, 103, 107-
  108
Beatles, The 175
Beaty, Douglas 10
Beaumarchais 87-88
Bel Canto Trio 16-17
Belafonte, Harry 99
Berdichevsky, Bertha 1
Berlin Opera 182-183
Bernhardt, Sarah 190
Bernheimer, Martin 20, 110
Bernstein, Leonard 146, 181
Berteau, Julien 88

Bing, Rudolf 34-35, 39, 83, 94-95,
  100, 186-187
Blair, William McCormick Jr. 176,
  178-179, 221
Blake, Rockwell 193, 206
Blatt, Joseph 17
Bliss, Anthony 189
Boheme 17
Böhm, Karl 21, 79, 98
Bolshoi Theater 31, 93, 108, 134-
  135, 138, 140, 142, 144, 150,
  183
Bonaparte, Felicia 3
Boris Godunov 11, 18, 28-31, 34,
  40, 49, 83-84, 86, 90, 93, 100,
  108, 110, 122, 128, 131, 133-
  135, 139,-141, 143, 146, 149-
  151, 159, 170, 183, 225
Borodin 27, 143
Bourgin, Simon 28, 75, 79, 173,
  219
Brahmssaal 29
Burnstein, Louis 1
Burnstein, Nat 15

C

Callas, Maria 96, 98
Carelli, Gabor 189
Carmen 10, 18, 27, 76, 86, 207
Carter, Amy 211
Carter, Chip 211
Carter, Jimmy 179, 211
Caruso 4, 163
Casa, Lisa Della 79, 86, 88, 92, 97,
Casablanca 13
Chaliapin 18, 41, 42
Chaliapin, Lydia 42
Champagne Aria *73, 80*
Chapin, Schuyler 188, 189
Civic Light Opera 13
Clark, Lincoln 200
Cliburn, Van 99, 182